PELICAN BOOKS

Concepts of the Man-Made Environment
General Editor: Alexander Tzonis

Critical multi-disciplinary investigations
of fundamental problems in our environment.

CONFLICT IN MAN-MADE ENVIRONMENT

Anatol Rapoport was born in Russia in 1911 and went
to the United States in 1922, where he attended public
schools in Chicago. He studied music in Chicago and
later in Vienna, where he graduated from the State
Academy of Music with degrees in composition, piano
and conducting.

He was awarded a doctors degree in mathematics from the
University of Chicago in 1941. During the Second World
War he served in the United States Air Force on overseas
duty in Alaska and India. Thereafter he was a member of
the Committee on Mathematical Biology of the University
of Chicago (1947–54), a Fellow at the Center for
Advanced Studies in the Behavioral Sciences, and
joined the faculty of the University of Michigan in 1955.
In 1970 Professor Rapoport joined the University of
Toronto where he is associated with the Departments of
Psychology and of Mathematics.

His major research is in mathematical biology and
mathematical psychology, and he is the author of
numerous books on these subjects. He has also edited the
Penguin edition of *On War* by Clausewitz, and has
contributed to a number of scientific, professional, and
news journals in the United States and abroad.
Anatol Rapoport is married and has three children.

ANATOL RAPOPORT

Conflict in Man-Made Environment

PENGUIN BOOKS

Penguin Books Ltd, Harmondsworth,
Middlesex, England
Penguin Books Inc., 7110 Ambassador Road,
Baltimore, Maryland 21207, U.S.A.
Penguin Books Australia Ltd, Ringwood,
Victoria, Australia
Penguin Books Canada Ltd, 41 Steelcase Road West,
Markham, Ontario, Canada

First published 1974

Printed in the United States of America
Set in Monotype Plantin

CONTENTS

6 *Contents*

PREFACE

Like all other organisms, man receives inputs from his environment and secretes outputs into it. Some of the inputs are life-sustaining; others are noxious, even lethal. The outputs modify the environment: some make it more livable, others less so.

Unlike any other biological type, man modifies his environment *cumulatively* so that now his environment is mostly of his own making. This man-made environment includes not only the technical artifacts, on which men have become dependent for survival, but also less tangible features, which we shall subsume under 'symbolic environment'.

To put the relation of man and his special environment into proper perspective, in Part I we shall examine systems interacting with their environments in more general contexts; these will include non-human and even inanimate systems. The man-made environment, including the symbolic, will then appear, like man himself, as a product of evolution of systems.

The nature of the symbolic environment is such that it depends in great measure on what men say or think about it. In particular, what men think or say about human conflict (an important component of the symbolic environment) has a great bearing on the nature of human conflict and its consequences. Therefore, in discussing conflict as a feature of man-made environment, we shall have to examine various *conceptions* of conflict, not only with the view of estimating to what extent the concepts are accurate (as one does with scientific theories) but also with the view of seeing how some of these conceptions make human conflicts what they are.

In Part II, we shall examine various 'theories' of conflict. We shall not take them up in chronological order, because we do not discern any clear line of development in these 'theories'. We find the dialectical formulation of conflict, as developed by Hegel, anticipated two and a half millennia earlier by Heraclitus; the social Darwinists of the nineteenth century, anticipated in the seventeenth by Hobbes. Strategic theories of conflict so prevalent today were anticipated by Machiavelli in the sixteenth century and even by Sun Tzu, who wrote *c.* 500 B.C. Themes of inner conflict pervade all literature, and the ideas of depth psychology were clearly inspired by those themes, the 'psychoanalysis' of the great tragic figures, Job, Oedipus, Hamlet, Don Quixote, and Faust, being undertaken as readily as if they were patients in the flesh.

To be sure, the central ideas of natural science have also been anticipated. The atomic theory of matter, developed systematically from the beginning of the nineteenth century, was anticipated by Democritus in the fifth century B.C.; the heliocentric theory, by Anaxagoras etc. Nevertheless, there is a fundamental difference between an anticipated scientific theory and an anticipated conception of conflict. The seed of a scientific theory, appearing ahead of its time, remains dormant; it sprouts and develops only when conditions become ripe. Philosophies of conflict, in contrast, often spring full-grown in the minds of their proponents, and they reflect attitudes or convictions rather than beginnings of a systematic accumulation of knowledge.

In short, general theories of conflict, whether ancient or modern, do not have the status of scientific theories. *Special* forms of conflict have at times been studied with a view to relating hypotheses to observations. Some of these studies deserve, perhaps, the status of scientific theories in the sense of having exhibited testable relations between conditions or variables. But the range of validity of every such theory cannot be safely extrapolated beyond what has been demonstrated.

It is likely that a 'general theory of conflict' is altogether impossible to construct, because 'conflict' may be no more than a word that expresses our interpretation of (and attitudes toward) a multitude of widely disparate phenomena, governed by entirely different principles. Even a 'general theory of war' (war being a narrower category than conflict) may be impossible to construct. A closer scrutiny often reveals that several unrelated phenomena are frequently subsumed under the same name because of superficial resemblance or because our attitudes toward the phenomena are similar. Examples of the former practice are the now discarded nosological categories like 'fever' that used to designate many unrelated diseases accompanied by a high temperature. Examples of the latter practice are reflected in terms like 'vermin' to designate all animals (especially insects and arachnids) that give us trouble. While the term 'fever' may still be useful in medicine, since the condition itself merits medical attention, the term 'vermin' is of no use in biology.

Similarly, while the term 'war' may be useful in discourse about a certain situation recognizable by its symptoms, it may not be useful as a category in a theory because many quite unrelated phenomena may have been subsumed under it.

Some speculations offered as general theories, or as philosophical systems purporting to explain the role of conflict in the scheme of existence, are by their nature formulated in abstract terms. Other schemes are highly specific, dealing with particular conflict situations (e.g., racial conflict circumscribed in place and time). Some seek sources of conflict in the psychology of individuals; others, in social arrangements. Among the abstract theories, some have been suggested by the so-called general theory of systems. In these 'systemic' theories we shall find an elaboration of the concepts discussed in Part I: equilibrium, steady state, stability, etc.

During the last decades many books on conflict have appeared, including works by individual authors, anthologies, and symposia, from which an overview of contemporary thought on conflict can be gathered. Our task here will be to select the ideas that have a bearing on the relation of conflict to man-made environment, in particular to point out the effect of conflict *upon* the environment (in addition to showing, or guessing, the effect of environment on conflict). This feedback effect is only occasionally discussed in studies of conflict, but it is an important one. In most causally connected events, 'causation' goes both ways. Unfortunately, in our search for 'causes' of events that affect our lives, we often lose sight of these reciprocal relations.

Toward the end of this book, we shall address ourselves to the problem of the so-called conflict between man and his total environment, or rather the perception of this conflict, as it is evidenced by expressions like 'mastery over nature', 'the conquest of nature', etc. Only quite recently has this conflict come to the forefront of men's consciousness as a major problem in itself. We shall inquire into the relation between man's intra-specific conflicts (wherein man is pitted against man) and man's perceptions of the 'conflict with nature'. The first has been traditionally the preoccupation of religion and philosophy and has been often identified with man's most conspicuous shortcomings and, hence, the source of most of his many misfortunes. The second, at least in Western thought, has been identified with man's special and privileged position in the scheme of life, and so the source of his success as an organism. This latter assumption has now been challenged. We shall examine the basis of this challenge and what it portends.

INTRODUCTION

To speak of conflict in any context, we must first identify the conflicting parties. These are not all of the same type. Individual organisms, human and non-human, enter into conflicts with each other; so do aggregates of organisms, especially human aggregates (tribes, social classes, nations). When we speak of conflicts among such aggregates, we tend to identify *them*, instead of the individuals comprising them, as the 'conflicting parties'. Moreover, we think of these aggregates not as mere collections of individuals but as entities in their own right, sometimes even endowing them with human psychological traits, such as ambitions, beliefs, or fears. This is the way we often think of nations interacting in diplomacy or war.

Non-human aggregates also sometimes appear to be in conflict with each other, an impression reflected in the phrase 'the struggle for existence'. This 'struggle' has been dramatically but often erroneously symbolized, as in Tennyson's phrase 'nature red in tooth and claw' and in the popular expression 'the law of the jungle', at times paraphrased also in human contexts: 'kill or be killed' (as in war) or 'that which stops growing begins to rot' (in international politics an aphorism attributed to an eighteenth-century Russian statesman).

What is left out of sight (and out of mind) in these images is that the 'conflicting parties' appear as units only when they are differentiated from the other parties to the conflict. *Internally*, a conflicting party is a *complex organized aggregate* of constituent parts. These constituent parts are not in conflict, at least not in the same sort of conflict that is 'waged' by the whole entity. On the contrary, success in conflict waged by the entity depends on how well its parts are integrated, i.e., 'cooperate' with each other. Therefore, every instance of external conflict implies internal 'cooperation'. If species engage in a 'struggle for existence', the individuals comprising them must cooperate at least in reproductive acts. An army fighting another army represents a high order of internal cohesion and coordination, that is, cooperation among its sub-units, down to the individual soldiers.

No form of conflict can be understood unless the internal organized structure of the conflicting units is understood. So long as the conflict continues, the conflicting units must maintain their respective internal organization, that is, must maintain themselves as *systems*. Indeed, as we shall see, the common feature of all conflicts is the tendency of the conflicting units to maintain their identity as systems. If 'the struggle for existence' has any meaning at all, it must be the tendency of systems to maintain themselves as such.

Therefore, in approaching our main theme, we must inquire into the meaning and characteristics of systems and what it means for a system to 'maintain its identity'. Since systems are of different orders of complexity and organization, we must distinguish between types of systems, and between the various meanings of 'conflict' when this term is used to describe their interactions. We shall first examine systems of different orders of organization, from the 'simplest' that occur in nature to those of which we ourselves are part, and also the environments in which these systems are immersed, from the simplest conceivable to that which we ourselves have created – the man-made environment.

PART ONE: SYSTEMS IN ENVIRONMENT

CHAPTER 1

The So-Called Struggle for Existence

The notion of 'environment' suggests a partition of a portion of the world into two regions, an inside and an outside. The environment constitutes the outside. The inside, that which is immersed in the environment, will be called a *system*. In the mind of someone who defines an environment, it is usually the system that is the object of interest. The environment is of interest to the extent that it has a bearing on what goes on in the system and what happens to it.

Sometimes a system and its environment occupy different regions of space. At other times, however, the system and its environment are 'diffused' through each other. For example, a solution consists of a solute dissolved in a solvent. Each can be considered as the environment of the other. Strictly speaking, the solution consists of minute particles of the solute surrounded by molecules of the solvent. However, since we cannot delineate all the minute regions occupied by the individual particles, we say that the solvent and the solute occupy the same region in space.

Characteristically, living systems, comprising many organisms, occupy the same gross region as their environment. Each individual organism may be geometrically compact, separated by a boundary from its environment; yet, the whole collection of organisms, say, a population consisting of a single species, is, as it were, 'dissolved' in its environment, somewhat as a solute is dissolved in a solvent. The absence of a clear geometric boundary does not, however, prevent us from distinguishing between the two. What we fix our attention on is the system. What is left over is the environment. It is important to note, therefore, that what is a system and what is environment is a matter of subjective preference, depending on what interests us most. If we are interested in an individual and what happens to him, everything outside the individual's skin is the environment. If we are interested in a family, a firm, an institution, a nation, humanity, or the entire biosphere, we define our environment accordingly.

The relation of system to environment is something like that of figure to ground in perception. The same visual image can be perceived as either a white circle on a black square or a black square with a round hole. We may fix our attention on a species and study what happens to it in the environment, or we may fix our attention on the environment (which thereby becomes the system) and study what happens to it when the species is 'dissolved' in it. The species is then the 'environment'.

A system and its environment interact, except in the very special case of *isolated* systems. These have boundaries impenetrable to either matter or energy. In this special case, we can study the system independently of its surroundings, which now do not deserve to be called 'environment' since they exert no influence on the system. In all other cases, what happens in or to the system depends on what happens in or to the environment. In particular, the interaction may be such that the system 'maintains' itself; or it may be such that the system 'ceases to be'. The phrases 'maintains itself' and 'ceases to be' are vague. Whether the one or the other can be asserted about a system depends on what we mean by 'itself'. In many cases, we feel that we know what we mean, and so can decide the question. In other cases, the situation is by no means so clear.

In the case of a living organism, we usually have no difficulty deciding whether the system 'maintains itself'. The organism that maintains its state of life is usually recognized as 'itself' over time. We attribute an identity to a living organism even though it changes radically, say, in growing from the newborn state to maturity. In some cases, however, we cannot be sure how far the 'identity' of an organism extends. An amoeba divides in two. Has it lost its 'identity'? Is the identity preserved in one of the daughter cells? In both? At the other extreme, no one seriously doubts that a man preserves his identity even as millions of his cells leave his body, one of which unites with another cell eventually to become another human being. Yet, the two processes, the procreation of the amoeba and the procreation of man, have a great deal in common.

The two examples just cited are extreme, but intermediate cases exist, such as reproduction by budding. Other examples readily come to mind. Is the butterfly the 'same' animal as the caterpillar from which it came, or did the caterpillar 'die' to become re-born as the butterfly? These cases may be troublesome to categorize but, in general, interest in problems of this sort may be limited to philosophers who ponder on the nature of identity. Such problems become of paramount importance when the identities involved are ourselves or beings with which we identify, even though some of the latter have little or no resemblance to 'us'. As an instance, if we are fond of a city, we may feel that it loses its identity when its character changes. Yet, on maps New York is still New York. Did Rome ever 'fall'? The city never ceased to exist, but hardly anyone would maintain that modern Rome is the 'same' as the city of the Caesars. Just what do people mean when they sing 'There'll always be an England'?

Indeed, a great portion of all our activities, both conscious and unconscious (e.g., physiological processes of which we are unaware), seem to be directed toward maintaining ourselves as living systems endowed with identities. As we project the inner experience of such maintenance processes of which we are aware to other living beings, we attribute to them similar 'goals'. Moreover, we note that these goals are often at cross purposes. The lion chases the antelope, apparently in an attempt to maintain *itself* as an integrated living system. The antelope probably sees the situation differently. Presumably, it does not occur to the antelope to see its own loss of identity as enhancing the continued identity of the lion, or to adopt a more cosmic view of the matter from which it appears that the proteins presently constituting its living cells will eventually be transmitted in a chain of chemical reactions into the proteins within the lion's living cells. The antelope seems to 'want' to remain an antelope, not become part of a lion, and behaves accordingly, attempting to escape from the lion.

We feel that the antelope and the lion are in 'conflict'. The feeling arises naturally, because we can imagine ourselves in either's situation. We too would run if we were pursued by a lion. And we too pursue animals to kill them for food, or at least our ancestors did, and those habits still persist among some of us. At any rate, we have an immediate internal appreciation of 'conflict', all of us having been in conflict situations. Using an ancient form of cognition, we project this appreciation onto phenomena we observe.

In some cases, the phenomena seem to resemble our own internal knowledge of conflict so vividly that we do not even raise the question of whether the projection is appropriate. Two bucks fight 'for' the posses- sion of a female. If we have experienced sexual jealousy, we feel we under- stand what we observe. To the positivists or the behaviorists among us, the quotation marks around 'for' are essential. All we are reasonably sure of is that if one of the bucks leaves the scene the other will take possession of the female. The word 'for', however, implies more. It reflects our readiness to place ourselves in the position of a buck and to imagine that he feels somewhat as we do in situations that we interpret as analogous. Of the buck's feelings we have, of course, no knowledge. Nor can we obtain *this* sort of knowledge.

Cognition by projection, analogy, and extrapolation is a deeply in- grained habit. Unhampered by the discipline of critical analysis, projec- tion knows no constraints. Primitive man readily ascribed goals, purposes, and desires to inanimate objects and forces of nature, as well as to animals. Fire is extinguished by water; therefore, fire and water must be 'in conflict'. Storms and earthquakes destroyed man's dwellings; hail killed his crops; plagues decimated his flocks. These were all interpreted as hostile acts perpetrated against him.

Such projections were not dissipated in 'rational' philosophy. Heracli- tus, the philosopher who emphasized the lack of permanence in nature, epitomized the principle of constant change in the aphorism, 'War is the father of all things.' That is to say, change, he thought, is the result of conflict. Twenty-four centuries later, Hegel pictured history as a succes- sion of conflicts between abstract opposites (thesis and antithesis), each conflict culminating in a synthesis (union of opposites) and the start of a new cycle. Marx followed Hegel's cue but, re-interpreting Hegel's dia- lectics 'materialistically', saw history as a succession of conflicts between social classes, each phase being a struggle of the oppressed against the oppressors. In fact, the idea of conflict pervades practically all human thought. It is a principal theme in myth, religion, philosophy, and literature. Luce and Raiffa, in the opening sentence of their book *Games and Decisions* (1957), surmise that more has been written on conflict than on any other subject, with the possible exceptions of God and love.

In science, however, conflict is not a dominant theme, except where conflict is specifically the object of investigation or analysis. It is instructive to see why this is so. Science is, among other things, an effort to understand the world *without* projecting onto it man's fears, appetites, or aspirations. The most distinguishing feature of scientific cognition is the separation of the idea of causality from the internal feelings of volition. The linkage of temporarily contiguous events is inherent both in our recognition of causality and in our internal feelings of volition. In prescientific thought, the distinction between the two is blurred. Our own acts seem to us to occur because we have willed them. We experience volition, then we act. In our conception of causality, we ascribe the occurrence of an event to the occurrence of another event, neither being necessarily a consequence of someone's volition. Appreciation of volition, however, precedes the concept of objective causality. Before the infant learns to link successive external events, he becomes aware of the connection between his intents and the resulting bodily movements. Science became possible only when man turned his attention *outside* of himself and learned to associate sequential events not in any way connected with his internal feelings or intents.

This objectivization (de-personalization) of the external world manifested itself most emphatically in modern physics. No longer did the universe appear as a manifestation of a Will or a fulfillment of a purpose. Instead, the universe appeared as a clock that ran by virtue of the arrangement of its parts, apparently destined to run forever without supervision.

The extension of this mechanical point of view to explanations of life processes met with considerably more difficulty. There were, to be sure, many incursions. Physiology, for example, became progressively more oriented toward seeking explanations of processes within living organisms in terms of known physical and chemical laws instead of in terms of the purposes they served. Nevertheless, the *function* served by an organ or a process remained central in the physiologist's inquiry, not only because of the persistence of habits of thought but also because the notion of function as 'the purpose served' continued to be a powerful unifying notion in physiological theory. Physiological processes fitted admirably into a 'purposeful' pattern.

The exquisite complexity of living behavior was another difficulty in the way of extending the mechanical point of view to physiology. Behavior seemed all too obviously to be guided by goals and purposes. Accordingly, vitalists persisted with considerable tenacity in their view that living systems were governed by principles different from those governing the behavior of inert matter. The dominant purpose attributed to the living organism by vitalists was that of maintaining itself alive. By extension, an analogous purpose was attributed to an entire species. Species were thought to adapt to their environment *in order* to insure continued existence in progeny. Consequently, the idea of conflict remained in biology long after it was banished as irrelevant from the physical sciences. The idea lives on in the popular conception of the 'struggle for existence'.

Ironically, this notion, intimately linked to the notion of natural selection, appears in the light of that theory to be merely a metaphor. For the theory of natural selection effectively *eliminates* purpose from biological evolution in quite the same way as celestial mechanics eliminated purpose from cosmic events. The theory of purposeful evolution is a pre-Darwinian theory. It is most closely associated with the ideas of Lamarck,[1] who pictured the adaptation of organisms to environment as an *active* process. Lamarck supposed that living things adapted to their environment by 'exercising' appropriate organs. For instance, the antelope was thought to have evolved into a swiftly running animal by virtue of the fact that for many generations antelopes exercised their leg muscles by running away from beasts of prey. Likewise, the giraffe presumably got his long neck by stretching for leaves on trees generation after generation.

How Lamarck's theory would apply to the evolution of plants is not clear. There is no evidence that plants 'exercise' any of their parts; with few exceptions plants are incapable of self-generated motion. However, for a philosopher, who readily resorts to abstract generalizations in formulating 'principles', Lamarck poses no difficulty. One can invoke a 'life force' as the principle that guides all living things along the paths of evolution: embryos in their development, individuals in their pursuits, etc. Philosophers are not required to cite *independent* evidence for the existence of principles postulated by them. It usually suffices to accept a principle if it helps one to imagine that by accepting it one has a better understanding of what is going on.

The scientist tends to distrust explanatory principles for which the only evidence is the phenomena to be explained in the first place. Accordingly, if a scientist can explain a phenomenon without invoking a principle specially tailored to explain it, he does so, guided by the principle of parsimony. Darwin's most important achievement was that his theory of natural selection made 'life force' or any analogous teleological principle superfluous in accounting for the adaptation of species to their environment.

The theory of natural selection assumes, first of all, that although, by and large, members of the same species resemble one another (at least more so than members of different species) there are none the less variations among individuals. No special mechanism was postulated to underlie the origin of these variations (such mechanisms were discovered later). Now, some of these variations have greater survival value than others. That is to say, the individuals characterized by 'favorable' variations will have a better chance to survive longer and so to have more progeny than individuals with handicapping variations, who may not even survive long enough to have any progeny. For instance, it stands to reason that antelopes with superior equipment for running will escape in larger numbers from pursuing lions than will slow-running antelopes. On the other hand, the swifter and stronger lions will be more successful in hunting, will provide more food for their cubs, and so will have more progeny growing up to procreation age.

The next assumption is that the variations among individuals are transmitted by heredity to the progeny. There is evidence that Darwin, at least at one time, accepted Lamarck's belief that variations acquired during the lifetime of the individual, as well as accidental variations present at birth, can be transmitted by heredity. This is now known not to be the case. Only some variations are inherited, and acquired characteristics, such as muscles enlarged by exercise, are not among them. However, the theory of natural selection does not stand or fall by the validity of inheritance of acquired characteristics. Natural selection works, whatever be the source of the variation, provided only that the variations are inherited.

We know there are two sources of inherited variations. One source is mutations, changes in the hereditary units, called genes, which carry encoded information, a sort of chemical blueprint that guides the development of the organism from its initial state, a fertilized egg. The other source of variation is characteristic of sexual reproduction. Here the organism starts its development from the zygote, a cell that results from the union of two sex cells, each of which contributes one half of the genes to the zygote. Because of prior mutations, the genetic composition of the sex cells of each parent is, in general, different. The genetic composition of the zygote, therefore, depends on which hereditary units happen to combine in the zygote. This is a matter of chance. The assortment of genes in the zygote is analogous to the result of shuffling a deck of cards.

The complex of genes in the organism is called its *genotype*. Variations of genotypes in general manifest themselves as variations of *phenotypes*, defined by the grossly observed characteristics of organisms, including physiological processes and biologically determined behavior patterns. Natural selection acts on the phenotypes: the better adapted ones survive longer and so tend to have more progeny. Even if the survival advantage is ever so slight, the consequent somewhat higher ratio of progeny in each generation soon becomes substantial, so that the better adapted phenotypes (and hence the genotypes associated with them) replace the poorly adapted.

This is what the 'struggle for existence' amounts to in nature. Actual struggles, as we understand the term (combats etc.), are not essential components of the 'struggle for existence'. To be sure, 'competition' for food, sunlight, water, etc., where there is not enough for all, does go on in the sense that the better adapted individuals or species get larger shares and so 'crowd out' the poorly adapted in a given environment. We may observe, for instance, that weeds 'choke' the grass on our lawns. But to ascribe 'aggressiveness' to the weeds on that account is to project our own feelings on beings totally incapable of harboring them. If weeds replace grass, this is a consequence of their being better adapted to the particular environment. They don't fight the grass; they just grow faster. If we sprinkle weed-killers on the lawn, we change the nature of the environment, making it less favorable for the weeds.

At times we observe 'cooperation' among organisms. Again, it is not justifiable to ascribe any intent or affect to organisms on that account, at least not to 'cooperating' organisms of different species. The flower nurtures the insect feeding on its nectar. At the same time, the insect helps the plant procreate by carrying pollen from a 'male' flower to a 'female'. Although each fulfills survival needs of the other, as it were, this mutual assistance is no more a manifestation of good will than competition is a manifestation of ill will. The sensorium and the behavior pattern of the insect attracted to the flower are evidence of natural selection that has resulted in the adaptation of the insect to its environment, of which the flower is part. The flower's bright colors and fragrance attract the insect and the nutrients of its nectar help to procreate the insect species. These, too, are evidence of natural selection that has resulted in the adaptation of the plant to its environment, of which the insect is part. Here natural selection acted not just on one species but on a *system* that includes the insect and the plant. Accordingly, the process that is commonly interpreted as a 'struggle for existence' has produced 'cooperation'. There is no contradiction here, and there is no need to invoke Hegelian dialectics to explain the result as something turning into its opposite. The 'contradiction' is only in our projection onto nature of our own concepts and affects. Whether one sees 'cooperation' or 'competition' depends on what one has singled out as a 'system' and what as 'environment'. The system 'insect' seems to be in cooperation with the system 'plant'. But taken as a whole, the system 'insect–plant' may have outcompeted other such systems less well integrated, that is, not so efficiently adapted to each other. In short, natural selection operates on systems, and these may comprise single organisms, or populations of similar organisms (species), or complex populations of quite different organisms – called eco-systems.

An eco-system is the totality of life in some region. The boundaries of such a region are sometimes clearly delineated, an enclosed body of water, for instance. Sometimes it is hard to say what the boundaries should be, as when one type of landscape passes gradually into another. In principle, the boundaries of a system separating it from its environment are a matter of the observer's choice. The portion of the world so delineated is populated by a vast variety of organisms that may range in size from microscopic to huge (e.g., tall trees). An eco-system will, in general, comprise representatives of many phyla of both plant and animal kingdoms. Except for plants, all of these organisms feed predominantly on living matter or matter that was once alive. In other words, the denizens of an eco-system feed on each other. Predation is, in general, not reciprocal. If species A eats species B, species B, as a rule, does not feed on species A. Nevertheless, if we trace the 'food chain' in the eco-system, we shall find cycles. Some animals feed on plants and, in turn, are eaten by other animals. The latter may be eaten by still others, etc. The corpses or excrements of animals, in turn, may act as fertilizers for the soil and so provide nourishment for plants. There is also the well known respiratory exchange between plants and animals: plants extract carbon dioxide from the air and, with the aid of chlorophyll and sunlight, manufacture sugars from the carbon, releasing the oxygen. Animals breathe oxygen and release carbon dioxide into the atmosphere.

An eco-system of this sort may persist for a long time. That is to say, the rates of transformations of all sorts will just balance each other. And even though changes go on constantly, a system may present the same appearance. For example, a state of balance may exist between a population of predators and their prey, both members of an eco-system. If the prey population increases, more food is available to the predators. Consequently, the predator population increases. Then, as the predators become more numerous, they eat more of the prey, so that the prey population decreases; this puts constraints on the predator population.[2]

The complex processes going on within an eco-system may seem to us to be manifestations of 'competition' or 'struggle for existence' or 'co-operation' or, perhaps, all of these simultaneously. The predators hunting prey may be perceived as an instance of the 'struggle for existence' ('nature red in tooth and claw'). The same process may as readily be perceived as an exercise in mutual population control. That, without prey, the predators would starve is clear; so might the prey, if, unchecked by the predators, they multiplied to the point of permanently depleting their own food supply.

In summary, cooperation and competition (along with their moral and affective connotations) are terms pertaining to human affairs. In the context of the non-human world, these words are at best metaphors, and their connotations shed no light on what is actually happening. A living system, whether a cell, an organ, an organism, a species, or an eco-system, neither competes nor cooperates. It simply exists, immersed in its environment with which it interacts. The question of scientific interest is, under what conditions does a system remain 'itself', given an explicit criterion for recognizing the identity of the system? Admittedly, the question has also a philosophical component: what are acceptable criteria of identity?

CHAPTER 2

Systems in Steady State

One unambiguous criterion of 'identity' of a system can be stated. A system certainly remains 'itself' if it persists in a *steady state*, but this criterion is too strict, as we shall see. Nevertheless, 'steady state' is a concept of prime importance in any discussion of systems in environments. Therefore, it will be examined in some detail.

Having said only that a system is some portion of the world singled out for attention as an object of interest, then, of course, if just anything at all attracted our interest, *any* portion of the world, whether geographically contiguous or not, whether its parts 'hang together' or not, could be called a system. For instance, if for some reason I am interested in all the typewriters in the world and all the kangaroos, I could call the totality of typewriters and kangaroos a system. However, it is difficult to conceive a situation outside of textbooks on logic or set theory in which the set comprising typewriters and kangaroos would be of substantive interest. The example is offered not facetiously but to illustrate the generality of the concept 'set'. Literally, any collection is a set if we can decide unambiguously whether a given thing belongs or does not belong to that collection. Every definition of system must involve a set, but not every set deserves to be called a system. And so, we would exclude the set 'typewriters and kangaroos' from the class of things called systems, not on logical grounds but on practical ones: we simply cannot think of anything interesting to say about this set.

In contrast, the set comprising all typewriters and all typists can with some justification be called a system, at least a class of systems, each comprising a typewriter and a typist who operates it. The justification is not far to seek. The typist and the typewriter interact. What happens to the one affects the other. Moreover, if we are interested in not just a particular typewriter-typist system but in all of them, we can speak of the typewriter-typist system as an *abstracted* system. Each concrete pair is a realization of the abstracted system, and the abstracted system itself is a special instance of a still more abstract class called a *man-machine system*.

Portions of the world attract our attention if they comprise such a set of interdependent parts. The interdependence of the parts of a system is manifested in their *interaction*. The most obvious kind of interdependence is one that assures the spatial contiguity of some portion of the world, for it is spatial contiguity that enables us to perceive objects and entitles objects to be named. All human languages contain names of objects. A tree, a typewriter, a kangaroo is an 'object' because it is sharply delineated from the surrounding space, whether it stays put like a tree or a typewriter or hops about like a kangaroo. Examination of these objects will reveal that their spatial continuity is insured by cohesive forces, binding their parts together. This spatial contiguity and relative invariance in size and shape define objects' identities.

There are other portions of the world that maintain a spatial contiguity without possessing forces of cohesion among their parts. A fountain presents itself to our eyes as an 'object', being delineated in space and having a definite shape. Yet, it is not a rigid object held together by cohesive forces. Its shape is determined by the trajectories of the streams of water that make up the fountain. But, although not held together by cohesive or elastic forces, the fountain maintains its shape against disturbances. A gust of wind may temporarily distort the shape of the fountain, but after the gust has spent itself the shape is restored.

The fountain is an example of a system in a *steady state*. The material constituents of the system are constantly changing. A drop of water is part of the fountain for only a few seconds, while it traverses its trajectory. In a few moments all the drops have been replaced by other drops. Yet, the fountain gives the impression of 'something' with a relatively permanent existence.

A flame presents a similar picture. A flame is not an object like a typewriter. It is a system of chemical reactions, in which released energy makes minute particles (say, of carbon) incandescent. The region in which the energy is sufficient to produce incandescence is fairly well delineated. Thus, the flame has a shape, which, like that of a fountain, resists temporary, not-too-strong distortions and so gives the impression of an object – another example of a system in a steady state.

On closer examination we find that living systems, although they are more 'object-like' than fountains and flames, nevertheless resemble them because they too are in a state of flux. The material particles of which living things are composed are being constantly replaced. Yet, we would say that these systems maintain their identity. Not only do they retain approximately the same shape and size but also certain recognizable patterns of behavior, certain definite ways of reacting to events in the environment. The same can be said of eco-systems. The individual organisms in them die and disintegrate, being replaced by other organisms of the same kind. As a consequence, the eco-system exhibits over a period of time the same recognizable characteristics. It maintains a more or less constant, steady state.

To define 'steady state' more exactly, we must define the state of a system. It turns out that the state of a system can sometimes be defined as a set of numbers. If this can be done, then the system can be said to be in a steady state if these numbers remain constant.

Consider a physical or chemical process going on in some circumscribed portion of space, say, within an organism. At a given time, the various substances of which the organism is composed are there in various concentrations. These concentrations will be, in general, different in various parts of the organism. We can, however, focus our attention on a small region, say, a portion of the blood stream, where concentrations of substances dissolved in the blood will have certain numerical values. This region will also be characterized by certain physical quantities, say, temperature. The region in question is not isolated; it receives inputs from its 'environment', e.g., the inflow of blood and heat from neighboring regions; it also produces outputs to the surrounding regions. At a given moment, the totality of the quantities of interest (concentrations of salts or sugars in the blood stream, the temperature, etc.) has a certain magnitude. The totality of these magnitudes (a set of numbers) defines the state of the system at that moment. If these quantities remain constant, the system is said to be in a steady state.

Returning to the eco-system, we see that its state also can be characterized by a set of quantities depicting, say, the proportions of various organisms in it. The quantities may refer also to the physical characteristics of the system: the temperature, the amount of precipitation, the chemical composition of the soil, etc. In this context, the concept of steady state must be somewhat generalized. For example, we may ignore the seasonal variations of temperature, precipitation, etc., and say that the system is in a steady state if the yearly averages of these quantities remain constant. Likewise, population concentrations may undergo fluctuations. However, as long as these fluctuations are cyclic, or cluster around their average values, we can say the system is in a steady state. The same applies to the individual organism.

From the foregoing it should be clear that 'steady state' is a more important system property than the material identity of its constituents. This is so because a steady state is maintained by the interaction of the system with its environment, and it is these interactions that make the existence and the fate of a system interesting and instructive. A system completely isolated from its environment will also eventually attain a steady state, in the sense that the quantities characterizing it will reach constant values. In fact, the Second Law of Thermodynamics states that eventually these quantities will be uniformly distributed throughout the isolated region, creating an equilibrium. An example is a mixture of gases in a container with boundaries impenetrable to both matter and energy. Eventually the concentration of each gas will be the same throughout the container, and so will the temperature. Such a system will no longer be differentiated in its parts and so nothing will ever 'happen' in it. We know also that a living organism isolated from its environment will die and so will cease to be interesting as an organism. A steady state differs from an equilibrium of an isolated system in that *non-equilibrium gradients* can be maintained in it – that is, *differences* in concentrations, electric potentials, pressures, temperatures, etc. If the system were isolated from its environment and thereby achieved a thermodynamic and chemical uniformity, these differences would disappear. It is precisely the *non*-uniformity within a system, its *structure*, that defines a system or a class of systems as distinctly organized entities (as the name 'system' implies) and thereby makes them interesting objects of study. Since a system in a steady state (or near-steady state) is most clearly identified as 'itself', the question naturally arises how the steady state is maintained in the system. This question has a bearing on how the system maintains its identity.

A system persists in a steady state if it is so organized that a departure from that state gives rise to 'forces' that will tend to bring the system back to the original state. 'Forces' is put in quotation marks because the word is used here in its loose sense; not necessarily in the strict sense of physical force. Sometimes, of course, the restoring 'force' is an actual physical force. Consider a marble resting at the bottom of a bowl. It is at rest because the forces acting on it add up to zero. The downward force of gravity is exactly balanced by the upward force of the surface at the bottom of the bowl. Suppose a disturbance moves the marble away from this equilibrium position. Now the forces are not balanced. Gravity is still acting downward, but the surface of the bowl now exerts a force that is not exactly upward. The force acting on the marble is now the resultant of these two forces, which is not zero (because the forces are not equal and oppositely directed). The resultant propels the marble toward the bottom of the bowl. The marble acquires a momentum and overshoots the equilibrium position at the bottom, whereupon the resultant force acts in the opposite direction. If there were no friction, the marble would oscillate forever, but because of friction its momentum keeps decreasing; eventually the marble comes to rest again at the bottom.

Consider now a chemical reaction in which a substance is produced at a constant rate and also disintegrates, the rate of disintegration, however, being proportional to the concentration of the substance. If the concentration is small, so is the rate of disintegration. Then the rate of production will exceed the rate of disintegration. Consequently, the concentration of the substance will keep increasing. If we add a large amount of the substance to the system, the concentration will become large, and the rate of disintegration will exceed the rate of production. In this condition, the concentration will decrease. If we remove a substantial amount of the substance, the rate of production will exceed the rate of disintegration, and the concentration will increase. There is, however, a level of concentration at which the rate of production exactly balances the rate of disintegration. Undisturbed, the system will persist in the steady state characterized by that critical level of concentration. Moreover, because the level of concentration must decrease if it rises above the steady state level and must increase if it falls below, we see that the system will 'resist disturbances'.

Such disturbance-resisting arrangements are said to operate on the principle of *homeostasis*.

Many physiological steady states – the concentrations of oxygen and of other substances in the blood, for instance – are maintained by homeostatic mechanisms more complex but in principle similar to the chemical one described. Such steady-state-maintaining systems give the impression of being guided by a 'goal', namely to return to their 'proper' steady state whenever they are disturbed. The discovery of homeostatic mechanisms has made such teleological explanations unnecessary in physiology just as teleological explanations of evolution were made unnecessary by the discovery of the principle of natural selection. Thereby the boundary between living and non-living systems appeared less sharp than it was once thought to be. It is now known that no special assumptions of a 'life force' or of 'goal-directedness' are necessary to account for at least some aspects of life, namely the maintenance of steady states, which is one of the fundamental principles of the life process.

One should not conclude, of course, just because the maintenance of a steady state was explained in a simple case without reference to goal-directedness, that the 'nature of life' has been thereby explained. Life-maintaining processes are enormously complex and only a minute portion of them are understood in terms of known natural laws. There is, however, an interesting lesson to be drawn from our illustration, coupled with what we know about natural selection. We can more properly say that a system is living because it includes steady-state-maintaining mechanisms than that it maintains steady state mechanisms because it is a living system. To put it another way, the answer to the question, why living systems maintain steady states, is that if they did not maintain steady states they would not be living systems and so would not be distinguishable as such.

This point of view can be extended to systems other than organisms, which can with some justification be called 'living'. A city continues to 'live' only if it possesses mechanisms for maintaining relatively steady states. Food must be delivered to it at a rate within certain limits, enough to forestall starvation but not so much that the storage capacity is exceeded. Sewage and garbage must be removed. Traffic must keep flowing, utilities must be maintained, etc. All these are 'life processes' of a city. Their serious and prolonged disruption can cause the 'death' of the city in a way quite similar to the death of an organism.

Clearly, the homeostatic processes that keep the city 'alive' are not merely manifestations of simple physical or chemical laws. Still, the difference between a steady-state-maintaining city and a steady-state-maintaining chemical reaction is only a difference in the degree of complexity. In what follows we shall examine more closely homeostatic mechanisms of increasing orders of complexity.

CHAPTER 3

From Tropism to Behavior

Consider once again the simplest steady-state-maintaining system described in the previous chapter. A substance is produced inside the boundary that separates the system from the environment. Production goes on at a constant rate. The substance also disintegrates at a rate proportional to its own concentration. The 'goal' of the system is to maintain a certain level of concentration of the substance. The system is able to do this by virtue of the relation between the rate of production and the rate of disintegration of the substance. In that description, however, we have not told the whole story. The fact is that a substance cannot disintegrate into 'nothing'. The law of conservation of matter requires that, in disintegrating, the substance turns into something else. Call this something else a waste product. The waste product must be carried away or else it will accumulate inside the system (which we shall now call an organism) and prevent it from maintaining the proper steady state.

If the boundaries of the organism are permeable to the waste product, the latter will diffuse to the outside, provided the concentration in the immediate vicinity is lower than the concentration inside. This might be so initially. But as the waste product continues to diffuse, it may accumulate in the vicinity until the concentration there equals that inside. Then the diffusion can no longer take place and the organism itself will become clogged with the waste product. Therefore, we must make additional assumptions in order to keep our system 'viable'. We could assume that the organism is immersed in a current that carries away the waste products. Or we could assume that the organism is endowed with a *tropism*. A tropism is a tendency to move along a gradient. A gradient involves asymmetric conditions on two sides of the organism. Such an asymmetry can give rise to a force that will propel the organism along the gradient. In particular, if the tropism propels the organism toward regions where the concentration of waste product is lower, its problem of waste removal will be solved. Such an organism will keep 'polluting the environment', but as long as there is enough unpolluted environment, it can go on living.

We have seen that species adapt to their environment in the course of evolution. This type of adaptation is extremely slow and is effective only if changes in the environment occur at comparably slow rates. Tropisms, on the other hand, enable *individual* organisms (not just the species) to adapt to changes in their environment even if these changes are comparatively rapid. Plants as well as primitive animals exhibit tropisms, the sunflower being a well known example. To a naive observer, the 'behavior' of the sunflower may seem goal-directed or voluntaristic. Actually, however, the motion is due to the fact that a gradient in the intensity of light produces a torque that turns the sunflower toward the sun.

Many insects exhibit tropisms: for instance, toward or away from light, along or against a gradient of temperature or the gravitational field, etc. The 'behavior' resulting from a tropism is motion. Natural selection insures that the tropisms selected for are of survival value to the organism; for instance, 'driving' the organisms along chemical gradients (e.g., scents) to regions of abundant food or to the presence of a mate. However, a tropism can also be fatal, as in the classical example of the moth and the flame. The light tropism of a moth operates by acting differentially on the rates of flapping of wings so that unequal rates on the two sides turn the moth toward the light. If the source of the light is a flame, the moth flies into it. The moth has no 'suicidal' intention; it simply can't help flying toward the flame. Tropisms act mechanically.

Since, as in the case of the moth, some tropisms manifest themselves as 'behavior', it will serve the purpose of our discussion to distinguish behavior from simple tropisms. A tropism involves some *physical gradient in the environment*, so that tropic motion is no different from the motion of water downhill or of an iron filing in a magnetic field.

Behavior, distinguished from tropism, involves an act of 'all-or-none' recognition. Gull fledglings exhibit *behavior* when they open their mouths wide in the presence of a parent. The recognition of something that identifies a stimulus as 'parent' triggers the behavior pattern, in this case a very simple one – opening the beak. To serve as a trigger, the stimulus must be *recognized*, that is, differentiated from all other stimuli.

Such all-or-none differentiation depends on the presence or absence of some crucial distinguishing feature of the stimulus. It has been found, for example, that fledglings' response (open mouth) can be triggered by a white object with a red tip and not by other objects. In nature, the only white object with a red tip that is likely to make its appearance at the gull nest is a parent's beak. The fact (established experimentally) that any other white object with a red top will evoke the same response pinpoints the distinguishing feature of the effective stimulus.[1]

The 'act of eating' is any behavior pattern that will result in food being put inside the eating organism. For the fledgling, the act of eating is opening the mouth in the presence of a white object with a red tip. In the natural state, the object 'means' that a parent is present. Moreover, for the parent the sight of the open beak is a stimulus for dropping food into it.

Complex behavior patterns can in principle be explained as sequentially triggered links in a chain of simple patterns. In proper season, birds start building nests. Projecting our own feelings in a similar situation, we attribute foresight to the birds. It seems to us that they build nests 'in order' to lay eggs in a safe place, 'in order' to hatch eggs, 'in order' to perpetuate the species. There is, however, an alternative explanation, independent of the attributed foresight. The 'proper' season is characterized by a complex of stimuli – temperature, duration of daylight, possibly the disappearance of snow, etc. – all of which constitute stimuli. The stimuli trigger a pattern of behavior that we recognize as 'nest building'. This pattern itself consists of many steps, such that the completion of one step stimulates the next. The presence of the nest triggers the laying of eggs; the presence of the eggs in the nest triggers brooding, and so on.

The concept of 'triggering' is crucial for understanding a sequence of behavior patterns. To trigger a process means to initiate it with the expectation that, once initiated, the process proceeds of its own accord. Thus, when a trigger of a gun is pressed, a process is initiated that is driven by its own dynamics which had been *pre-arranged*. The spark produced by the stroke of the hammer ignites the power in the cartridge, the explosion propels the bullet, the barrel guides the bullet along the direction of the aim.

An organism with a repertoire of behavior patterns can be conceived as passing from one state to another, each state corresponding to one of the patterns, the passage being triggered by appropriate stimuli. Each pattern is analogous to a steady state of a system.

So far we have associated the 'identity' of a system with the persistence of a steady state. However, a system can also remain 'itself' while it passes from one steady state to another, especially if the transitions are reversible. Consider a marble on a surface where several 'valleys' are separated by ridges. Initially the marble is at rest in one of the valleys. In case of small disturbances, not sufficient to push the marble over a ridge, equilibrium will be restored and so the marble will eventually come to rest in the same valley. However, if the disturbance is sufficiently large to push the marble over a ridge, then when it comes to rest it will be in a different valley. The system 'marble on a landscape' has passed from one equilibrium state to another.

Now consider organisms whose physiological mechanisms maintain a steady concentration of sugar in the blood stream. Small fluctuations will be corrected by the homeostatic mechanism, provided deficiencies can be replenished from some source inside the organism. When the source is depleted, the level of blood sugar sinks. If it sinks below some critical level, certain behavior patterns are triggered. The organism passes from, say, a resting state to a 'food seeking state', then to an 'eating state', until the proper blood sugar level is restored. The whole cycle, then, is analogous to homeostasis. It serves to re-establish a steady state but does so in virtue of a sequence of pre-arranged events set off by triggering mechanisms and in virtue of the organization of the nervous system which keeps each activity 'going' until the next one is triggered. Like simple homeostasis, the complex homeostasis of behavioral chains makes teleological explanations of life-maintaining activities unnecessary. There is no need to suppose that the bird carries around in its 'mind' an image of future fledglings, the way an expectant mother pictures her future baby. There is even less need to suppose that the bird is 'concerned' with the survival of its species as we are concerned with the survival of our own, or, for that matter, as some of us are concerned with the survival of some *bird* species and guide our actions accordingly.

It might seem that I have gone to great lengths in 'debunking' goal-directedness, purpose, and providence from nature. The reason for doing so is not to show that 'purpose does not exist' in nature, even less to reserve the faculty of prescience and providence to ourselves. The arguments were derived from epistemological considerations. What is important to establish here is that whether or not 'purpose' is seen to govern a chain of events depends, not on the events themselves, but on how we view them. When we view our own actions 'from the inside' they may seem purposeful to us, that is, guided by a future envisaged goal. When we attribute similar feelings to other living beings (or even to non-living ones), purpose seems to govern their behavior also. But if we examine a chain of events, each a consequence of the preceding, or even if we can imagine such a chain, explanations in terms of goals and purposes no longer seem necessary. In fact, explanations dispensing with purpose have frequently been found for events originally supposed to be governed by wills and purposes. Thus, it may serve us well to seek such 'causal chain' explanations for our own actions, specifically actions involving conflict. Frequently this shift of point of view will enable us to understand conflict and its relation to environment in a new, enlightening way.

To return to our discussion of living systems and their repertoire of (generalized) homeostatic mechanisms, the significant difference between tropisms and behavior is that genuine behavior, governed by recognition – especially recognition of configurations and patterns of events – provides the organism with many more and far-reaching means of maintaining its identity (keeping alive) than do tropisms. A tropism is only a 'passive' adjustment to the environment, say, going to where the environment is physically more 'comfortable'. Genuine behavior involves as a rule a sequence of rather complex acts, in particular, acts producing a change in the environment. To illustrate, a tropism away from light may put an insect in an environment where it is less likely to be seen by a predator. However, the burrowing of a hole *creates* a protective environment where there was none before. Burrowing, nest building, web spinning, etc., are all forms of behavior that *make* changes in the environment – changes conducive to keeping the organism alive.

To this point we have identified one line of evolutionary change involving the following levels of homeostatic mechanisms for maintaining the 'identity' of living systems.

1. On the most primitive level, the mechanisms are confined to the permanent structures of an organism. These structures establish and insure gradients within the organism, maintained at a steady state as long as the environment remains constant. Example: a single cell suspended in a medium with a constant supply of nutrients from which the cell's waste products are removed. Many cells in living organisms are in just such conditions. They 'cannot do anything about their environment' and so are entirely dependent on it.

2. On the next level are organisms with tropisms. They usually possess some mechanism of locomotion that enables them to move into more favorable locations of the environment. Examples: single-celled animals, such as amoebas, paramecia, etc.

3. Animals with sufficiently developed nervous systems can recognize *patterns* of events in an all-or-none fashion to which they respond with 'acts' (patterns of responses) like eating, escaping, catching prey, mating, etc. The acts serve to re-establish the steady state in the organism and also in the species, as in replenishment by births of population removed by death.

4. On the next level are animals capable of behavior that results in more or less permanent changes in the environment, making it more favorable for survival. Examples: nest weaving (birds), web spinning (spiders), dam building (beavers), food storing (squirrels). Some ants actually engage in a sort of agriculture.

In principle, natural selection can account for this line of evolutionary development. The qualification 'in principle' is necessary, since it is at times very difficult to imagine how natural selection might have produced the exceedingly complex behavior patterns of animals. This very complexity is sometimes invoked in arguments against the natural selection theory of evolution. Some critics have even undertaken calculations purporting to show that the probability of some complex mechanisms arising 'by chance' is vanishingly small. While it remains difficult to explain the appearance of such mechanisms 'by trial and error', as it were the rejection of natural selection by arguments based on probability calculations is not justified. Such arguments make a tacit assumption that complex mechanisms appear all at once. Actually, they evolve quite gradually, each step being a minute 'improvement' on what has already been established. Thus, the exceedingly complex mechanisms of vision in birds, mammals, and some molluscs, involving schemes of pattern recognition, might well have evolved through progressive refinement from initially quite primitive sensitivity to light differences.

Evidence of gradual evolution of behavior patterns is found in the traces sometimes left by these patterns. For instance, the termite hill is a material trace left by the behavior of termites. Examination of fossil termite hills reveals lines of evolutionary development of these artifacts, quite as clearly as the lines of anatomical evolution evidenced by fossil skeletons.[2] Natural selection does what its name implies: it selects more viable forms, whether of anatomy or physiology, or 'psychology' (that is, neural mechanisms governing behavior patterns), from what already exists.

Our own artifacts go through a similar evolution. The jet passenger plane was not built and could not have been built in 1903. The plane that flew at Kitty Hawk could, and was built, because the internal combustion engine and the propeller already existed. Another important thing that existed was the kite, an illustration of the principle that an inclined plane facing the wind can be supported by the upward component of the force acting on the plane, suggesting the idea of an airplane. The internal combustion engine supplies the torque to the propeller; the rotating propeller supplies the wind for the inclined surface (the wing); the wind provides the lift. The idea does not yet make an airplane, for there are many problems to be solved – those of stability, control, etc. But the idea in a proper environment becomes realizable through trial and error. In this case, the environment consisted of men determined to fly and a cultural climate hospitable to inventions. In this way, men could experiment, that is, produce a whole population of would-be airplanes, on which a principle analogous to natural selection could act. Models that failed were not repeated. Models that *almost* succeeded were retained to be modified and repeated with the modifications. Once a flying model was produced, the invention 'took off' figuratively as well as literally.

An even more exact illustration of how selection 'directs' evolution can be seen in animal breeding. The pedigreed cow that gives several times the volume of milk that her ancestor gave did not appear all at once. She is the product of many generations of selective breeding. Not only physiological characteristics can be selected in breeding. Behavior patterns also can be bred. Hunting dogs are an example. In fact, the dog in general is an example of selective breeding, although the selection may have been 'unconscious' for many thousands of years. The creature that at one time attached itself to man as a source of sustenance (food scraps) may have been allowed to remain in man's vicinity because it gave warning of approaching beasts. Thus, the dog found a 'niche', that is, an environment conducive to survival. Thereafter the survival of the descendants depended on the presence of behavior patterns that man found useful, such as those of a watch dog or of an assistant in hunting. The animals with attractive characteristics were cared for; others were driven off or killed. In this way, the evolution of the dog was 'directed' long before systematic, selective breeding became a practice.

Can we identify selective breeding with natural selection? Yes, if we extend the concept of environment. The presence of man and his behavior can be conceived as the environment of the animal species undergoing selective breeding. The 'desired' characteristics have a survival value for the domestic animal just like any other characteristics that adjust an organism to its environment. Most domestic animals could not survive in a wild state because in the process of their evolution they have become adapted to a specific environment, of which man is a part. Thus, no distinction needs to be made between selection exercised by man and that exercised by 'nature'. Man is after all a part of nature. Even non-domesticated animals have evolved in a way that has made them dependent on man: for example, city pigeons and certain species of body lice that can live only on man.

In the same way, it makes perfect sense to speak of the evolution of machines in an environment that includes man. To be sure, machines do not reproduce in the same way as living organisms, by fission or by union of sex cells, but 'reproduce' they do, in the sense that copies of a machine are constructed by man. Whether copies are constructed, and how many, depends on man, more properly on the interaction between the machine and man. But then, whether or not an organism reproduces also depends on the interaction between the organism and its environment.

One important difference between organic and technological evolution can be pointed out. While changes in the genetic complex of organisms (even of those bred selectively) occur by chance, according to the theory of natural selection, the changes introduced into successive generations of machines appear to be systematic, directed by man. Whether this difference is essential or only apparent will be seen when we examine the other line of evolutionary development – the development of learning capacity.

CHAPTER 4

Learning

By learning is meant a more or less permanent modification of a behavior pattern as a result of experience. We have defined behavior as grossly observed 'acts' of an organism. These primarily characterize animals with well developed nervous systems. We have assumed that these acts occur as responses to recognized configurations of events called stimuli. It can be posited that there exist linkages between stimuli and behavioral acts, supposedly in the channels of the nervous system. Evidence of such channels is provided by the phenomenon of the simple reflex. An electric shock applied to a frog's toe results in a contraction of a leg muscle, which draws the leg away. The chain of events that determine this response can be traced. The shock initiates an excitation in the nerve fibers that terminate in the toe. The excitation propagates along these nerve fibers (called *afferent*) to the spinal cord, where the cell bodies to which the fibers belong are situated. These cell bodies form connections with other cell bodies, from which nerve fibers (called *efferent*) extend to the muscle cells. The excitation passes across the connections (called *synapses*), then along the efferent fibers, finally causing the contraction of the muscle cells and so the withdrawal of the leg. The homeostatic purpose of this arrangement is clear: it protects the frog from noxious stimuli.

Ideally, we might suppose that any behavioral act, described, say, as a pattern of muscle contractions, consists of a sequence of such reflexes, each triggering the next. Thus, behavioral acts can be considered as 'mechanically' determined responses to external stimuli. (There are serious limitations to this model of behavior, but for the moment we shall by-pass them.)

If in the course of an animal's life the linkages between stimuli and responses change, learning is said to have occurred. For instance, if initially the sound of a refrigerator door being opened produced no identifiable response in a dog but eventually brings the dog running into the kitchen, we say the dog has 'learned'. Projecting our own feelings, we say that he has learned to expect to be fed when he hears the sound.

Simple, experimentally controlled changes of responses to stimuli can be produced by so-called *conditioning*. Three kinds of conditioning have been distinguished by psychologists: classical, instrumental, and operant. In classical conditioning, a response is linked to a stimulus (to which it had not previously been linked) if in the experience of the animal the stimulus is followed a sufficient number of times by the stimulus that 'naturally' evokes the response. As an example, if an electric shock is applied to a dog's paw, the paw will be withdrawn. This is the 'natural' (unconditioned) response to the electric shock. Now, if the electric shock is preceded a sufficient number of times by a whistle, the dog will withdraw the paw when the whistle sounds even if no shock follows. This withdrawal of the paw has been conditioned to the whistle. We can say that the dog has learned to withdraw his paw when a whistle sounds.

In instrumental conditioning, the animal is compelled to choose between two or more alternatives, say, between a right and a left turn in a maze. One of these responses is systematically 'rewarded' (say, by food at the end of the turn), the other is 'punished' (or simply not rewarded). In repeated trials an animal is observed to choose the rewarded turn more frequently, and finally, exclusively.

In operant conditioning, the animal is comparatively free. It is desired to have the animal learn a certain act, say, pushing a lever. The experimenter simply waits until the animal accidentally pushes the lever, then rewards the animal.

The interesting feature in operant conditioning is that the animal may be taught to perform quite complicated acts by successively rewarding a *partial* performance of the act to be taught. Suppose the act to be learned is pushing a lever just three times, no more and no less. At first, the experimenter may reward the animal for just approaching the lever. When this act has been learned, the reward is withdrawn until the animal touches the lever (which is now more likely, because the animal spends more time near the lever). Later the animal is rewarded only if the lever is pushed, then only if it is pushed repeatedly. Finally, the rewarded response is narrowed down until it becomes the desired one. B. F. Skinner, who explored this technique of conditioning, succeeded in teaching pigeons 'to play ping pong'. One sees two pigeons stand at opposite ends of the 'ping pong table' and push the balls with their beaks as it comes rolling to them. If a pigeon misses, the ball rolls off into a trough, and the *other* pigeon gets rewarded. It is astonishing to see the pigeons batting the ball back and forth, faithfully simulating the game.[1]

Note the similarity between operant conditioning and natural selection of complex behavior patterns. Had the experimenter waited until the animal performed exactly the required act before rewarding it, he might have to wait a very long time, perhaps longer than the life of the animal or his own. It is extremely unlikely that the complex act would have occurred 'by chance' in a reasonable time. Similarly, if the evolution of a complex behavior pattern depended on a chance mutation establishing the entire pattern, the act might never have appeared in the animal's repertoire. (Recall the 'probability argument' against natural selection discussed in Chapter 3.) In effect, operant conditioning occurs by stages. First some crude approximation to the desired act appears by chance and is rewarded. Then successive, progressively more refined variants of the act are 'selected' until the prescribed act emerges. It is quite likely that in learning complex motor skills, like skiing or playing a musical instrument, we undergo operant conditioning. Initially our motor responses are more or less random. Progressively some of these responses are 'selected for' as the results become more and more 'successful' until we reach the limit of our skill. Also, the entire evolutionary process can be compared to learning by operant conditioning. The system comprising a whole species 'learns' in the sense of tending toward a genetic complex (by trial and error) from which deleterious genes have been eliminated by 'punishment' (non-procreation) and genes contributing to survival have been fixated by 'reward' (procreation).

All three forms of conditioning may occur in the life of an animal and contribute to its repertoire of homeostatic mechanisms. In classical conditioning, the animal may learn to respond to a *sign* of an event, that is, to an event that portends another one that is important to the animal's survival. For instance, an animal may learn to hide at the sound that ordinarily precedes a dangerous situation, or to approach an object if it portends food. (Gulls learn to follow ships, because ships discharge debris containing food.) In instrumental conditioning, an animal may learn to choose among alternatives which at previous times have led to different-ially rewarding (or punishing) situations. ('A burned child dreads fire.') In operant conditioning, an animal may learn complex skills.

All three forms of learning have survival value in that they enable the animal to *change* its behavior pattern in a changing environment. Recall that our primitive cell with its internal homeostatically maintained gradients is at the mercy of its immediate environment. An animal with tropisms can drift until it finds a suitable environment. An animal with complex built-in forms of behavior reacts to *events* in the environment, but always in the same way. This survival mechanism, therefore, still depends on certain constant characteristics of the environment. An animal able to learn adjusts its behavior to a *changing* environment. Its behavior is plastic. While built-in ('instinctive') forms of behavior, reflecting the cumulative result of interaction between an evolving species and its environment, are the result of a very slow process, lasting for hundreds, thousands, or even millions of years, the learned forms of behavior reflect the accumulation of experience within a single animal's lifetime.

It is said that man is the most 'plastic' of animals, least dependent on rigidly established and genetically determined behavior patterns, and that this plasticity is man's specific survival mechanism. This may be true, but it is not the whole truth. There is another form of learning, unique to man, that confers on him an even greater independence from his physical environment. But this form of learning also makes man increasingly dependent on another kind of environment, which is a product of his own activity. This environment is called culture. It is a moot question whether this new and unique kind of dependence en-hances or jeopardizes the long-term survival potential of the human species.

CHAPTER 5

From Signal to Symbol

Learning, we have seen, establishes new linkages between events in the environment and behavior patterns. Thereby the events become stimuli for *learned* behavioral responses. Learning enables an organism to anticipate changes in the environment and so enlarges its repertoire of homeostatic mechanisms. Events that evoke conditioned responses become for the organism *signals*, and thereby acquire 'meaning'. 'Meaning' of this sort is not to be confused with 'meaning' that ordinarily we associate with language. The fundamental differences between the many possible meanings of meaning are worth elucidating.

No two events are ever exactly the same. Likewise, no two instances of the 'same' behavior pattern are really the same. Yet, when we observe that a dog lifts his paw when a whistle sounds, we say that he has been conditioned to 'lift his paw' at the sound of a 'whistle'. In recognizing this phenomenon, we identify all the instances of the whistle sound as a single event and all the liftings of the paw as a single event. Actually, the events differ. One whistle sound may be longer or louder than another. One lift of the paw may involve a slightly different sequence of muscle contraction from another. In our recognition of the two events, these differences are ignored. They appear to be ignored by the dog also. At least so it seems to us when *we* identify the 'lifting of the paw' as the 'same' reaction whenever it occurs, ignoring differences that do not interest us. In the process of conditioning, the dog may learn to distinguish between different whistles so as to lift his paw when just the right kind of whistle sounds. This will happen if various whistles appear differentially (e.g., followed or not followed by a shock) in the conditioning process. The dog may also learn to lift his paw in a peculiar way. This will happen if in operant conditioning the experimenter differentiates between the various ways in which the dog lifts his paw, rewarding only the 'correct' way. This sort of learning involves *discrimination*. But the opposite can also be achieved. The dog may learn to respond to a larger variety of stimuli and with a larger variety of responses. This feature of learning is called *generalization*. That is to say, we call it generalization by analogy with a highly abstract *logical* process to which we give the same name. Initially some 'generalization' is already present in the conditioned response, because, as remarked above, variations in the events are unavoidable: no two can be exactly alike. We can, however, ask to what extent the dog 'himself' generalizes. Suppose, for example, that in the conditioning procedure we are careful to keep the signals as nearly similar as possible by keeping the duration and the loudness of the whistle nearly constant. Then, after the dog has learned to respond to the whistle, we change the stimulus. Will he still respond in the same way if the duration is considerably longer or considerably shorter? If the pitch of the whistle tone changes? If the whistle is replaced by a buzzer? If the whistle is replaced by a light signal? The range of stimuli that will still produce the conditioned response (assigned by the experimenter) is a measure we assign to the dog's ability to generalize.

By and large, an animal's ability to generalize a signal seems to be limited by the physical similarity of the events that elicit a similar response. Having learned to respond to a particular whistle, the dog may still respond to different whistles, perhaps to buzzers, but not generally to stimuli that are physically quite different. This dependence of the stimulus on its *physical* features in evoking a learned response characterizes it as a *signal* and distinguishes it from a *symbol*. The 'meanings' of symbols can be generalized to an incomparably greater extent than the 'meanings' of signals. The behavior of human beings depends *primarily* on the recognition of *symbols* and their generalized meanings; that is to say, on the comprehension of language. Language is what makes culture possible, and culture is what distinguishes man from every other form of life.

Possibly every form of life is in some sense 'unique', but ours seems to us to be *essentially* so. This is not surprising, because we are the sole judges of our 'uniqueness'. It is natural that language should be for us the most distinctive of human traits, because our identification with other human beings is most reliably cemented by verbal communication. The most common criterion that distinguishes 'our own' from strangers is language. How much more of a chasm gapes between us and non-humans with whom we cannot communicate by words except in limited, trivial ways.

Words can, of course, become signals to some animals, particularly to those that live with man. Dogs can be conditioned to respond to words with specific acts. What dogs cannot be taught to do is to link word meanings into larger, verbally determined meanings – meanings of assertions. A dog can be taught the meaning of 'jump' in the sense that he will jump when the word is spoken. He can be taught the meaning of chair in the sense that he will approach the chair when 'chair' is spoken. But from simply these two meanings he cannot derive the compound meaning of the command 'Jump on the chair.' If he learns the meaning of 'Jump on the chair' (which he can do) and the names of other objects (showing his understanding by approaching them), he still will not be able to shift the response to the command 'Jump on the chair' so as to make the appropriate response to 'Jump on the sofa.' Finally, when a dog learns the meaning of a word denoting an object, the meaning resides for him in the particular object that he has been taught to associate with the word. As a rule, he will not be able to generalize this meaning (in our sense of generalization) to other objects to which we have given the same name.

On that account, we tend to deny 'intelligence' (as we conceive it in our language-centered sense) to the dog. It is a sobering thought to imagine our predicament if we had to associate meanings with smells, not just single, clearly distinguishable smells but intricate combinations of exquisite nuances of smells, a 'smell grammar', as it were, which is second nature to the dog, the matrix of his perception of 'meanings'.

For us, on the other hand, generalization of verbal meaning is second nature. In fact, learning vocabulary is for us as much a process of broadening meanings as of narrowing or refining them. The young child, having learned to call the cat 'kitty', will often call other furry animals or even toys 'kitty'. At the start, 'kitty' has for him a broad meaning, perhaps anything animal-like and furry. Later he will learn to apply 'kitty' to cats but not to dogs or teddy bears. Here, learning has narrowed the meaning of a word. Still later the child will learn to apply 'animal' to a large variety of living things quite unlike the animals in his early encounters. Here, learning will broaden the meaning of a word.

The crucial feature about the human language is its tremendous power for identifying *abstract* features of situations. All human languages are metaphorical. In English, we say that an animal dies when it has ceased to live, and also that a fire 'dies' when it has ceased to burn. We use 'flow' to refer to both a river and a speech; 'sharp', to both an edge and a pain; 'stoop', to both the bending of the back and the compromise of principle. All these are instances of metaphorical references, of singling out some common feature in phenomena of widely differing contexts, an abstracting power unique to human languages and common to all of them.

The other, equally unique, feature of human language is that of syntax. The content of our speech is more than naming. We speak in assertions, questions, and commands. Assertions refer not merely to objects or situations but to the *structure* of situations. The prototype of an indicative sentence, with its subject and predicate, calls attention to a relation between classes of events, agent and action, object and property, cause and effect. A question is an invitation to another to make an assertion. A command is an attempt to elicit an act from another.

Communications among non-humans that are most conspicuous to us are primarily of the command type – signals that elicit acts. Possibly an extra-terrestrial observer trying to make sense of our communications would get the same impression; for the communications with the most immediately perceived meanings would be those that are consistently associated with definite elicited acts of others. Recent investigations primarily of communications among primates have revealed a much broader range of meaningful 'messages', encompassing a recognizable repertoire of gestures, bodily contacts, etc. In a way, these continual exchanges can be said to generate a 'non-material environment' for all social animals, somewhat analogous to human culture. Still, one can suppose that mating calls and warning cries are among the most pervasive forms of communication among co-members of non-human species if only because of their obvious survival value. By analogy with human language, these signals could be considered as instances of the imperative mode. In a very limited sense they can be likened to utterances in the declarative mode, that is, giving information. Still, the only information that such signals can give is about a state of affairs immediate in space and time and relevant to immediate action to be taken: the presence of danger, the location of a mate, sometimes the availability of food. No information can be given that can be stored in the memory for *future* use.[1] Nor can specific information be elicited, as in an answer to a question.

Above all, no information can be given by a non-human organism about causes and effects. An individual animal can learn that one event will follow another, as in conditioning. But *this* information cannot be transmitted to another animal. Thus whatever learning occurs is accumulated only in the learning animal. It cannot be shared except in quite limited ways. And, most significantly, it cannot be accumulated over several generations. Human beings, on the other hand, are unique in that they can share learned information and can transmit it to succeeding generations. This accumulation of experience and knowledge over generations constitutes an environment with which only human beings can interact. This is what is called culture.

Culture, then, can be defined as the peculiar environment in which human beings live and to which they adjust, as any animal adjusts to its environment. It consists of both material things (dwellings, tools, weapons) and non-material components (language, customs, laws, beliefs, attitudes, ways of perceiving the world). In a limited way, some animals also create their own material environment. We have mentioned nests, webs, dams, etc. Some of these artifacts – for instance, a termite hill – serve several generations. However, as far as we know, no animal creates a *non*-material environment comparable to that of man, certainly not one that accumulates over many generations. No animal creates a culture in the full sense of the word.

The non-material components of culture comprising accumulated knowledge and beliefs are made possible by symbolic language, because a symbol has no *necessary* connection to what it symbolizes, whereas a signal does have. For an animal to learn a conditioned response to a stimulus, the stimulus must have appeared at least at one time in some connection with an event that naturally elicits the response. In other words, the signal must have been, at least at some time, a *true* portender of the signaled event. Not so with symbols of language. An assertion can be false and still elicit a response which would be appropriate if the assertion were true. It can also be stored in the memory as true. This is because assertions can be made not only about events here and now but also about past events, expected events, hypothetical events, and events that never occurred.

The human being reacts to language as promptly as he does to events. What is more important, the human being reacts to the world about him through the screen of language. He does this even if he is confronted with an event directly. As a rule, except when the reaction is instantaneous, as in a reflex, the human being first *tells himself* what he experiences, then how to react to it. The mediation of language need not be explicit, but just the same, language mediates practically all our reactions.

It turns out, then, that, unlike other organisms, man lives in two environments, a physical one and a symbolic one. The physical environment is not much different from that in which other organisms live. It comprises the atmosphere and certain resources from which man by his activities extracts the necessities of life. These activities are vastly more complex than corresponding ones of other animals and result not only in providing man with the necessities of life but also in introducing modifications of the environment which at times enhance and at times jeopardize future procurement of these necessities. On the whole, however, man's interaction with the physical environment differs only quantitatively, not qualitatively, from corresponding interactions of other animals with their environment. A house is but an elaborate nest. A super-highway is an improved cow path. A hydroelectric dam is like a beaver dam magnified many-fold. A fishing net is analogous to a spider web.

The other environment, the symbolic one, has no real analogue in the non-human world. There are no precursors among animals of epic poems, monuments, preferred stock, protest marches, confessions, astronomy, or astrology.

Clearly, the degree to which man has been able to modify his physical environment (for better or for worse) is intimately related to certain features of his symbolic environment, to science, for example. The symbolic environment deserves careful examination in its own right as, perhaps, the most important determinant of the human condition.

CHAPTER 6

The Symbolic Environment

We have now described three kinds of environment and three correspond-ing types of adjustment mechanisms that enable a living system to 'main-tain itself', that is, essentially, to restore a steady state after a disturbance or to guard against disruptive disturbances.

1. Every system (except isolated ones) is in a physical environment. The events of this environment that impinge on the system are changes in the physical states, such as in temperature, in concentrations of substances in the surrounding medium, etc.

Correspondingly, within living systems there are physical and chemical mechanisms that respond to such changes, both external and internal. These mechanisms are inherent in the physical and chemical properties of the material constituents of the living system. Their operation depends on these properties alone.

2. Organisms endowed with nervous systems respond also to a 'signal environment'. Certain events that would not by themselves elicit adjust-ments by virtue of the system's physical and chemical responses do elicit adjustments by virtue of being external stimuli to which the nervous system responds. These responses are triggered by pre-arranged channels of excitation, along which nervous impulses travel, finally stimulating glands or muscles. There is no necessary relation between the energy of the signal and the energy released. To be sure, signals, being physical, are energy inputs, but it is not to the energy inputs that the elements of the nervous system respond. They respond to *information inputs*, that is, to configurations of events. Very minute quantities of energy carried by signals can release very large amounts of energy, as in the case of a machine that may put out large amounts of work in its performance but can be started by a very weak signal. The crucial circumstance is that the signal has been properly coded to be 'accepted'.

Responses to signals, especially responses that can be modified by learning, enable the organism to 'anticipate' physical changes portended by the signals and so greatly enhance its repertoire of homeostatic adjustment. Still, the signal environment, at least in the state of nature (without human interference), bears a direct relation to the physical environment. The animal is not ordinarily 'deceived' by the signals it receives from its environment. (Man can, of course, deceive an animal by baited traps, simulated mating calls, etc. But in doing so, he uses signals to which the animal normally responds in an appropriate way.) Nor can an animal be deceived by a 'false assertion' (e.g., 'Lady bug, . . . your house is on fire, your children will burn') because an animal can respond only to signals, not to symbols.

3. Man lives in a symbolic environment fashioned entirely by himself. Symbols, like signals, elicit responses that depend not on penetration of matter nor on the quality of energy inputs but on configurations of events. The symbols of language differ from signals in that they can elicit 'appropriate' responses even if no specific connection had ever been established between them and the responses elicited.

Recall that a signal elicits a more or less specific response under two conditions. (1) A neural mechanism that 'processes' the signal and triggers the response is part of the organism's inherited make-up. (2) The neural mechanism has been established as a result of experience (learning). In either case, the response will be elicited by a range of *physically* similar events.

The amazing process of abstraction and the consequent tremendous advantages conferred on man by symbolic language deserve to be described in more detail.

Consider the following question, presented either orally or in writing. How much is 84 times 1117? Under appropriate conditions, virtually all people (at a certain educational level) will answer 93,828. Yet, the question is a combination of symbols which it is unlikely anyone has seen or heard before. To be sure, the *elements* of the combination are familiar. But the ability of people to give the 'right answer' depends in no way on their having learned this particular answer. Furthermore, the answer may be given in different, physically quite dissimilar, forms (in English or in Japanese, for instance) and still be recognized (by people familiar with these languages) as the 'correct' (that is, appropriate) answer. Here the appropriateness of the answer is not in its physical characteristics but in its 'meaning', and the 'meaning' of a symbol (as distinguished from that of a signal) is quite independent of its physical manifestations. Witness the complete physical unrelatedness even of the two forms in which the question above can be presented: spoken or written.

The unique feature of symbols is their power to elicit responses without the necessity of associating 'meaning' to each symbol or to each set of symbols separately. While it can be argued that the 'meanings' of at least some words are learned by the usual kind of association between the words and the situations in which they are likely to be spoken, the notion that the meanings of sentences are learned in this way is untenable. This can be seen from a simple calculation. The information content of an average English word is about ten bits. A ten-word sentence, accordingly, carries about 100 bits of information. This means, roughly, that the probability of encountering a particular ten-word sentence is about 2^{-100} or about 10^{-30}. During the course of a lifetime a person cannot encounter more than 10^8 sentences, assuming even that he is bombarded with words from the moment of his birth to the moment of his death. Therefore, excluding the simplest clichés, like 'How are you?', 'What's the matter?' etc., the probability that anyone will encounter the same sentence twice in his life is vanishingly small. Every sentence you are reading now is in all likelihood new to you. Yet (I hope) somehow these combinations of symbols, never before encountered by you as such, have a 'meaning' for you.

It is, of course, not enough to assume that the meanings of sentences are simply compounded from the meanings of the words that compose them. Anyone can convince himself that this is not so by trying to read a foreign text by looking up every word as he goes along. For that matter, the meaning of a sentence in a discourse on a technical subject will usually escape an untrained reader or listener, even if he knows the meaning of every word. It follows that association of words with 'situations' is only a very small part of learning a language (including one's own). This sort of learning is, within rather narrow limits, accessible even to some non-humans and accounts for their ability to perceive some words as signals.

The true symbolic significance of language functions by imparting *emergent* meanings to combinations of words. These emergent meanings encompass considerably more than the single words. In fact, the meanings of assertions are to a certain extent quite independent of even the words that compose them. Two sentences may be almost identical in sound and in appearance when written, yet have practically unrelated meanings. Compare

'We gave him a gun for his money'

and

'We gave him a run for his money.'

Contrariwise, two sentences unrelated in sound may have practically the same meaning. Compare 'We gave him a run for his money' and 'He found that it was not easy to beat us at this game.' Or 'We gave him a gun for his money' and 'We discharged our debt by presenting him with a revolver.'

Besides having meanings that do not depend on the physical characteristics of the signals, symbols can have meaning dissociated from the situation they represent. This property is a derivative of the combinatorial potential of symbols. As a simplest case, consider the word 'horse'. The word has referents in the real world, namely horses. Similarly, the word 'wing' has referents. But the phrase 'a winged horse' has no referents in the real world, yet it has a 'meaning' in the sense that it can evoke a mental image of a horse with wings. This power to evoke an image does not depend on previous experiences with, say, pictures of winged horses; the phrases 'a horned horse', 'a talking horse', 'a six-legged horse' can also easily evoke mental images even though (unlike winged horses) they may never have been pictured.

In the same way, assertions may evoke mental images of events that never took place, events expected to take place, desired events, feared events, etc. A vast amount, perhaps by far the most, of what we know or think we know comes to us via words rather than via direct experiences with the situations depicted. Even the knowledge that comes to us via experiences becomes 'knowledge' only after the experiences have been somehow categorized. The established categories depend to a great extent on the verbal descriptions of experiences. Words abstract particular features common to the events subsumed under the same verbal description, and these, then, become the distinguishing features that make categorization possible. Without categorization, experiences could not be stored for future reference, for every experience is different from every other. Verbal descriptions *identify* experiences and relate them to each other.

Let us follow Mr A (a human being) on his daily routine and see how practically everything he does is a consequence of 'proper' responses to symbolic inputs. Moreover, if he does something 'improper', for the most part it is improper by virtue of the symbolic environment surrounding him and the people with whom he interacts.

Mr A wakes up. Whether he was awakened by the sound of an alarm clock or by his wife's voice, or by the light shining through the windows (quite different events, physically) matters not nearly so much as the fact that he woke up at a particular time. His behavior upon waking depends quite a bit on the exact time of awakening, as shown on his clock, which has been synchronized with signals issuing from an astronomical observatory. In fact, all over the world millions of people keep track of time in this manner. They pay more attention to this conventionally defined time than to its physical manifestations, such as the amount of daylight, or to their physiological state, whether they are sleepy or wakeful, hungry or sated, etc. So it is with Mr A. Whether he gets out of bed immediately or tarries depends on the position of the hands on his clock. Whether he hurries or performs his morning rituals leisurely also depends on what his clock 'says'.

The rituals themselves are performed largely through force of habit, but the habit itself was established by learning, which was accomplished primarily by attending to spoken words.

Mr A is shaving. One might ask why he is shaving, but this would be an unusual question. One ordinarily does not ask why a regularly occurring event occurs. One asks why such an event does *not* occur. If Mr A failed to shave on that particular morning and if the result were observed, he might be asked why he did not shave. One of the reasons why Mr A shaves even if he is not inclined to do so is to avoid such a question.

And so it goes with Mr A's subsequent activities. He puts on a pair of socks, two foot coverings made of the same material and of the same color. If he should put on socks of different kinds and colors, he might be asked why he did this. He certainly would be asked questions if he failed to put on some kinds of usual attire. If he walked out of his house nude, for example, he would be arrested, and his plea that the day was blistering hot would not have sufficed to free him from unpleasant consequences. His arrest, incidentally, although resulting in a physical restriction of his movement (e.g., possible confinement in a jail cell), would most likely be accomplished by spoken words (symbols), provided they were spoken by a person wearing an appropriate uniform (another symbol).

Mr A eats his usual breakfast. (If it were unusual, *he* would ask questions about it.) The food he eats is an input from his physical environment. It helps keep Mr A alive by supplying the energy necessary to keep his homeostatic mechanisms going. While eating, Mr A reads a newspaper. The patterns of black marks passing through Mr A's exquisitely complex visual apparatus are also an input, this time from the symbolic environment in which Mr A also lives. The patterns he sees will make substantial physiological changes inside Mr A's skin – when you think of it, a most astonishing fact, because the 'symbolic input' involves no material substance (like food) and quite trivial amounts of energy. Here is a pattern that started a complex physiological process in Mr A:

WstAir 2.19 f 63 30–1/4 28–5/8 30–1/4

Mr A's pupils dilated somewhat; his heartbeat quickened. He experienced a momentary sense of elation (had the last symbols been 28–5/8, Mr A would have experienced a sense of depression with attendant physiological changes). Note that the symbols perceived by Mr A do not portend any immediate change in Mr A's physical environment, as we might suppose in view of the physiological reactions. They do not even portend significant future changes. For Mr A can become considerably richer or considerably poorer without substantially changing the physical aspects of his life. The effect of the symbols on Mr A's psychological and physiological state is due to the way Mr A has learned to respond to symbols quite apart from what these symbols portend about Mr A's physical environment.

We shall continue to keep Mr A company on this day, which will turn out to be an important one in his life. He is now at the station, waiting for a train to take him to the city where he works. If the train does not arrive within a minute or so of a specified time, he is likely to comment on the fact. He may be disturbed, and physiological changes would occur inside his skin that are in no way helpful to him in making the train arrive. If he arrives at his place of work within a certain time interval, no one will ask why. But if he does not, comments and questions are likely to follow. Moreover, if he arrives late several times, conversations may ensue, or written messages (symbols) may be initiated, as a result of which Mr A's whole pattern of life (as he perceives it) may change.

We see here the operation of a 'steady state'. The system, however, is not a living organism with its usual homeostatic mechanisms of control. The system is a larger one of which Mr A is a part, and it is a social organism. The entities of that system are themselves organisms, like Mr A. The system's mechanisms of adjustments are symbols exchanged between its component organisms. When someone notices that Mr A did not shave and comments on the fact, he or she is responding not so much to the sight of stubble on Mr A's cheeks as to the thought 'Mr A did not shave.' When Mr A is disturbed by the fact of his being late, it is not the absence of the train that disturbs him but the thought of possible consequences – mostly spoken words, which, in turn, may have consequences, most of them symbolic. For, when after several late arrivals a person designated as 'Mr A's superior' fires Mr A, the act is not a consequence of changes in this person's physical environment. Mr A's superior is, rather, reacting to keep his *symbolic* environment in a steady state. He wants employees to come at the time prescribed to them because in this way they give evidence of being 'dependable', 'steady', 'loyal', etc. And if we press him to tell us what these words mean, we will probably get explanations in terms of other words. While he may also make references to acts, the acts referred to will in all likelihood be symbolic ones. Few, if any, references will be made to the actual physical environment.

A social organism in a steady state is one whose members act in accordance with the expectations of other members. The steady state of the social organism's physical environment is only part of the picture, and only a small fraction of the 'organism's' actions are directed toward affecting this physical environment. For the most part they involve the production, manipulation, processing, reception, and interpretation of symbols. The maintenance of a steady state with respect to the physical environment, in which Mr A, his boss (Mr Z), and all the other members of that social organism live, depends *crucially* on the proper interaction of symbolic behavior.

To keep alive, Mr A needs food. For the most part, food is where he expects to find it. It is put before him at home and in restaurants. It is delivered to his home and to the restaurants from larger stores, and at the proper times, as a consequence of symbolic exchanges (words spoken, pieces of paper transferred). It is initially delivered to these larger stores in consequence of still more symbolic exchanges. The pieces of paper which induce people, strangers to Mr A, to give him food when he asks for it come into Mr A's possession by still other symbolic exchanges. In fact, almost everything that is done in Mr A's environment that insures his steady state is a result of fulfilled expectations expressed by symbols, either uttered when the occasion demands, or stored in people's memories.

To be sure, behind all this there are also acts affecting the physical environment. But, overwhelmingly, even these acts involve stored symbolic experience. Somewhere the food eaten by Mr A, the materials from which his clothes and his house are made, etc., are produced. In this production, machines are involved, which, in turn, were made. Their making involved knowledge, and this knowledge was accumulated and transmitted by symbolic interactions.

For the most part, Mr A and all the other members of the social system do what is expected of them. Deviations are corrected largely by the use of words. Only in some instances are people forced to do what they are expected to do or prevented from doing what they are not expected to do by the application of physical force. In fact, no human society could function if physical force were required to elicit expected actions. For one thing, physical force can be used only to prevent actions, not to realize them. Actions are realized by complex, coordinated movements of muscles, and this coordination must be effected within the nervous system of the actor, which is not accessible to direct manipulation. Next, even if it were possible to effect coordination by force, there would not be enough enforcers to do this on a substantial scale. 'Subjugation' of some people by others marks almost the entire history of organized society. Yet, typically, the subjugated always outnumber the subjugators. How, then, is it that slaves, soldiers, prisoners, and other people who perform forced labor do what is expected of them? One ready explanation is, of course, fear of reprisals, including death. But the physical force available to the relatively few subjugators could hardly take effective reprisals against all of the many subjugated. Compliance is also explained, oppositely, by hope of reward. Yet compliance is observed in situations where it does not substantially improve the lot of the compliers, and even where, by complying, individuals and groups have made their continued existence hopeless, as in slavery, for example.

Subjugation of the many by the few is made possible through the control of symbolic interactions. Coordinated resistance by the subjugated is effectively prevented by blocking communication among them. For instance, in recruiting slaves for American plantations, care was exercised to mix captives who spoke mutually unintelligible languages. Tyrannies depend to a very large extent on restriction of communication and expression and, in our age, on the control of mass media.

In short, subjugation, even in its crudest, most naked forms, depends almost entirely on the control of symbolic processes. In 'free' societies this control is much more diffuse than in totalitarian states. It may even seem to be entirely absent, as when no overt restrictions are placed on communication and expression. Nevertheless, control does operate, whether it is centralized or not, whether it is applied consciously or not. Where a population is not overtly subjugated by authorities, steady state is maintained by internalized notions of what is expected and proper, and, for the most part, what is expected is proper responses to symbols. Diffuse control is exercised by innumerable cues (also symbolic).

Mr A is not a typical representative of the human race. He belongs to a portion of it, vaguely called 'the middle class', which, in turn, comprises a substantial portion of the population of the so-called Western civilized society, which, in turn, comprises a not very large portion of mankind. The reason for singling out Mr A is that he represents the portion of the human race that is today most completely 'insulated' from the physical environment of this planet. How effectively Mr A is insulated is a question that will be raised in the proper place. It is, nevertheless, a fact that for the moment Mr A enjoys almost complete protection from unfavorable variations in the physical environment. Throughout his life he has never been in danger of dying for lack of food or from exposure to the elements, or from ravages of plagues. He is also reasonably protected from violence on the part of others of his species. At any rate, Mr A has gone through life without having to give much attention to his physical safety, unlike many others who do not belong to this portion of humanity. Except for occasional illness and occasional sensual experiences, the sources of Mr A's comforts and discomforts are mostly symbols produced by others and by himself. He is concerned with what other people have said or will say to or about him and with what he himself will say to other people. His deprivations are often a lack of symbolic inputs, as when he is bored or when he feels that he has no friends (interactions with friends being primarily verbal). He may feel hurt because his sex life is unsatisfactory. But, if so, this is because he must inhibit certain forms of sexual behavior or because his sexual partners do not give him the symbolic cues he desires, not because the actual physical sensations of his sexual activity are much different from those that might give him intense satisfaction if accompanied by different symbolic cues. His pleasures, aside from gratification of physical needs, are also predominantly derived from reception and production of symbols. He likes to read. He likes to play cards and gets pleasure from 'winning'. His fears are engendered by what information he gets about 'world events', which he 'experiences' via symbolic inputs. Except for the threat by weapons of mass destruction (not yet experienced and therefore also perceived symbolically), Mr A is not aware of any threats to his physical existence. He expects to complete his 'normal' life span (which is nearly twice the average for his species) in the same state of comfort and actually gives this matter little thought. His situation does not usually seem to him anomalous.

Besides pleasures and displeasures, actual or anticipated as hopes or fears, Mr A's inner life is compounded of attitudes and beliefs. The former categorizes things, people, events, and situations roughly along a good-bad dimension. The latter arranges assertions along a true-false dimension. By far the greatest portion of his attitudes and beliefs were imparted to Mr A by words. This is not to say that he simply absorbs everything that he is told or reads, nor that the source of every attitude or belief was some explicit assertion addressed to him. The formation of Mr A's attitudes and beliefs is a complex process of accepting and rejecting the symbolic inputs that impinge on him. But whether he accepts or rejects these inputs, and how, if accepted, they are incorporated; whether they change, modify, or reinforce his system of attitudes and beliefs, depends in large measure on previous symbolic inputs. Mr A's personal experiences may certainly have played a part in this process, but these experiences themselves have been largely symbolic, so that it is not in-accurate to say Mr A's inner life is almost entirely the result of symbolic inputs. The structure of Mr A's body and the physiological processes in it are products of genetic evolution. The structure of his 'mind', how-ever, is a product of a very different sort of evolution, to be discussed presently.

The use of quotation marks around 'mind' is a quasi-apology made to dissociate the ideas developed here from 'dualism' that still pervades much of our thinking – the notion that man is composed of two onto-logical aspects, the 'physical' and the 'spiritual' or 'mental'. The dichotomy is no help in understanding human behavior. Nevertheless, a sharp distinction must be made between the sources of man's 'physical' make-up (which includes his anatomy and the material manifestations of his homeostatic processes, such as digestion, respiration, etc.) and his propensities to act as he does (his 'psychological' make-up). The bases of these propensities may well be as 'material' as his physical characteristics, being incorporated in the structure and processes of his nervous system. However, it is next to impossible to trace these propensities to physical states, and so for this reason they are lumped under 'mind'.

The social system of which Mr A is a part is composed of individuals of whom most are, in some crucially important respect, of the 'same mind' as Mr A. For instance, most of them speak and understand the same language – an obvious common denominator. There are many other common properties, in spite of a multitude of variants, without which the 'living system' represented by Mr A's society could not maintain itself, that is, would not persist in a relatively steady state.

Mr A's social system and culture is only one of many. Each is 'held together' by a symbolic environment, a common language, common expectations, common values. It is not possible to delineate these social systems and cultures precisely, as can be done in the case of biological species. Unlike biological species, which, as reproductive systems, are virtually isolated from each other, social systems and cultures are criss-crossed by currents of mutual influence. The extent of inter-penetration depends both on the individual characteristics of the systems (for instance on their degrees of 'openness') and on how far the symbols of one fit those of another. And yet, in spite of the fact that cultures can cross-fertilize each other, while biological species cannot, the 'ways of life' in different human cultures are much more disparate than modes of existence of closely related species. This can be taken as evidence of the profound differences between biological and cultural evolution. We shall examine both these differences and the similarities between the two processes in the next chapter.

CHAPTER 7

Evolution and Survival

So far we have identified the maintenance of a system with the persistence of a steady state or with reversible passages from one state to another. We have also discussed evolution, which can be conceptualized as a relatively slow change continuing for some time in the same direction, as distinguished from, say, short-term fluctuating changes.

The clearest examples of evolution are changes that species undergo over periods of time exceedingly longer than the average life span of the individuals comprising the species. These changes are often in the 'same direction' at least over some stretch of time. For instance, the individuals may over many generations increase in size. Some of their organs may become progressively more complex and specialized, etc. By extending the meaning of evolution, we could subsume under it the entire development of the individual organism from the fertilized cell to maturity, the changes in the behavior patterns of a mature organism as the result of experience, etc.

The seemingly contradictory notions of steady-state-maintenance and evolution can be reconciled by keeping in mind that the maintenance of steady state refers to relatively short-term and fluctuating changes, while evolution (in whatever context) refers to relatively long-term and 'secular' (that is, unidirectional) changes. Then every living system can be said to both maintain a steady state and evolve.

The 'direction' of biological evolution is not easy to establish except with reference to specific, clearly identifiable and quantifiable variables. For example, body mass is a well defined quantity, and progressive increase (or decrease) of body mass in some line of descent can be traced over a long period of time. If the evolution of a class of life has been going on for some time in the same direction, we can surmise that the direction represents progressive adaptation to the environment (provided the environment remains relatively constant). Degree of adaptation may be reflected in the number of individuals comprising a given species. Some biologists discern a steady increase in complexity of living things. It is important to note that none of these changes in a prevalent direction is without exception. Some evolutionary lines are toward smaller size. Some parasites have become more simple, not more complex, than their self-supporting ancestors. In fact, 'complexity' is itself a complex concept, not easily defined. In a way, animals are more complex organisms than plants. In another way, plants, with their photosynthesizing apparatus, which animals lack, are more complex. The only sure thing that can be said about the 'direction' of evolution is that at any given time it is toward a better adaptation to the environment in which a class of life is immersed *at that time*, the adaptation being insured by natural selection. (The environment is to be understood as including the presence of other organisms.)

Typically, in the course of the evolution of a species, at first the number increases, reflecting a progressively more successful adaptation to the environment. Eventually the population may persist in a steady state for a time, perhaps some millions of years. Then it may start to decrease, as it loses 'the struggle for existence' to better adapted competitors, until the species becomes extinct.

Another variable, reflecting, perhaps, the degree of adaptation of a taxonomic category larger than a species, such as a family or a class, is the number of species in that category. If the type of adaptation achieved by, say, a class (fishes, mammals, insects) is a 'theme', the species in it are the 'variations' on the theme. A 'good' theme provides a rich source of variations and insurance against the extinction of the entire class. For instance, the class Insects in the phylum of Arthropods comprises over a half million known species. Since that class did not always exist, we must suppose that at least at one time the numbers of species in it kept increasing. Whether the peak has been reached or passed is not known, but there is no question that the growth in diversity reflected some specially successful adaptation of that class to the terrestrial environment. Evidence of successful adaptation of some insect species is suggested by the observation that among these are found some of the most 'conservative' types of life. Ants and cockroaches have remained virtually unchanged for about 40 million years. We note that the average total life span of a bird species is about 40,000 years and of a mammalian species, about 20,000 years.[1]

Our own species, homo sapiens, is known to have existed at least 40,000 years. Cro Magnon men, who lived in Europe about that long ago, are clearly recognized as our species. The genus, homo, is older, perhaps a half million to a million years old; but now this genus comprises only one species. On the face of this evidence alone it is difficult to estimate the 'success of adaptation' of our species.

On the basis of numbers, however, there is strong evidence of man's successful adaptation. The total numbers of individuals comprising our species has been steadily increasing for at least 10,000 years, and, moreover, at an accelerated rate. While it took an estimated 200 years for the human population to increase from half a billion to a billion, it took only 110 years to increase from one billion to two. At present, the doubling time of the human population is only 35 years.[2] It is quite likely that other species at the time of their population explosions showed comparable or even greater rates of increase.

Man has been traditionally supposed to be incomparably more 'intelligent' than any other animal. Moreover, the 'evolution of intelligence' in the descendent line culminating in man seems demonstrable, especially since there is evidence for evolutionary growth of complexity of the nervous system, particularly of the brain. The mammalian brain is the most complex of vertebrate brains; the primate brain is the most complex of mammalian brains; the human brain is the most complex of primate brains.

'Intelligence' has often been cited as an index that establishes a direction in evolution. There is no evidence that the human brain has increased, either in size or in complexity since the time of Cro Magnon men. Yet, the idea of 'evolving intelligence', while encompassing biological evolution, really comes into its own in the context of human history, during which no dramatic biological changes in man are demonstrable.

Accordingly, the idea of evolving intelligence was linked to a non-biological context, namely that of cultural evolution – presumably the accumulation of *collective* intelligence through the accumulation of experience across generations, the process that Alfred Korzybski once called *time-binding*.[3]

The outstanding fact about cultural evolution is that it is much more rapid than biological evolution. It is difficult to make this statement precise because no 'unit of change' has been established for either type of evolution. However, precise or not, the meaning of the statement should be intuitively clear. Two human beings, born 10,000 years apart, would be anatomically and physiologically practically indistinguishable. However, if the later specimen were properly chosen, their ways of life would present a dramatic contrast. Physical similarity and cultural contrast are observed even in the comparison of contemporaries.

Biological evolution also exhibits fluctuations in rate. Before the 'invention' of sexual reproduction, evolution must have been much slower than afterwards. This is because the only source of genetic variation in asexual reproduction is mutations, which are comparatively rare. In sexual reproduction, on the other hand, the most important source of hereditary variation is the re-combination of genes in the mingling of hereditary material from each parent. This vastly greater range of accidental variation through re-combinations provides an immensely wider store of 'raw material' on which natural selection can act.

As George Simpson pointed out, evolution is 'opportunistic'.[4] Variations can occur only in whatever already exists. Moreover, the variations that will survive natural selection are those that enhance the survival potential imparted by already existing structures and mechanisms. The general rule of changes in adaptive mechanisms is 'more and better of the same'. That is, changes are selected for only if they contribute to the already existing mechanisms. Thus, to take a fanciful example, a variation in the brain of a non-swimming bird that might have meant an improvement of swimming ability would not survive natural selection: it would not 'fit'. On the other hand, a variation that would improve coordination between distance vision and rapid air diving (as in swooping down on prey) would be selected for if this activity were already part of the bird's way of life.[5]

The pace of cumulative effects of biological evolution is limited by the spacing of generations. Each innovation must wait until the next 'deal' of genetic material. To be sure, improvement of performance can take place also in individual organisms (through learning), but these individually acquired characteristics cannot be genetically transmitted to the succeeding generations. As for transmitting experience by 'teaching' the progeny, although occasional instances may be observed in animals, this sort of transmission plays only a minor role in the life of non-humans.

Cultural evolution combines independence from genetic changes with the possibility of transmitting cumulative effects to succeeding generations. As explained in Chapter 6, this combination is made possible by symbolic language, which also makes possible the acquisition of knowledge independently of direct experience. Thereby the rate of accumulation of collective knowledge (previously dependent on genetic changes) increases by several orders of magnitude.

The accelerated rate of cultural evolution (in certain of its aspects) can be related to another feature that cultural evolution shares with biological evolution, namely its 'opportunistic' character. What is already present in a culture is likely to evolve further if its variations are selected for. (We shall examine the mechanisms of selection below.) Completely new features must depend for their survival on fortuitous combinations of circumstances. Thus, in cultural evolution we observe the same kind of 'inertia' – a tendency to continue along directions taken – as in biological evolution, particularly if the direction is 'successful', that is, if further developments along it are selected for.

It remains to examine the mechanisms of selection that operate in cultural evolution. Analogies are always helpful in speculations. They can also frequently be seriously misleading. Following the ideas of natural selection in biological evolution, it would be tempting to single out cultural types as analogues to species and to assume that cultural evolution is a result of the survival of the fittest. Upon closer inspection, this analogy will not hold up. Natural selection operates on species via the variations in and re-combinations of genetic units of millions of individuals. Nothing remotely resembling this process can be observed in the context of cultural evolution. In any given historical moment there are at most some scores of cultural types in existence. Further, we do not know what 'survival of the fittest' might mean if cultural types are taken as analogues to species. A species attests to its survival potential by persisting for many (perhaps thousands of) generations in a more or less steady state. The mere existence of a species is not evidence of its 'fitness', because many existing species are already doomed to extinction. If they are not *yet* extinct, this is only because it takes many generations for a species to disappear through non-renewal. Cultures have been known to persist in a steady state for centuries; that is, over a score or so generations. We might generously take this span of survival as evidence of fitness, but these are exceptional cases. In our day, hardly any culture is in a steady state. Whether the more or less rapid changes that go on in existing cultures are signs of 'progressive evolution' or, on the contrary, of impending demise is a matter of conjecture. Nor are cultures as readily identifiable as are biological species. A culture is an abstraction, which anthropologists and historians have found convenient for organizing their ideas about patterns of human existence. There is no unambiguous way of delineating a particular culture to differentiate it from other cultures. Moreover, regardless of the most serious efforts at objectivity on the part of historians or anthropologists, value judgement must perforce enter the method of description or comparison. And so what will appear to some as a 'corruption' of a culture will appear to others as an enrichment; what will appear to some as development will appear to others as decay. Consequently, whether a culture 'dies' or survives in a descendant will be a matter of judgement, unlike the question of whether a species dies or evolves into another. The lines of biological descent are, in principle, clearly traceable. Those of cultural descent are not.

It appears, therefore, that a culture or a culture type is not a good analogue of a species in the context of 'survival of the fittest'. None the less, the similarity between cultural and biological evolution is too striking to be dismissed as a superficial analogy. The similarity is especially suggestive in certain special aspects of culture, language being a major example. The taxonomy of languages is structurally almost identical to that of biological types. Closely related dialects can be considered to be variants of the same language just as subspecies are variants of the same species. Closely related languages are grouped naturally into families (Romance, Teutonic, Balto-Slavic); families, into larger classes (Indo-European, Semitic, Sino-Tibetan). The evolutionary pattern of languages is similar to that of biological types. Both result in bifurcations from common antecedents in consequence of isolation. If science is concerned with general principles governing wide ranges of phenomena, then certainly a search of general principles governing the evolution of biological types, of languages, and, perhaps, of other aspects of culture falls within the scope of a scientific discussion. How far can the analogy be carried and where does it break down?

It is, of course, futile to search for an analogue of sexual reproduction in the analysis of cultural evolution. Sexual reproduction is not an essential feature of evolution. It is only a particular mechanism that speeded up the rate of biological evolution. We have also seen that 'survival of the fittest' is not a concept that can be easily applied to culture (or, in particular, languages), because the objective criterion of 'fitness' (the survival potential of progeny) does not apply. Neither a language nor a culture 'gives birth' to progenies on which natural selection acts. To say that the 'struggle for existence' reflects itself in the competition of cultures or languages is to succumb to the metaphorical meaning of that phrase, to treat it as a metaphysical principle instead of inquiring into its concrete, demonstrable mechanisms, as was done when the biological struggle for existence was shown to be a by-product of natural selection without reference to any 'struggle'.

Is there, nevertheless, a genuine analogue of natural selection in the evolution of cultures or of any aspects of cultures? I think there is, but it can be brought out only if we appropriately re-define reproduction.

Man-made environment is our main area of interest, and culture is but another name for it. Just what units of a culture are reproduced? How are they reproduced? Does the reproduction involve variations (analogous to phenotypes), and does natural selection act on these variations? If it does, then we ought to be able to define the 'fitness' of a variant. We shall take as an example the evolution of a language. Although it is only one aspect of a culture, the analysis may suggest ideas applicable to the evolution of cultures as wholes and so to the area of our principal concern – the man-made environment.

Languages certainly 'exist' but not as material objects. A language is said to exist if there are speakers or writers that produce units (utterances) recognizable as units of that language. If it were not for written records, these utterances would be ephemeral events. (Written records are simply material traces of events, just as footprints are material traces of an animal's passage.) The events occur as long as speakers or writers have a propensity to make them occur. This propensity is reinforced by the occurrences themselves. We can, therefore, consider each utterance (say, a word) as an individual in a population called 'language'. This 'individual' exists only for a moment. But it has a 'progeny': the fact that the word was uttered contributes to the likelihood that it will be uttered again by the same speaker or by others, and as long as the repetitions continue, the word 'lives' in the language. If it is uttered infrequently, it will stimulate fewer repetitions (that is, will have fewer 'progeny'), which, in turn, will further reduce the frequency of subsequent utterances until the word 'dies', that is, drops out of the language, becomes obsolete.

Having suggested the meaning of reproduction in the life of a language, let us look to the sources of variation and the analogue of natural selection. It stands to reason that no two repetitions of a word will be exactly alike, just as the progeny of an organism are not its exact replicas. However, variations in the pronunciation of a word do not usually persist. Random fluctuations are 'corrected' by the tendency of the speakers to pronounce the word according to the standard of their dialect. It may happen that over a long period of time the pronunciation will undergo a cumulative drift because of the slow but directed changes in speech habits. Thus, shifts in the direction of the changes in speech habits will be 'selected for', that is, imitated by other speakers. The progeny of the variant will eventually displace the old form.

It is known that language changes are most evident when different language communities come in contact, especially when they mingle as a result of mass migration, conquest, and so on. It is further known that under these circumstances language changes are in the direction of simplification. For instance, inflected languages tend to lose their inflections, as did English during the centuries marked by invasions and mingling. The reason for the simplification seems clear. In trying to communicate with someone whose knowledge of our language is scanty, we tend to avoid complexities. American pioneers, in addressing Indians, would say, 'You tell chief white man come make trade', etc. Similarly, when people try to understand a language they do not command, they ignore grammar and concentrate on key words. The two procedures are complementary and reinforce each other. Now, speech habits become incorporated, and the language undergoes pressure for change. In short, variants in pronunciation and in grammar will replace the old forms if they are repeated by other speakers. They will be repeated if they are accepted, and they will be accepted if they 'fit' into some new scheme that is better suited to the needs of the speakers.

The same applies to changes in the meanings of words. That words change their meanings over time is a matter of record. The coinage of new words is a response to new needs. When I ask a secretary to have a letter 'xeroxed', I am aware that a few years ago I could not have used that word. That I now use it as a matter of course and that she immediately understands me is a consequence of the fact that English nouns may be used freely in the role of verbs, even if such usage is not formally sanctioned (to 'radio' a message, to 'research' a problem), and of the fact that in industrialized societies brand names often are absorbed into the language as common nouns (aspirin, vaseline, IBM-card). So, 'to xerox a letter' fits into the language habits of office workers. Since the verb 'to xerox' was heretofore unknown, it must have been used for the first time by some particular person on some particular occasion. Because 'have this xeroxed' is easier to say than 'have this letter reproduced on a photocopying machine', the progeny of the new verb multiplied rapidly and the word was established in common usage.

I think that this view of language evolution provides a clue to cultural evolution in general. Culture is the totality of man-made objects, rules, expectations, patterns of behavior and interaction, attitudes, and beliefs that constitute a man-made environment (very largely symbolic) of a group of human beings. The items of culture can be defined in many ways, but we are not here concerned with singling out the 'proper units' with a view of constructing a theory of culture. For our purpose, it is sufficient to note that, however these items are defined, the culture exists only as long as the items that comprise it are *reproduced*, just as a species exists only as long as its members reproduce themselves. Further, the culture evolves by virtue of the variations in its items and by virtue of the fact that a process analogous to natural selection acts on these variations. The items may be material (dress, houses, weapons) or behavioral (speech patterns, customs, rituals) or 'mental' (attitudes, beliefs, aspirations). All of them are reproduced. Material items are reproduced by being copied; behavioral items are reproduced by being imitated; attitudes and beliefs are reproduced by being symbolically transmitted to the young.

The distinction made here between material, behavioral, and mental items of culture is only for the sake of clarity of analysis. It would be a gross error to conceive of a culture as a simple catalogue of such items, just as it would be futile to conceive of a language as the contents of a dictionary or even of a grammar. Culture lives and evolves through the interaction of all these modalities of its contents: Mr A's riding a train to work reflects the existence of a train (a material item), proper behavior on the part of the operator and on Mr A's part (buying a ticket), his expectations (that the train will come and take him to the proper destination), and a set of attitudes (that people regularly employed should appear at their places of work at specified times). This interdependence of cultural items is a direct analogue of the interdependence of anatomical structures and behavioral patterns in organisms. It selects the possible directions of evolution and provides for acceleration along the 'successful' directions.

Here I must remind the reader of what I mean by 'successful' directions. The meaning of 'success' in this context is related to natural selection, which, in turn, depends on how well the evolving item 'fits' into established patterns. The 'success' of an item in this context has no necessary relation to the survival potential of the culture in which it is embedded. In fact, as I have said, we cannot speak of the survival potential of cultures, because there is no way of telling whether a culture has 'died' or 'lives on' in another guise. However, even if we do make this distinction, we must further separate the 'success' of a new cultural item from the continued existence of the culture.

The importance of separating these concepts can be seen when we identify the patterns of life in, say, medieval Europe as a culture. Late in the Middle Ages gunpowder appeared as a new material item. It fitted into the existing patterns and attitudes: the feudal princes were carrying on almost continual warfare against each other, and the potentials of fire power were appreciated by them. With the introduction of artillery, the walled castle ceased to give protection to the feudal lords and their serfs and so ceased to perpetuate the loyalty of the serfs to the lords. Thus, an innovation that 'succeeded', that is, was accepted and reproduced, led to the demise of the culture in which it became embedded.

The success of a cultural item is particularly likely if its introduction stimulates changes which, in turn, stimulate the reproduction of the item. The introduction of roads and automobiles is a clear example of this mutual reinforcement. The acceptance of the automobile as a common means of transportation (as in the United States) stimulated the construction of hard-surfaced roads; the availability of roads, in turn, made the automobile even more acceptable. The automobile interacted in this mutually reinforcing way also with other items in American culture. Availability of automobiles changed people's attitudes toward distance, particularly, the distance from home to place of work. A distance of 30–40 miles no longer appeared as an inconvenience. Accordingly, people spread out in a radius of tens of miles around city centers, which then made the automobile indispensable as a means of transportation – or so it was thought. And because of this conviction, reliance on public transportation declined; thus, public transportation services were curtailed, which still further increased dependence on the automobile. Many, if not most, of the material items in industrialized cultures owe their 'success' to such mutually reinforcing interactions.

This is true also of non-material items. Recall the example of language change resulting from the introduction of a new verb, 'to xerox' (p. 72), which, as explained, could be introduced naturally into English because many English nouns can be used as verbs without changing their form, and also because massive advertising has established the practice of converting brand names into common nouns. The changes reinforce each other: each innovation makes successive innovations easier.

The principle of mutually reinforcing interactions is the direct antithesis of the steady-state-preserving principle of homeostasis. Systems engineers call homeostatic devices 'negative feedback', and anti-homeostatic devices, 'positive feedback'. The simplest example of a negative feedback device is the ordinary thermostat. When the temperature in the vicinity of a thermostat falls below the set temperature, the dropping of the mercury column triggers a switch that turns the furnace on. In consequence, the temperature begins to rise. If the temperature rises above the setting, the rising column of mercury triggers the switch to turn the furnace off. Thus, the temperature is kept within certain limits (a steady state).

It is easy to turn the thermostat into an anti-homeostatic device simply by switching the connections. Then the falling mercury column will turn the furnace *off*, and so the temperature will keep falling. If the initial temperature happened to be above the critical level, the furnace would have been turned *on* and the house would become still hotter.

An important concept related to positive feedback is that of *threshold*. To demonstrate, consider a system comprising two teams playing tug-of-war. Suppose that initially the two opposing forces are in equilibrium. Eventually, for whatever reason (say, a slight relaxation on one side), the forces become unbalanced. Motion in one direction will start; that is, the soles of the feet of one team, instead of being dug in, will start to slide along the surface. To restore equilibrium, a greater force is required than merely to maintain it, because the force of sliding friction between two surfaces is generally smaller than that of resting friction. If the losing team cannot exert the greater force required to stop the sliding motion, the momentum of the system will increase, since an unbalanced force results not merely in motion but in *accelerated* motion. The more momentum the system acquires, the more difficult it becomes to restore it to equilibrium. That is to say, an initial disturbance of a certain critical or 'threshold' magnitude gives rise to forces that tend to make the disturbance still larger. Here positive feedback is operating.

As in the case of negative feedback, the 'forces' acting in positive feedback need not be physical forces. Consider again a chemical reaction, this time one wherein the rate of production of a substance is proportional to its own concentration. That is, the substance acts as its own catalyst. The more the substance is produced, the larger will be the rate of production. The system will be moving *away* from a steady state until other conditions, say, depletion of the substrate from which the substance is formed, put an end to the process.

Positive feedback can be surmised to be operating in many social phenomena. The so-called bandwagon effect may be an example. Consider a social movement that wins adherents on the strength of its inherent appeal. Originally there is a 'substrate' of susceptible individuals in the society, comprising those to whom the aims of the movement are appealing and who will therefore join it. There may, however, be another factor operating – the tendency of individuals to join the movement because others have already joined. Now the more people join, the larger the concentration of 'converts' in the population, and the more willingly others become converted. This is the bandwagon effect that may be responsible for accelerating recruitments frequently observed in fads, riots, rapidly growing new political parties or religions, etc.[6]

Actually, all 'explosions', whether physical, biological, or social, are manifestations of positive feedback. A 'population explosion' is a consequence of the fact that, if the birth rate exceeds the death rate, the more born, the larger the population becomes; and the larger the population becomes, the more are born.

We are now living in an age of technological explosion. Technological innovations are mutually reinforcing, which accounts for the accelerating growth of technology.

Biological evolution, being 'opportunistic', in the sense mentioned (p. 68), may also be driven by positive feedback. However, the direction of biological evolution is always under the control of the adaptation of the evolving type to the environment. A particular form of adaptation may lose its survival potential because of changes in the environment. If so, a species may become extinct or 'change direction' to adapt to the new environment. But a sustained counter-adaptive direction is not possible in biological evolution.

In cultural evolution no such control operates. Changes are incorporated into a culture, not necessarily because they enhance the survival value of the culture. They may be simply the result of positive feedback, since cultural change produces *its own* (man-made) environment. Adaptations are made to *it*, and there is no guarantee that these adaptations enhance the survival potential of the culture.

In fact, whether innovations within a cultural matrix have a survival value for the culture is difficult to decide, because, as has already been pointed out, it is difficult to decide whether a culture has survived or has died or has changed into another culture. Unlike species, 'culture' is a vague concept, dependent on what aspects of life have been singled out as defining it. The concept comprises roughly what is generally understood as a 'way of life'. But the importance assigned to different aspects of a 'way of life' varies with what is particularly valued. Thus, culture changes cannot be unambiguously related to the survival of cultures. We can, however, raise the question as to what cultural changes – particularly the rapid, now explosive ones – portend for the survival of man. The question has become of pressing importance because the very changes that have been taken for granted (at least, in technically advanced societies) as continually enhancing man's survival potential are now seen as threats to man's survival.

CHAPTER 8

The Idea of Progress

Cultural evolution is channeled into certain directions and accelerated along those directions by mutually reinforcing interactions among material, behavioral, and attitudinal items. The interaction of science and technology, and of the attitudes engendered by them, is the most pronounced example of this process. And it is the evolution of culture along the direction charted by these particular interactions that has provided the strongest impetus to modern ideas concerning the uniqueness of man.

The mutually reinforcing interactions that have determined this direction are obvious and conspicuous. The use of tools and of symbolic language marks the appearance of Man. At first, technology advanced quite slowly. Many thousands of years elapsed before the practice of domesticating plants and animals spread throughout the human race. Once dependence on domesticated plants and animals became established (probably along the great rivers of the Middle East, India, and China), corresponding changes in the character of human societies followed rapidly. Since agriculture insured enough food to support large numbers of people in a small area, social organization based on factors other than immediate blood kinship could come into being. Now also possession of arable land became a requisite of survival, and organized warfare began. The practice of organized warfare stimulated both technological and social innovations.

Agricultural practices made men aware of their dependence on seasonal cycles. Because noting the regular motions of heavenly bodies provided methods of keeping track of time, an incipient science appeared. Empirical generalizations were stimulated also by animal breeding practices and by medical practices. Soon accumulation of experience transmitted over generations made the body of available knowledge and of developed skills too vast to be retained by a single mind. Specialization appeared and with it the stratification of human society according to occupations.

Religion appeared as a foundation for social solidarity and as a crystallization in symbols of men's fears, desires, and aspirations, now no longer limited to the welfare of a small, familiar band but extended to a whole 'people' bound by language and a common past. Note that now the binding force itself became symbolic. Not direct familiarity with a person now marked him as 'one of us', but the symbols he used and responded to – his language, his awareness of the past, his practice of ritual – even if he was never seen in the flesh. The recognition of 'one's own' produced its obverse as a matter of course: the concept of 'enemy', too, was defined in abstract terms, the 'enemy' now becoming an enemy by virtue of belonging to another group identified as hostile.

Awareness of 'man', transcending group identification, seems to have emerged during the first millennium B.C., the period marked by the appearance of 'universal' religions (as distinguished from tribal religions). We can only speculate about the impetus that gave rise to the idea of 'the brotherhood of man'. It may have been an extension of the idea of solidarity with one's own kind. Or it may have been a response to the frightful devastations and suffering brought about by organized warfare, which appeared along with 'civilization' (that is, with large, organized societies).

The first millennium B.C. witnessed also the appearance of philosophy, in part, perhaps, a by-product of generalized religions, in part, a consequence of writing.

In recounting the history of civilization, the invention of writing (about 3000 B.C.) is often cited as the second 'take-off' point, or threshold (cf. p. 39), following the domestication of plants. The importance of written records, as depositories of knowledge accumulated beyond the capacity of individual memory, is obvious. Writing performed another important function. Being slower and less spontaneous than talking, writing served to organize ideas and so was conducive to the development of generalizations and abstractions.

As symbolic language permits a dissociation of communication from what is immediate and present (cf. Chapter 5), written language does so even more. Additionally, written records make possible direct communication over many generations, facilitating intimate contact with the past and fixing more firmly the awareness of the past. A writer, realizing that he addresses not some particular person but an *audience*, including generations still unborn, is motivated to generalize, to speculate. Thus, along with the awareness of Man in general, his nature and fate (the concern of universal religions), there emerged an awareness of the world and attempts to understand it through *articulated* generalizations of experience.

In classical Greek philosophy we find perhaps the first explicit concept of man as the reasoning animal, and, in Aristotle's writings, a formal exposition of the reasoning process, logic. There and then we find also the first remarkably full flowering of the original deductive science, mathematics, systematically constructed by formal logic.

This new conception of man as a reasoning animal differed fundamentally from the conceptions offered by universal religions. Where the latter depended on introspective appreciation of soul, immortality, kinship to the Deity, and the like, the ability to arrive at truth by reason was presumably demonstrable by an *experiment*.

Such an experiment (whether actually conducted or invented) is reported in one of Plato's Dialogues. A young slave is brought into the company of intellectuals and is guided in the demonstration of a theorem of geometry.[1] The most remarkable thing about this scene is that it was meant to illustrate man's ability to arrive at a truth by his own power. Truth is here represented not as something revealed to man by a Deity and thereafter passed on through authority, but as something that exists apart from any authority and is to be discovered by intellectual effort. Moreover, truth is shorn of mystery. It becomes accessible to the humblest mind. The role of teaching is shown to be that of directing the human mind to certain questions. The answers are not given by the teacher. They occur to the student who enjoys the autonomy of his own reasoning power. Here is the germ of the scientific conception of truth.

Systematic reasoning is only one half of the 'fertilized cell' from which science grew. The other half, the experimental method, took almost two thousand years in making its appearance. The union of the two in the late Renaissance is usually cited as the next important 'take-off' point of civilization.

The scientific revolution in the sixteenth and seventeenth centuries and the industrial revolution in the eighteenth mark the beginning of so-called 'modern' civilization. From that time on, unidirectional cultural change becomes clearly perceptible in the West and the concept of evolution begins to dominate man's awareness of himself and of the world. The period is marked by accelerated growth of population, of areas under centralized political control, and, above all, of science and technology spreading from Europe to all parts of the world where the Europeans had extended their dominance. The mutually reinforcing interactions of material, behavioral, and mental items of culture become conspicuous. The commonplace observation is that science gave birth to modern technology (via the harnessing of energy sources). However, as someone has pointedly remarked, it is possible that the steam engine has done more for science than science has done for the steam engine.

Technology is older than science, and, until science matured as a systematic and organized social activity, theories grew out of practice rather than the other way around. Once the mutually reinforcing interactions set in, however, the 'substrate' and the 'product' could be easily reversed. By then, technology was stimulated not only by 'practical' needs but also by the needs of pure scientific investigations; for example, in electrodynamics and chemistry. Coupled to both were entirely new patterns of behavior and entirely new attitudes.

Consider the following excerpt from Goethe's *Faust*. The scene is the Emperor's Court. The treasurer has just declared that the Empire is on the verge of bankruptcy. Mephistopheles in the guise of the Jester gives advice:

> Where in this world doth not some lack appear?
> Here this, there that, – but money's lacking here.
> True, from the floor you can't at once collect it,
> But deepliest hidden, wisdom may detect it.
> In veins of mountains, under building bases,
> Coined and uncoined, there's gold in many places:
> And ask you who shall bring it to the light?
> A man endowed with Mind's and Nature's might.

This proposal *to go after* what is wanted, by application and ingenuity, is not easily accepted by the medieval mind. The Chancellor resists the suggestion:

> Nature and Mind – to Christians we don't speak so,
> Thence to burn Atheists we seek so.
> For such discourses very dangerous be.
> Nature is Sin, and Mind is Devil:
> Doubt they beget in shameless revel.[2]

The battle is joined and Mephistopheles prevails, anticipating the outcome of the struggle between conservatism and dynamism, between negative feedback, seeking to keep a culture in a steady state, and positive feedback, seeking to propel accelerating cultural change through acquisition of power.

The victory of dynamism was complete. Europe embarked on an open-ended program of conquest. The scientific age was launched in a climate of unbridled appetites. The rationalization of science as a profoundly humane and humanizing enterprise was to come later.

It could not have been otherwise, for the so-called 'scientific method' is the fusion of reason and action. Reason alone could not effect the launching. Pure reason, disciplined and precise, can lead at most to the flowering of mathematics, as it did in classical Greece. If it is free-wheeling, following all the metaphorical ramifications of its symbolism, it leads to scholastic philosophy and theology, as it did in medieval Europe and in India. The true beginning of modern science is the experiment – a fusion of reason and action. In the experiment, the scientist does much more than 'listen' to what nature chooses to tell him, as he does in observations. In the experiment, the scientist puts a direct question to nature, that is, *compels* nature to answer a question which he, the scientist, has formulated. Reason guides the formulation of questions so that the answers do not pile up in an untidy heap but are fitted into a logical scheme, called a theory.

Reason coupled with action implies an organization of *sequences* of actions, hence a choice of direction, hence the vision of a goal. The modality of the scientist's activity, therefore is conscious goal-directedness and the rationalization of actions in terms of how they serve goals. It is the *instrumental* modality, as distinguished from, say, expressive modality, where actions are results of immediately felt inner needs regardless of whether they bring the satisfaction of those needs. Thus, the scientist who designs an elaborate experimental program and a chain of deductive reasoning with a view to 'establishing truth' acts in the same modality as the military strategist who designs an elaborate plan of campaign in order to destroy an enemy force, or as Machiavelli's model Prince who weaves an intricate web of intrigue in order to destroy potential rivals and challengers to his power. The moral dimensions of these various types of actions are not being compared here; only their modalities. They are all of the instrumental type, where choices of actions are determined predominantly by anticipated consequences. At any given time, the consequences are evaluated in relation to (usually, clearly specified) goals. But the goals themselves typically turn out to be but stepping stones toward further goals. The dynamism of this modality is absolute; no steady state is envisaged.

As we examine the history of any system that resembles a living system by the criteria discussed in Chapter 2, we see a period of growth that culminates in a steady state and eventually a decline and extinction. In the case of the individual organism, extinction (senility and death) occurs as a consequence of the 'wearing out' of the mechanisms that maintain the steady state. (The nature of this process is far from being completely understood.) In the case of a species, extinction is usually a result of changes in the environment (which may include the appearance of competing organisms, predators, etc.). The species previously adapted to the environment now becomes maladapted and the population can no longer be maintained in a steady state. We see similar processes in cultural evolution. Certain items of culture 'grow' (by being copiously reproduced), then decline when they are no longer adapted to their environment, i.e., man and his perceived needs.[3] This is clearly the case with specific items of technology. The sailing ship underwent a steady development, reaching a high degree of perfection and a peak of its 'population' just before steamships appeared, then declined, remaining only as a 'vestige' in modern technology, serving recreational but not utilitarian functions.

Cultures and entire civilizations have seen their days of growth, full flowering, and decay. Various art forms and styles exhibit the same sort of life cycle. Styles of painting, architecture, music, literature, all resemble the branches of an evolutionary tree. Each has had a 'golden age', fol-lowed by a period of extreme elaboration and, finally, extinction.

The idea of 'progressive evolution' pictures the process as a growing tree, the branches terminating but the trunk continuing to grow. Whether this model can be applied to, say, the arts is an open question. To do so would imply a continuity in art, a process of development in which new art styles or art forms *include* the earlier ones in the sense that the later artists can do everything that the earlier artists have done. That such is the case is doubtful. It is unlikely that sculpture identical in style and equal in quality (whatever this may mean) to classical Greek sculpture can ever be produced. Nor will Beethoven's Tenth Symphony ever be composed; nor the sequel to *War and Peace* about the Decembrists that Tolstoy once thought of writing.

Science is a conspicuous exception to this rule. Unlike art styles, ways of life, states, or empires, no part of science has ever died. *All* scientific knowledge available to our predecessors is available today. Mathematics offers the foremost example of this ever-cumulative process. There is not a single problem of mathematics which a mathematician of the previous generations could solve that some mathematicians (usually many, some-times all) of the present generation cannot solve. Moreover, the larger the time span, the more disparate becomes the power of contemporary mathematics compared with that of the earlier period. The most complex problems of antiquity are within the grasp of any competent student of today.

The case of technology is more complicated because much of techno-logy includes specialized skills, which may be lost or which may be developed in unequal degrees in different cultures. Thus, not all of contemporary technology 'includes' all previous technologies in the way that all contemporary mathematics includes all of previous mathematics. Therefore, in comparing two technologies, we cannot decide quite as easily as in the case of mathematics which is the more 'primitive' and which the more 'advanced'. Nevertheless, if we accept the measuring stick usually applied to technologies, namely the extent to which a technology 'makes man independent of his *physical* environment', a case can be made for a unidirectional, 'progressive' development of technology for the past 10,000 years, with a discontinuity about two hundred years ago that resulted in a fantastic explosion.

It is easy to see that acceleration of technological growth provides an impetus for even greater acceleration. At first, natural forces were harnessed to move things (flowing water to turn millstones, steam to propel vehicles). Then power was harnessed to tap new sources of power (gasoline engines to drill oil wells, electric power to release atomic energy). At first, machines were used to make things – cloth, for instance – then designed to make other machines. The same self-propelling processes occurred in science. At first, physics inquired into the 'physical' properties of matter; chemistry, into the 'chemical' properties. Then the two were fused so that the insights of physics unlocked the secrets of chemistry. At first, the methods of physical and biological sciences had little in common. Later they were fused in biophysics and biochemistry. Mathematics as the general tool of deduction (a tremendous extension of logic) came to be applied in every science where theories had reached a certain level of maturity.

Even more important than the mutually reinforcing interactions within the sciences, and the interactions of science and technology, was the influence exerted by science on the general outlook of men living in scientific-industrial societies. The prevailing outlook became that of activism and dynamism already mentioned in connection with the ideology of the Renaissance. Central in this outlook is the conscious, goal-seeking actor, who is not a god but a man. This actor pursues his goal by manipulating the world about him. He is able to do so because he knows the connections between causes and effects. Consequently, he knows that in order to bring about the desired effects, he need only bring about conditions that will lead to them.

It may seem that this is the outlook of any rational man, and that there is no need to relate it to a particular historical period or to a particular culture. But this is by no means the case. The objections to Mephistopheles' advice voiced by Goethe's Chancellor represent a once pervasive outlook. The attitude of passivity or resignation is also central in certain religions, in the original forms of Christianity and Buddhism, for example. It has found also distinct and eloquent expression in the late writings of Tolstoy, who expressly rejected the idea that man should individually or collectively intervene in the course of events in pursuit of specific goals, no matter how worthy these goals appear in consequence of rationalization. And, of course, fatalism, the idea that attempts to avoid predestined events invariably fail, permeates Greek tragedy and must reflect, at least in part, the outlook of that age and culture.

In the context of politics, the 'actor' appears either as an individual seeking power (like Machiavelli's Prince) or a social organism (such as a State). In the context of economics (preoccupation with which became intense following the Industrial Revolution), the actor is the entrepreneur seeking profit. In the context of scientific humanism, the actor becomes Man seeking to improve his condition by transforming his environment to suit his needs.

The idea of evolution fitted admirably into the conception of 'progress' that dominated Western thought in the nineteenth century. Typically, evolution appeared in the philosophy of the period as progress toward perfection. Biological evolution culminated in Man. With man another evolutionary process began, namely the 'progress of civilization' marked by ever-increasing mastery of nature through applications of science and the perfectibility of man, a parallel moral progress. Lapses of morality were ascribed to ignorance or to misery. With the improvement of material conditions (achieved by ever-increasing technology) and the spread of education (necessitated by the new methods of production and made possible by decreasing the burden of labor), men were expected to become more civilized, that is, more reasonable, less ridden by superstition, better behaved. This betterment was thought to go hand in hand with greater democratization of the political process (a principal 'progressive' cause in nineteenth-century Europe), and, in time, the blessings of civilization would be extended to the 'primitive' people. Democratization should put the interests of the majorities foremost on the political agenda, and these would supplant the ambitions and rivalries of princes. Thus, eventually mankind could anticipate being delivered from the plague of wars, from drudgery, ignorance, and disease.

Mastery over the environment and enlightenment were not the only blessings expected from the unimpeded growth of science. The practice of science suggested, in addition to the conquest of environment, also a way of establishing truth independently of the commitments, prejudices, or pre-dispositions of men. The enmity between the Catholics and the Protestants, erupting in the religious wars of the sixteenth and seventeenth centuries which devastated much of Europe, seemed to stem from a clash of beliefs. Persecutions of heretics and other religious dissenters had marked the entire history of Christian Europe. It seemed that science, by establishing universal criteria of truth, provided a common ground for agreement among all men. Conflicts among men, however, have not always been about what is *true*. Many arise from disagreements about what ought to be, whereas scientific truth is concerned with what *is*. In the nineteenth century, this distinction between what is good and what is true was not always sharp. The distinction continues to be blunted by the instrumental outlook. This means that if an act is evaluated primarily in terms of its consequences it appears as if the discovery of what is good depends upon knowing the consequences of acts; therefore, it appears that such knowledge should fall within the area of scientific inquiry.

Faith in science as an instrument of progress was not limited to its application in manipulating the non-human environment. In 1822, Auguste Comte, sometimes called the Father of Sociology, wrote:

It is clear that scientific men alone constitute a really compact and active body, all of whose members throughout Europe have a mutual understanding and communicate easily and continuously among themselves. This springs from the fact that they alone, in our day, possess common ideas, a uniform language, a general and permanent aim. No other class possesses these powerful advantages, because no other fulfills the above conditions in their integrity. The industrial classes, even, so eminently disposed to union by the character of their labors and habits, are still too much influenced by hostile inspirations of a savage patriotism to allow of their establishing as yet a real European alliance among themselves . . .

To resume then; the necessity for confiding to Scientific Men the preliminary theoretical labors recognized as indispensable for reorganizing society is solidly based upon four distinct considerations, each of which would have sufficed to establish it: 1) scientific men are by the character of their intellectual capacity and cultivation alone competent to execute these works; 2) from the nature of the case, this office is reserved for them as constituting the spiritual power of the system to be organized; 3) they, exclusively, possess the moral authority requisite in our day to determine the adoption of the new organic doctrine when formed; 4) and finally, of all the social forces in existence, that of scientific men is alone European. Such a combination of proofs should without doubt place the great theoretic mission of scientific men beyond question and controversy.[4]

It is interesting to observe that Comte does not assume that everything is right in nineteenth-century Europe. In fact, the opening sentence of his essay is 'A social system is in decline, a new system arrived at maturity and approaching its completion – such is the fundamental character which the general progress of civilization has assigned to the present epoch.'

He goes on to describe the crisis that resulted from the disorganization of the old system: '. . . society is hurried toward a profound moral and political anarchy which appears to menace it with a near and inevitable dissolution.'

The danger is great but the remedy is available – Science, the application of factual knowledge and sober, dispassionate reasoning, unencumbered by 'savage patriotism', applied to the business at hand – the reorganization of European society after the upheavals of the French Revolution and its aftermaths.

The essentially cooperative and rational spirit of scientific activity gave rise also to the idea of socialism, the principle of organizing the productive forces of a society along cooperative lines so that the incentive for production would be the satisfaction of human needs rather than profit, as under private enterprise. The idea of a communist society was inherent in early Christianity, but its rationale had been a purely ethical one – the brotherhood of man. In the nineteenth century, the abolition of private ownership of the means of production was argued (for instance, by Robert Owen) as a way of organizing society more rationally, specifically to eliminate the waste of competition and to avoid social tensions by a more equitable distribution of wealth.

Karl Marx rejected this approach to socialism as 'utopian'. He did not argue that society 'ought' to be organized along socialist lines but that it *will* be so organized eventually, because of the forces already at work in capitalist society. We shall be examining the Marxist theory of the class struggle in Chapter 13. Here we shall only remark that Marx, like the 'utopian' socialists, also placed complete faith in Science as the instrument of human progress. In fact, he sought to extend the activist component of science to encompass revolutionary action. Just as natural science was able to 'take off' only when men put direct questions to nature by manipulating it (experimenting), so a genuine social science would emerge, according to Marx, only when men, instead of contemplating the nature of society, take active steps to change it in accordance with their interests. This role was assigned to the 'proletariat', the new class produced by capitalist society and preparing its doom.

Especially pertinent to our discussion is the view emerging in the nineteenth century, that continued progress guided by science will eventually lead to the abolition of war, which, in this view, is pictured as an anachronism. Sheldon Amos wrote:

... the teachings of history certainly are to the effect that practices and institutions, which at one time seem to be necessary conditions of social and political conditions of all people, and yet which stand condemned as counter to principles of morality, justice, and political expediency, vanish in an almost inconceivably short space of time, and become so far obsolete as to be with difficulty revived, even in imagination.[5]

Amos goes on to trace the progressive 'humanization' of war among 'civilized states'.

... the modes of conducting Wars between such States have been steadily undergoing changes *in one continuous direction* [emphasis added], the object of these changes being the diminution of miseries inherent in warfare, the limitation of its area, and the alleviation of the evils incidentally occasioned by it to the Neutral States.[6]

To be sure, these rules and considerations seldom apply to wars waged against 'primitive people'. Nevertheless,

... it may be expected ... that these Wars will decrease as the knowledge of the Science and practice in the Art of Government progresses ...[7]

The key to the abolition of war is the application of control guided by knowledge.

... even if there are those who regard all hopes for a time of permanent Peace as utopian, it is not denied in any quarter that there are general causes which produce both Peace and War, and that these causes can, to some extent, be controlled so as to foster the one and not the other.[8]

In short, the nineteenth century was dominated by an almost unbounded faith in progress, with science as its instrument and activism as its motivating force.

The trauma of World War I shook not so much this deeply internalized faith in science as the conviction that man is a 'rational being' without qualifications. For it was not enough to explain the cataclysm by pointing to the intrigues in the chancelleries, the struggle for markets, or the machinations of munition makers. Somehow the fact had to be explained that, at the outbreak of that war, people in Europe's capitals shed tears of happiness and embraced strangers on the streets, and that the slaughter continued for four years although it was clear after a few months that a cheap decisive victory was out of the question and that the cost in blood and treasure would far exceed any gains that a 'formal' victory could bring.

Questions asked about World War I included, significantly, questions about what induced pecpl: to fight. In the past, armies fought because that is what armies were for; it made as little sense to ask why soldiers fought as to ask why farmers sowed and reaped. After the Napoleonic Wars, European military establishments abandoned the professional army in favor of the conscripted 'citizen' army. During that century, the democratic ideas stimulated by the French Revolution spread and penetrated the popular consciousness. After World War I, the question – what made ordinary people kill other ordinary people whom they had never seen or heard of – opened a host of entirely new questions about the nature of man and of human society and about the meaning of 'progress'.

During the succeeding two decades a great deal of attention was paid to the uses of language for the purpose of manipulating the behavior of large numbers of people. 'Propaganda' became a household and newspaper word. It was commonplace to explain that the European masses were seduced by 'propaganda' into harboring strong feelings of solidarity with the rulers of their own nations and even stronger feelings of hatred for both the rulers and the people of enemy nations. Revolutionaries in the belligerent countries, particularly in those that suffered defeats –

Russia, Austria, and Germany – used the disillusionment of the masses to good advantage. Similar propaganda techniques, symbols of solidarity and of hatred, were employed in bringing the resentment of the disillusioned populations – particularly of the working classes and, in Russia, of the peasantry – to the ignition point. As a result, these three imperial dynasties of continental Europe vanished.

For a while it appeared to the Russian Marxists that the proletarian revolution prophesied by Marx had begun at last. Although, to their own surprise, it started in a country least suited for it (industrially the weakest of the European powers), it seemed then only a matter of months until the war-weary working classes of the other belligerents, particularly of Germany, would follow the example of the Bolsheviks and establish their own proletarian dictatorships, the springboards to socialism constructed on scientific principles. This, however, did not come to pass. The rest of Europe settled down to the same system of sovereign capitalist states except for replacing some monarchical regimes with 'republican' ones.

Yet, something had changed fundamentally. The old faith in continual, unimpeded 'progress' vanished, at least in Western Europe (it lingered for another generation in the United States). The hatreds fomented by militant nationalism, temporarily diverted against the ruling classes in the aftermath of the war, smoldered on, particularly in Germany, and within a few years broke out in another manic holocaust.

It seemed clear that Science, which conferred on man power over the 'forces of nature', was not sufficient for 'progress' if these forces could be turned by man against himself. It became fashionable to repeat that 'unless man learned to control himself as well as nature, he will destroy himself.' And some put it positively, as Comte had, that 'scientists' should be called upon to construct a 'scientific theory of society' that would open the way to a rational organization of human affairs. Yet, the use of such a theory as a key to a better society did not now seem as straightforward as it had to Comte. To Comte, it appeared as if 'all resolve[d] itself into establishing, through the combined efforts of European savants, a positive theory in politics . . ., which shall bring our social system into harmony with the present state of knowledge.'[9] Perhaps Comte was still not sufficiently far removed from the age of absolute monarchies, when 'reforms' could be instituted by edicts. It is difficult otherwise to understand what he meant by a 'positive theory' bringing our system 'into harmony with the present state of knowledge'. Is 'theory' an agent that can enact changes in a social system? Or did he suppose that the rulers would act as agents of change, once the savants discovered and disclosed the 'positive theory'?

At the time Comte wrote, the idea of 'people's sovereignty' was a pillar of political faith in the United States. 'The people' were the supposed ultimate authority in all matters pertaining to the conduct of human affairs. The problem of multiple wills and interests was considered neatly solved by the mechanisms of representative government. In a way, this doctrine was a variant of the old one that the king can do no wrong, with 'the people' substituted for the king.

The salutary effect of progressive democratization has been an article of faith in scientific humanism. Scientific knowledge, being knowledge of objective truth, is supposed to be accessible to all minds not fettered by dogma. At the time when it was still a revolutionary ideal, democracy was invariably associated with freedom of thought, speech, and press; with the right to challenge established beliefs by which privilege was rationalized. It was thought that the democratization of political power together with its correlates, the spread of popular education, social equalization, and civil liberties, would usher in an age where scientific knowledge could be utilized to the fullest to improve the human condition.

Alexis de Tocqueville, a contemporary of Comte, already foresaw with impressive insight the ambivalent effects of democracy on human society. Tocqueville viewed the development in the United States (which he called 'the first new nation') with serious misgivings. He saw the paradoxical correlation between democratization and the centralization of power. The centralization results from the erosion of traditional authority – the family, local community, and morality. 'Authority' and 'power', it should be noted, are not synonymous. The former rests on the inner nature of association, on functionally rooted allegiance. Power is exercised by coercion. In fact, power is exercised most openly and ruthlessly precisely when authority is eroded. Centralization of power attendant with democratization occurs, according to Tocqueville, as a result of the erosion of 'intermediate' social authorities standing between the individual and the emerging bureaucracy in which power in democratic societies is vested.

Tocqueville wrote about 'the tyranny of the majority', anticipating the hegemony imposed by mass culture, whether in formal democracies (as in latter-day United States) or in mass-supported totalitarian states. The extent of Tocqueville's farsightedness can be appreciated from his anticipation of race conflicts in the United States. In the South, he noted, where slavery still existed, questions of status (and the malaise induced by class mobility) did not arise. Once the Negroes were freed, however, and once their aspirations (stimulated by formal avowals of social equality) were aroused, intense conflicts would become inevitable.

. . . once raised to the level of free men, they will soon revolt at being denied all their civil rights, and as they cannot become the equals of whites, they will speedily show themselves as enemies.[10]

Paradoxically, the erosion of faith in the twin blessings of science and democracy had already begun even as this faith was becoming the source of a new religion (scientific humanism). For a while the faith seemed to be gaining ground, at least in the Western world, the fountainhead of both science and democratic ideals. From the second half of the nineteenth century to World War I, futuristic novels were still utopian (Edward Bellamy, *Looking Backward*; H. G. Wells, *A World Set Free*) and the unbounded potentialities of technology still inspired romance of adventure, as in the fantasies of Jules Verne and Wells. Eventually, however, the anti-utopian novel became predominant (Aldous Huxley, *Brave New World*; George Orwell, *Nineteen Eighty-Four*).

Today the sense of confidence in the future, once the dominant mood in the West, has given way to despair and anxiety, the companions of loss of faith in God. By 'God' I mean here not The God (or gods) worshipped in traditional churches but the gods by whose imagined commands people guide their everyday secular activities. In the West, Progress had been a God of this sort, first and foremost technological progress, the source of abundance and of protection against the physical environment. Another God has been social progress, worshipped by both liberals and revolutionaries. To the former, the will of this God was to be revealed through social evolution toward ever greater realization of freedom via democratization, public education, and rationalization of institutions. To the latter, the will of the God of history was to be revealed in social revolutions, the last of which would abolish all social stratification by ending private ownership of resources and machines. Social evolution and revolutions have occurred but, instead of the promised millennia, new tyrannies have emerged, derived neither from hereditary privilege nor from private ownership of the means of production.

Can hope persist without faith in *some* God? The humanists attempted to raise man to the status of God. Man's faith in himself, however, has not taken root. The pessimism of our age stems from the conviction that man, either because of inherent inadequacy of his nature or because of the environment he created for himself, has only a grim future (if any) to look forward to. The two presumed sources of man's plight are, of course, inter-related. As to which is the primary source, the answer is not of the 'either-or' type. Man may have created the environment in which he finds himself because 'he is what he is'. But he may have become what he seems to be because of the environment he created. If so, then the view that man has attained freedom from the tyranny of nature by shaping his environment 'to suit his needs' must be critically re-examined. Indeed, judging by the ground swell of lamentation and despairing prognoses of impending doom that now dominate the 'collective voice of civilized man', the opposite view is already in ascendance: that the man-made environment is enslaving man, perhaps dooming him to extinction, by endowing him with the power to destroy himself.

CHAPTER 9

A Day in the Lives of Mr A and Mr Z

We left Mr A waiting for a train that was to take him to work in Pluto-polis. The train came exactly when expected. (Mr A glanced at his watch, synchronized with the clock in the astronomical laboratory.) In the car, he saw Mr Z, his superior, on whose good will his present pattern of life (as he pictured it) depended. Mr Z cordially returned Mr A's greeting and invited his subordinate to sit down beside himself.

Mr Z had boarded the train at the preceding station. The train carried a car reserved for passengers of Mr Z's standing, a sort of private club car, where a group of them, by paying extra, enjoyed their exclusiveness, played cards each morning, and drank each afternoon. Mr Z, however, did not join the club. He prided himself on his democratic views and rode to work with ordinary passengers.

Mr Z's income was twenty-six times larger than Mr A's. His house was accordingly larger than Mr A's, but, of course, not twenty-six times larger. It cost only about three times as much as Mr A's house. The suit worn by Mr Z cost twice as much as Mr A's. He had three cars to Mr A's two. His breakfast, however, was exactly the same as Mr A's.

The difference in appearance and in mode of living between Mr A and someone with an income one twenty-sixth of Mr A's was vastly larger than that between Mr A and Mr Z. People living on that fraction of Mr A's income, or less (in comparable units), constituted on that day over one half of humanity. Mr A had often seen pictures of those people and their emaciated children, published in advertisements appealing for help, and occasionally he contributed to appropriate agencies. However, he was much more aware of the difference between his condition and Mr Z's. He saw himself at the beginning of a career, of which Mr Z represented the epitome. Mr A's semantic environment was almost completely spanned by the two positions, analogous to the lowest and the highest ranks of an officers' corps.

At work, Mr A's role corresponded approximately to that of a lieutenant in the army, and Mr Z's to that of a general. Their familiarity was a consequence of the fact that Mr A was a sort of aide-de-camp to Mr Z. Mr Z made operational decisions. Mr A was the link between the high command and the subordinate 'line officers'. He also had some special knowledge that was valued by Mr Z.

Mr Z's decisions were ramified through a network of echelons, and the resulting actions were considered of the utmost importance by all concerned with their effects. The actions started or stopped the production of a great variety of commodities, hired or laid off thousands of workers. The market prices of the commodities produced (or not produced) rose and fell. In consequence of these fluctuations, which were quickly and accurately reported in the press, other prices fluctuated, not so much of commodities as of pieces of paper, which thousands of people bought and sold *because* the prices fluctuated. Sometimes in the process of these transactions people became very rich or comparatively poor. This, however, happened only occasionally. For the most part, the fluctuations had no effect on the physical environment of the people actually involved in the transactions. They continued to live in the same houses, to eat the same food, to ride the same trains, and to suffer the same diseases. Nevertheless, the fluctuations made a great difference in the way those people felt. Mr Z had seen the cryptic line of print that had put Mr A in a good mood, and he too was immensely pleased to see it. For a while, Mr A and Mr Z discussed this topic. Both of them judged the policies of their government and even the state of the world by the way numbers published in newspaper columns increased or decreased.

Actually, the state of the world *was* affected by those numbers. Through long chains of events, about which Mr Z knew a great deal (for which Mr A admired and respected him), the upward and downward fluctuations affected world-wide transactions. These, in turn, were linked (both as causes and as effects) with the world prices of several commodities on which the man-made environment depended: steel, petroleum, manganese, sugar, copper, wheat, etc. The price levels of such commodities influenced the flow of capital and so the allocation of resources and of production capacity throughout the world, hence the mode of living in far-flung regions. However, Mr A and Mr Z were concerned not with these effects but with others, purely symbolic ones, of which they became aware only through spoken or printed combinations of words. Awareness of these words occupied most of their waking hours.

The flow of capital in the world depended not only on the price levels and the demand for commodities but also on government policies in different countries. The government of Plutonia, of which Mr A and Mr Z were citizens, was interested in the widest possible access to exported capital. To a considerable degree the attitude of this government to other governments depended on the hospitality extended to Plutonian investments. In fact, for some years, the governments of the world were categorized by the Plutonian government as friendly or hostile, depending on whether Plutonian investments were welcome in the respective countries or not. The Plutonian government was also deeply concerned with the safety of Plutonian investments abroad and was constantly apprehensive of political changes that would endanger these investments.

Plutonia was considered by most Plutonians to be the political leader of the 'Free World', comprising the countries where Plutonian capital could be invested. The strongest power outside of Plutonia's economic and political orbit was Neptunia.

On their way to the city, Mr Z explained to Mr A that he had an overnight bag with him because he was to catch a transoceanic plane late that afternoon. He was going to Neptunia for a couple of days. Trips of this sort were within the normal range of Mr Z's activities. He had flown across oceans on similar missions eight times in the past five months. At one time it amused Mr Z to think that his grandfather would have been astonished at the idea of crossing an ocean in a few hours, just as *his* grandfather would not have believed that continents could be crossed in a few days. But Mr Z had long stopped thinking of these matters. The first-class airplane cabin had become simply his 'other office'.

Neptunia and Plutonia had been enemies for thirty years. They had never waged war against each other but had been in a constant state of readiness for it. Rocket-launching devices of both countries were aimed at their respective cities and known rocket sites. In both countries, communication networks had been organized with a view of initiating in a matter of minutes a sequence of events over the entire planet, designed to maximize the destruction wreaked on the 'enemy' and to minimize the damage inflicted by 'him'.

Most citizens of both Plutonia and Neptunia considered this state of affairs to be anomalous and deplorable but unavoidable. If Mr A and Mr Z were asked why Neptunia and Plutonia were enemies, they would explain that this was because the Neptunian leaders wanted to conquer the world, or at least to extend their influence over the world by imposing on others the Neptunian form of government and the associated ideology. This ideology, Mr A and Mr Z would go on to explain, was inimical to the Plutonian way of life, which Plutonians were determined to defend. If asked whether the Neptunians were preparing to impose their ideology on Plutonia by destroying Plutonian cities, Mr A and Mr Z would reply that this was not the point. The point was that Plutonian might was a bulwark against Neptunian domination of the rest of the world, and for this reason Neptunia was preparing to destroy Plutonia if the opportunity ever arose, which was why Plutonia had to remain in readiness to wreak destruction on Neptunia.

It might be said that for three decades Neptunia and Plutonia *had* been at war, but this war was fought only on the symbolic level with words as missiles. There were practically no casualties, except for a few individuals killed by their own governments. They were killed because, it was said, they had given the enemy information that could be used in a real war.

The war of words was itself fought on two levels. On one, the words referred to concrete things, namely the rocket-launching devices, their range and accuracy, and other accoutrements of military might. On the other level, the words referred to ideas. Each side disparaged the other's interpretation of history, conceptions of man and of the nature of freedom, the belief (or disbelief) in God, etc. The barrage of words was aimed by the media of both countries at their own as well as at the enemy's populations. The references to the weaponry warned the enemy of the dire consequences of overstepping certain bounds of politico-military behavior. At the same time they were meant also to reassure the home populations that the devices of destruction were actually *protective* devices, insurance against the similar devices of the other. The references to ideas (for the most part 'ways of life') were ostensibly also directed at both populations. Essentially, however, the purpose of extolling one's own 'way of life' was to maintain the conviction within one's own population that the enemy was indeed an enemy, and that readiness for war was indispensable for maintaining peace.

In the early years, while the lethal systems of the two countries were being developed, the war of words had been extremely intense. Many, especially among the military of both countries, believed that a sudden unprovoked attack by the other was imminent, and so the two systems were kept in a state of perpetual alert. There had been a number of crises, some triggered by political events, others by misinterpreted signals. Eventually, the symmetry of the positions of the two powers led to an attenuation of sorts. Cautious approaches were made now by one side, now by the other, aimed at exploring paths to a possible modus vivendi.

Slowly and cautiously, the two powers established business relations of increasing scope. Each step facilitated the next (positive feedback) until there was a lively exchange of missions, joint endeavors of environment control (e.g., regulation of fisheries), exchange of innocuous scientific information, and so on.[1] Concurrently, the war of words abated, and few people on either side (except in the military, whose business it was) gave much thought to the two lethal systems.

Mr Z's journey to Neptunia was not the first. Negotiations between his firm and representatives of Neptunia's concerns had been going on for some months. His passport had been stamped with a special visa, which entitled him to come and go at will. Sometimes he would take off a few hours after a transoceanic telephone conversation. On this day, however, Mr Z would be traveling for the first time in a Neptunian plane, where room had been made for him with admirable dispatch on short notice. It was this circumstance that brought home to Mr Z the strangeness of the situation against the background of recent history.

The day at the office was a usual one for Mr Z, except that he had to arrange for Mr A to accompany him, since it turned out that Mr A's special knowledge was needed at the meeting. The arrangement went smoothly. A messenger was sent to Mr A's home to pick up his passport and an overnight bag. A few telephone calls, including one overseas, expedited the affixing of proper symbols to Mr A's passport at the local Neptunian consulate, which again prompted Mr Z to comment on the changed circumstances. In doing so, he waxed eloquent on the subject of One World, from which age-old enmities would be banished.

'They're coming around now,' Mr Z explained to Mr A at lunch. 'We would have done business with them years ago if they had taken off their blinkers and realized that business has nothing to do with politics. Doing business is cooperating for the common good. Sure, each tries to get the biggest hunk of the pie, but without business there would be no pie to cut. It's business that brings people together. All businessmen speak the same language.'

Mr Z was right about the language. He found that he and the Neptunian businessmen understood the same language of production schedules, returns on investment, world prices, labor costs, and transportation problems. They shared the same symbolic environment. The implications of any change in that environment (say, in the world price of steel) would be clear to all of them, and there would be considerable agreement among them on what constituted rational decisions and actions under the circumstances.

The military of the two powers had also established a cooperative relationship. They too had a common semantic environment and understood each other when they talked about the 'capabilities' of their respective arsenals, about offensive and defensive strategies, and such matters. Like the business establishment, the military also shared a common interest. The military leaders had long abandoned the mode of thought in which war was conceived as a wellspring of glory or even as a means of conquest. Both, however, had a stake in the continued prosperity of the military establishments, because their professional competence was involved in it, just as the professional competence of businessmen was involved in the prosperity of business establishments. The growth and sophistication of the war machines was as much a source of psychic satisfaction to them as the growth and complexity of enterprises was to people like Mr A and Mr Z. Since, in the minds of the political leaders, military capability continued to be identified with 'national security', the question of dismantling the war machines was never seriously considered. The existence of each was amply justified by the existence of the other. It is in this sense that the military leaders of the two powers 'cooperated'. Each provided the other with powerful support for continuing to demand and to get generous allocations of resources.

'Arms control' had been instituted, and the arms race 'leveled off'. However, each side had complete and elaborate plans for wreaking destruction on the other whenever the situation should make it mandatory. The military leaders of each side knew that their opposite numbers had such plans. Although the details of the plans were closely guarded secrets, each side had considerable knowledge of the other's strategic commitments, because all the leaders were competent practitioners of the same profession. They all knew the 'proper' responses to the anticipated events. The anticipation generated no resentment. The military leaders' feelings toward their opposite numbers (many of whom were cordial acquaintances) were rather similar to those of competent chess players toward each other.

Both the business world and the military world were unified by the same technology of communication and transportation, served by technicians and operators who could function as readily in one system as in the other. At the time that the messenger was fetching Mr A's passport, another messenger was carrying a briefcase full of coded messages to a control center. At the time the telephone conversation across an ocean facilitated the fixing of proper stamps to Mr A's passport, another telephone call confirmed the content of the coded messages.

At four o'clock in the afternoon a cab pulled up to the entrance of the building in which Mr A and Mr Z had their offices. They had come down with their bags thirty seconds earlier. They had never seen the driver of the cab, and he had no idea who they were. But two words were sufficient to explain to the driver everything he needed to know. The driver had been pre-conditioned to respond to these two words with a complex sequence of actions. His drive to the airport was a feat of virtuosity. Naturally, it was also aided by the intricately synchronized system of traffic lights, without which the streets would become impassable.

At the same time, an army general and his aide were being driven to another airport by another driver. Two words sent the driver on his way, and he delivered the two men at the proper destinations safely and on time.

At the one airport, Mr A and Mr Z presented pieces of paper to a man they had never seen and would never see again. He, too, knew exactly what to do and did it. At the gate they again presented pieces of paper, without which they could not pass the gate, not because of a physical obstacle but because they would have been told so by a young man, whose income was one ninetieth of Mr Z's, but without whose permission Mr Z and Mr A could not pass the gate.

Elsewhere, the general presented his credentials, and was allowed to pass through a door by an armed sergeant. Had he tried to force his way in without showing a proper piece of paper, he would have been shot.

The airplane boarded by Mr A and Mr Z was a 'species' of a long evolutionary line, a result of natural selection and a realization of thousand-year-old dreams, until recently fulfilled only in legends. However, this marvel made no more impression on Mr A and Mr Z than the cab they had left a few minutes earlier. Actually, the cab, too, was a result of centuries of thought, experimentation, and organized enterprise, which trained thousands of men to work with regimented precision.

Aboard they were served dinner by a young woman very much like hundreds of other young women in uniform who had served them on other occasions. Mr Z had been served this way in the stratosphere over five continents by young women of all the major 'races' of mankind, speaking all the major languages. They all had been trained to do exactly the same things – to demonstrate the oxygen masks and the life jackets, to serve food, drinks, and pillows, to send every de-planing passenger on his way with a smiling good-bye.

The young women in uniform who worked in the control center where the general made his appearance were also attractive, poised, efficient, and cheerful.

It was now dark, and the airborne ship was over the ocean between two continents. Mr A and Mr Z were dozing in their reclining seats. Inside their skins was an environment remarkably similar to ocean water. Their ancestors lived in that environment. When those fish-like ancestors left the oceans to become reptiles, they took the ocean environment with them inside their bodies in the form of fluids in which their cells continued to be immersed, as they had been in the ocean, and with which they interacted in order to maintain a steady state. Hundreds of millions of years later, the descendants of those reptiles learned to *surround* their bodies with an artificial environment and to take it with them under the sea, miles above the surface of the planet where no living thing could survive, and to the moon.

The inner physiological environments of all the other passengers were practically identical. Their mental lives, however, differed. Many shared the conceptions, concerns, and aspirations of Mr A and Mr Z. But others did not; for instance, the members of a returning Neptunian ballet company. These young people were completely absorbed in intricacies of body movements. The purpose of their journey to Plutonia was to exhibit virtuosity and grace in these movements, for which they were justly celebrated. The preoccupations of Mr A and Mr Z would seem incomprehensible or boring or even wicked to these youngsters, while their preoccupations would seem childish or somewhat absurd to Mr A and Mr Z. Nevertheless, both they and the two belonged to the same 'subspecies' of the human race – a class of people who traveled in airplanes, slept between sheets, were careful not to eat more than was good for them, read books and newspapers, and used contraceptives. Like the airplane itself, all the passengers except the very youngest, who was eight months old, were products of a broad semantic environment that enveloped one third of humanity.

The airplane, too, was immersed in an environment to which it was adapted through an evolutionary line of its own – rarified air at a temperature lethal to all life, rushing past at over a thousand miles per hour. The body lines of the airplane were just right for this environment. It also had a delicate sensory apparatus that enabled it to maintain a steady state – constant velocity on a pre-set course.

Besides the sensors that maintained its steady course, the airplane had another sub-system inside its body – a human being with sensors and an input-processing apparatus of its own. This sub-system reacted to the symbol inputs, which the airplane in its present stage of evolution still did not understand. Thus, the man-machine system, airplane-man, possessed not only the necessary tropisms (proper responses to gradients in the physical environment) and a nervous system that responded appropriately to signals, but also a 'brain' by means of which it recognized symbols. It could receive messages from all over the world, and these messages informed it about everything it needed to know in order to achieve its goal – to come down smoothly on the Neptupolis airport.

The airplane was not the latest product of its evolutionary line. A later product passed it, traveling at a speed ten times as great. Its goal was also Neptupolis. This object had no human 'brain'. Its motion was guided entirely by its own receptors, responding to messages sent from a place deep in Plutonia.

For a while after the airplane left Plutopolis, its 'brain' was active, receiving and processing messages from Plutonia. Then the 'brain' was disengaged and the craft depended only on its physical homeostasis. Eventually, it was expected, the 'brain' would be engaged again to receive messages from the point of destination. However, it was not to be this time. No messages addressed to the airplane were coming from Neptunia, nor from anywhere else, as if the world had forgotten about the airplane's existence. The world did, in fact, forget, because all foci of communication in the world were sending and receiving messages related to only one sequence of events – the rapidly developing crisis which within a few hours exploded in the dreaded nuclear war.

How this sequence of events could have occurred remains incomprehensible from the point of view of the expectations of informed and responsible people: they had all been convinced that the international situation had been 'stabilized'. However, the sequence of events followed its own built-in chain of causation. All the links in that chain had been carefully pre-arranged. The preparations were as meticulous as those that put Mr A and Mr Z ten miles above an ocean ten hours after they ate their identical breakfasts in the suburbs of Plutopolis.

The events of those ten hours that decided the fates of Mr A and Mr Z seemed commonplace: the packing of overnight bags, the stamping of passports, the cab driver's competent performance, the gate keeper's recognition of the boarding passes, the clearance given to the Neptunian pilot by the Plutonian control tower. Even the incredibly complex interplay of aerodynamic forces that lifted the flying ship into the stratosphere were taken for granted by Mr A and Mr Z. Yet, when we view all these events from the outside, as it were, their perfect meshing seems miraculous. Only our knowledge of the way they had been pre-arranged makes this meshing seem commonplace.

The events that destroyed most of the urban population of Neptunia and Plutonia and of eight other countries had also been pre-arranged. They needed only a triggering mechanism to be set into implacable motion. To be sure, 'safeguards' had been built into the lethal systems to guard against 'accidental war', as the military experts called 'unwanted nuclear exchanges' that might occur because of errors in the transmission or interpretation of signals. In this case, however, there were no errors and no misinterpretation. All signals were correctly sent, received, and acted upon. They originated in another part of the world where Neptunia and Plutonia respectively supported two countries at war with each other. There had been a secret agreement on the limit of the support, and this limit was overstepped by either Neptunia or Plutonia, neither of which had any choice in the matter, because other secret agreements had been made by both with their respective protégés. These provided for action in case certain guarantees were violated. A violation did occur, which called for an instantaneous response by one of the principals; which called for an immediate ultimatum by the other principal.

The ultimatum was delivered over the 'hot line' (which had been installed to prevent just this sort of chain reaction). Receipt of the ultimatum called for putting into operation one of a dozen contingent 'plans', of which the other side was aware, thanks to its reliable espionage system. Realization that the 'plan' was about to be activated made it imperative to activate a corresponding plan, prepared for just such an eventuality. The war occurred not because something went wrong but, on the contrary, because everything went according to pre-arranged plans, all of which were perfectly executed. Everyone knew exactly what he had to do in specified circumstances and did it.

The crew of the Neptunian airplane, however, had not been told what to do in these circumstances. Their first efforts were to get some information about what was happening. When they finally pieced together some scraps of broadcasts, the pilot realized that Neptupolis was a raging inferno. While he was weighing the possibility of returning to Plutopolis, that city also became a raging inferno. (The strategy of hitting the capital instead of the enemy's missile-launching sites in the first strike had been only recently adopted by the Plutonian general staff on the basis of sophisticated calculations. The Neptunian general staff, reasoning from the same assumptions and calculations, had adopted the same strategy.)

The pilot thought he could try to land in one of the countries that had been called 'neutral', and consulted with the navigator. The navigator, however, could not go along with this plan. Part of his job was to forestall any 'lapse of loyalty' on the part of the crew. That under the circumstances 'loyalty' might have lost its traditional meaning did not occur to the navigator. He had a strong sense of duty. He knew only that deflection of a plane from the prescribed course, except as directed by proper authorities, was 'hijacking'. Contrary to practice in other countries, Neptunian navigators were ordered to resist hijacking even if it meant risking the lives of all concerned.

A heated argument ensued between the navigator and the pilot, in the course of which the navigator produced a pistol. In the end, however, he yielded and authorized landing in a neighboring country allied with Neptunia. Neither he nor the pilot knew that this haven, too, would cease to exist just as the pilot was getting ready to make the approach.

In the grey morning the passengers were informed that, because of bad weather, they would be landed at another airport. The news was accepted philosophically. This sort of annoyance had happened before. The events followed their usual morning routine. The passengers were given damp cloths to freshen their faces and were served tea and coffee. The youngest passenger was sucking a woman's breast. A few of the men and women queuing up for the washrooms smiled as they passed the nursing mother, and she shyly returned their smiles.

Mr A and Mr Z, however, being in the first-class compartment, died without having seen these two.

PART TWO: SOURCES AND STRUCTURE OF CONFLICTS

CHAPTER 10

The So-Called
Aggressive Instinct

The actions of people are commonly attributed to their wills, preferences, or pre-dispositions – a projection of our own feelings of desire or intent that ordinarily precedes conscious acts. 'Why do people fight?' is a question that invites the trivial answer 'Because they want to.' But the question suggested by that answer is not trivial: 'Why do people *want* to fight?'

Ancient philosophy, later reflected in medieval proto-science, sought the causes of events in the nature of the behaving objects, animate or inanimate. Although 'will' or 'drives' are no longer attributed to inanimate objects, concepts of this sort still abound in explanations of the behavior of living beings. 'Instinct' is one such concept. As the ultimate answer to the question why an animal behaves as it does, instinct is a vacuous explanation, a catch-all to mask our ignorance. When properly defined, 'instinct' may be a useful term to denote the ability of animals to perform complex survival-enhancing acts, apparently unlearned. That there are such acts appears to have been demonstrated at least in non-humans. *How* they are performed, that is, the question of underlying neural mechanisms generally supposed to be responsible for the triggering and organization of such acts, poses an important problem to ethology, the study of animal behavior.

Instincts have been attributed to men also, to denote the roots of certain persistent patterns of behavior. For example, the tendency to accumulate worldly goods has been attributed to an 'acquisitive instinct'; the practice of covering certain body parts and reticence about certain physiological functions, to a 'shame' instinct, and so on.

Wider observations having revealed that most such practices are by no means universal, 'instinct' in man has been deprived of its explanatory power. Today many psychologists refuse to recognize the existence of *any* instincts in man. Indeed, if the sharp definition of instinct (a manifestation of steretoyped, complex, and unlearned patterns of behavior) is strictly adhered to, it is virtually impossible to attribute any form of human behavior to 'instinct'. Human behavior is remarkably plastic, subject to a multitude of variations in different conditions and in different milieus. That all human behavior is a result of learning, that is, of specific experiences varying from individual to individual and from culture to culture, seems to be an inescapable conclusion.

Nevertheless, it would be rash to deny that some forms of human behavior are rooted in man's biological heritage. All human newborn babies are able to feed by sucking; all their cries are similar. Even if we exclude from consideration forms of behavior that we share with other animals, one specifically human form of behavior that might be attributable to man's biological make-up remains, namely talking. All normal infants in the company of talking adults begin to talk in the second or third years of their lives. To be sure, the human child invariably learns the dialect of his speech community; that is, the *particular* speech patterns that he will utter he learns by virtue of his particular experiences. But the pre-disposition of the human being to learn to utter and to respond to certain patterns of sounds must be there to begin with. The fact is that no other animal, not even man's closest biological relative, the chimpanzee, reared as a human child, will of its own accord learn human speech.[1] It could be ventured that a human child reared in a non-human family or tribe would *not* learn the 'language' (that is, behavior patterns serving as communication) of his adopted kin. A human child can learn only human speech. Mowgli never existed.

Defining instinct vaguely but suggestively as a pre-disposition to perform certain types of behavior patterns, we can pose the question whether an 'aggressive instinct' can be ascribed to man. But to make the question concrete, we must first define the type of behavior patterns toward which the hypothetical aggressive instinct pre-disposes. Therein lies the difficulty. In other animals, the complex behavior patterns that are apparently unlearned, hence attributable to an instinct, are typically stereotyped and so all such occurrences can be easily recognized as belonging to the type. In man, behavior patterns vary radically, and to subsume a class of such patterns under the single term 'aggression' requires an act of imagination on the part of the observer, a presumption of what behaviors belong together to constitute a 'type'.

Take sexual behavior. Although in many animals its forms are elaborate, as in courtship rituals, and so on, the patterns characteristic of a species are easily recognizable and as a rule follow a prescribed sequence culminating in mating. In man these patterns vary extensively with culture and are so vastly elaborated that it requires a 'theory' to categorize them all as 'sexual behavior'. The human scientist, aided by his own projected feelings, might construct such a theory. But whether a Martian scientist would conclude that preoccupation with dress, the writing of poetry, and the adornment of maypoles are all manifestations of the same urge is an open question.

The same observations hold with regard to theories about 'aggressive instinct'. Here too the formation of the concept is aided or limited by the projection of our own feelings and by imaginative acts of recognition. In common parlance, we subsume under 'aggression' acts intended to cause destruction or harm. But this 'definition' is no help in categorizing behavior patterns as 'aggressive' or otherwise. How is one to understand intent? Is destruction or harm perpetrated on something or someone as a by-product of *another* purpose to be attributed to 'aggression' or not? Some say yes, others say no. For instance, when a man kills an animal in order to eat its flesh, is he committing 'aggression'? Arguments in support of either answer can be given. On the one hand, the killing appears to be incidental to another purpose – eating. If we disregard the instrumental aspects of this 'destruction', we shall not be able to circumscribe the kinds of destruction that can be related to aggression. For instance, the act of uprooting a carrot in order to eat it is also 'destroying life'. Of of course, such formalistic extensions do not serve the theory well. It is far-fetched to say that man is 'committing aggression' when he eats plants. But are we, then, to draw the line between preying on plants and preying on animals? Surely it is not the physiological distinctions between plants and animals that are relevant to the definition of aggression. Clams and oysters are animals, but it is difficult to associate eating them with aggression.

All creatures with locomotion must be caught in order to be eaten. Is this aggression? The question poses a problem for psychologists and anthropologists who relate the presumed aggressive instinct in man to predation. Derek Freeman, for example (in *The Natural History of Aggression*), traces the presumed instinct to the predatory adaptation achieved by the Australopithecinae, thought to be the African progenitors of man.[2] He infers a 'behavioral transition from a retreating to an attacking pattern'. In this conception a manifestation of aggression must include 'attacking' – which would presumably exclude catching insects (hardly a form of attack, yet a form of predation practised by non-carnivorous primates) and would include the sort of predation that involves a separate act of killing the prey. Still, the relevance of killing to aggression is difficult to establish even here unless one associates killing with emotional states that we know are involved in fighting. In predation, this association cannot be made as a matter of course. It does not appear that the hunter necessarily harbors hostile feelings toward his prey nor the butcher toward his victim. Granted, we cannot on that account dismiss altogether any possible connection between predation and aggression in the sense of an urge to harm or destroy, but this is a separate problem, to be discussed below. The only point to be made here is that there is no *necessary* connection between predation and aggression.

Some ethologists (notably Lorenz and Fisher) would exclude predation altogether from behavior patterns that are accepted as evidence of the aggressive instinct. They draw a distinction between *interspecific* and *intraspecific* aggression. Lorenz has examined the biological bases of the latter.[3] Fisher gives examples of the former, none of them instances of predation. According to him, interspecific aggression is typically a response of the *prey* against the predator or, in some cases, of the host against the parasite. Birds often 'mob' members of species that prey on them, such as snakes, weasels, owls, etc.[4] Hartley reports experiments in which birds attacked *mounted* owls.[5] Some species of owls even have developed false eyes in the back of the head, possibly as a protective adaptation against mobs of birds attacking their eyes. Impressive evidence of this sort of 'aggression in self-defense' is seen in the mobbing of cuckoos (including stuffed specimens) in Europe by birds victimized by the cuckoo's parasitic habits. But United States birds pay no attention to stuffed cuckoos put in their territories. American cuckoos are not parasitic.[6]

If these are offered as instances of 'interspecific aggression' while predation is excluded, the criterion applied is clear: destruction, killing, or elimination must be a *goal*, not simply a necessary intermediate step. If we are interested in aggression in the context of ethical or moral analysis, the distinction presents a ticklish problem. In the examples cited, the predator is not charged with aggression, but the prey, acting 'in self-defense', is. And this is in consequence of the fact that the predator destroys the prey only incidentally, because he wants the flesh, whereas the prey destroys the predator because the *destruction* serves its needs. Carried to its logical conclusion, this approach would not fix the label of 'aggressor' on the conqueror who destroys a population simply because he wants the land, but would fix it on the resisting population who want only to get rid of the conqueror. To protest that this is what comes of mixing ethical questions with scientific ones misses the point. The scientific analysis of aggression may well be motivated by a hope that such analysis might shed some light on ethical problems.

If so, then it seems advisable, in following the biological approach to the phenomenon of aggression, to confine attention to intraspecific aggression, since human conflict is of this type. Instances of intraspecific aggression, as these are recorded by ethologists, are behavior patterns of members of the same species toward each other that are somehow recognized as 'hostile interactions', analogous to corresponding interactions among human beings in face-to-face contact. The fact of *recognition* is in itself remarkable and deserves scrutiny. Just *how* do we recognize 'fighting', or hostile interactions even in the absence of fighting, in animals? Somehow we do. 'Anger' is reflected in a dog's or in a cat's posture and physiognomy as clearly as in man's. How far in the animal kingdom these interpretations are justified is anybody's guess. At any rate, when bodily contact occurs and natural weapons, like horns, teeth, or claws are used to inflict injury, there is no question in our minds that 'fighting' occurs, and we assume that this process is somehow analogous to fighting or other hostile interactions among humans.

Which animals fight? What are the occasions for fighting? How do they fight? What are the outcomes? Here the ethologist provides rich and detailed information. The following instances of intraspecific conflict are frequently and generally observed.

1. The males of many mammalian species fight apparently for the possession of females.

2. Certain animals fight when confined in a constricted space.

3. Many animals will fight to keep an intruder out of 'their' territory.

4. 'War', that is, fighting between two 'armies' of animals, is observed among ants but in hardly any other species. Ants engage also in interspecific 'wars' with two species arrayed in mass formations against each other.[7]

Next it is noted that intraspecific fighting, except among ants, is seldom fatal to the participants. The encounter typically ends in the flight or 'submission' of the defeated contestant. The 'submission' of a defeated wolf has often been cited as evidence of inhibition against intraspecific killing, particularly among 'ferocious' beasts, the large carnivores. The defeated wolf exposes his neck to the victor as if inviting him to give a coup de grâce. The latter refrains from doing so, and the fight is over. Among apes, the defeated male sometimes indicates submission by inviting a homosexual act on the part of the victor, perhaps evoking a reaction to a female, thus inhibiting aggression.

Finally, 'hostile' intraspecific encounters often do not develop into actual fighting at all. They are confined to 'threatening gestures', which continue until one of the parties flees or 'submits'. Submission may be manifested in abandoning claim to a bit of food, as when a 'low-status' chicken gives way following a pecking gesture by a 'high-status' one.

All of these observations point to a reasonable conclusion. The behavior patterns that are recognized as intraspecific aggression among animals have specific survival value and so can be assumed to have been selected for in the evolution of the species. Fighting among males for the possession of females contributes to the likelihood that the more vigorous males will have more progeny and so add to the vigor of the species. Fighting for the possession of territory prevents crowding and so guards against depleting available food supplies. Finally, the inhibition against intraspecific killing is of obvious survival value especially to animals equipped to kill easily, since uninhibited killing would favor the 'survival of the fiercest' and eventually would lead to species suicide. If inhibition against intraspecific killing is a result of natural selection along with intraspecific fighting itself, then it is clear that in this instance the 'fittest' were the 'strong and merciful'.

Note that the 'demonstration' of the existence of an aggressive instinct in several species, as developed by ethologists, depends on two lines of evidence. First, patterns of behavior that are somehow recognized as 'aggressive' are observed in several species. Second, and most important, it is shown that these patterns can be reasonably assumed to be of survival value to the species. Therefore, in order to extend the concept of 'aggressive instinct' to man, the second argument must also be involved if the same validity is claimed for the demonstration. Here we get into formidable difficulties. Intraspecific aggression of the sort observed among animals is seldom observed in 'civilized' men. Actual fighting for the possession of females is a rare occurrence among men, and even where it does occur the defeated male, unless he is killed (as in duels), is not thereby relegated to a life of celibacy or sterility. The 'weak' have as much opportunity to have progeny as the 'strong'. Competition for females does go on, of course, but 'victory' cannot be demonstrated to be correlated with physical vigor. If it is correlated with anything, it is rather with characteristics that are not transmitted genetically: for example, wealth, social position, etc. Anyway, mate selection has nothing to do with the number of surviving offspring, which is the principal determinant of evolutionary direction on the basis of natural selection.

Next, while fighting over territory certainly takes place, as in conquest and defense of land, the issue is by no means always the limiting of population density. On the contrary, man is a social animal and bunching together to live in close proximity has been going on since the agricultural revolution. To be sure, cities in order to be fed must have access to an area under cultivation, and these areas are conquered and defended. But warfare for acquisition of land is a very different thing from territorial fighting. The latter is triggered by the mere presence of the intruder on one's territory; the former involves conscious actions guided by the anticipation of consequences. Fighting for land cannot be attributed to an 'instinct for defending territory' any more than planting, sowing, and reaping can be attributed merely to a 'hunger drive'.

In this connection, it is interesting to note that even in animals the so-called 'territorial imperative'[8] has been challenged. It has been shown that fighting over territory is in many instances closely related to the scarcity of available food supply.[9]

The most glaring disparity between intraspecific aggression in animals and in man is, of course, the apparent absence in man of inhibitions against intraspecific killing. Man kills members of his own species as readily as he does members of other species, and this fact alone should raise doubts about the presumed 'instinct for intraspecific aggression' in man. For, if such an instinct were selected for, certainly one would expect that it would have been saddled with inhibitions to reduce the danger to the species.

To this objection, the following counter-argument can be offered. There may well be inhibitions in man against intraspecific killing, similar to those in other fighting animals. A gesture of submission may have inhibited primitive man from killing his defeated adversary just as it does in the wolf or in the ape. Or running away may have kept fatal outcomes of fighting to a minimum. However, man's specific adaptation – the use of tools – radically changed the situation. With weapons man can kill at a distance. This extension cancels running away as the automatic termination of the fight. It also removes the victim from contact with the killer and so cancels whatever inhibitory mechanism may depend on such contact. The murderous potential of modern war probably depends essentially on the complete severance of contact between the killers and their victims.

One might ask why the inhibition against intraspecific killing did not keep pace with the lethal potential of the weapons. The answer that suggests itself is that the psychological evolution of man was arrested as soon as cultural evolution and its peculiar mechanisms replaced biological evolution as the principal determinant of man's psyche.

In summary, the ethologists have demonstrated that in many animals, particularly in mammals, intraspecific aggression serves a biological purpose. Thereby it becomes plausible to argue that a corresponding instinct exists in many animals and possibly in man. Next, it appears that the inhibitory mechanisms that keep intraspecific aggression within bounds are for one reason or another inoperative in man. Thereby the aggressive instinct becomes a danger to man, and this danger increases in proportion to the lethal nature of man's weapons and his ingenuity in using them.

The weak point in this conclusion is the tacit assumption that the wholesale killings concomitant to aggressive behavior in humans are simply monstrously exaggerated manifestations of this (originally functional) instinct.[10]

The existence of an aggressive instinct in man has been argued on other than biological grounds. The evidence offered by psychologists and psychiatrists is typically of the extent of destruction and harm perpetrated by man against members of his own species especially. Moreover, so the argument goes, since aggression in man often seems to serve no survival purpose, evidently it is undertaken for its own sake, presumably for the psychological satisfaction it offers. The appalling history of man's cruelty to his own kind is too well known to need reviewing. It is clear that in associating atrocities with an 'aggressive instinct' psychologists refer to something quite different from what the ethologists have singled out. Cruelty for cruelty's sake does not appear to serve any biological purpose.

Or does it? One ought to be cautious in dismissing any characteristic of a living system, whether structural or functional, as superfluous or useless. Sociologists and anthropologists of the 'functionalist' persuasion go to great lengths to find a rationale for any existing cultural feature. In doing so, they follow the practice of the physiologist, who persistently seeks to discover the function (as a survival mechanism) of any structure or process that he may observe in a living organism. This approach makes sense. If we assume that an existing living organism is a product of long-term adaptation, it is natural to suppose that whatever characteristic is observed in the organism is there because it was selected for. Occasionally, we find so-called vestigial features, those that once served survival functions in the progenitors of the organism but do so no longer and continue to exist because they have not yet been eliminated. In man, such may be the vermiform appendix or the muscles once used to cock the ears. Still, it seems advisable to avoid the conclusion that any existing feature is 'absolutely useless'. (Haphazard surgery has revealed many an unsuspected function of apparently useless parts.)

Following the cue of the 'functionalists', and keeping in check for the moment feelings of repugnance that may arise in some of us against the exercise, let us look for possible biological use of 'cruelty'. Here it is advisable to examine the behavior of animals because the innate nature of a behavior pattern is easier to establish in them.

If by 'cruelty' is meant the inflicting of pain or distress on others for its own sake rather than incidentally to, say, predation, instances of cruelty are difficult to find in non-humans. A possible example is the 'cruelty' of a cat that plays with a mouse it has caught instead of killing it immediately. Clearly, the verdict of 'cruelty' is here a consequence of projection, as is any inference about the inner psychological state of a non-human, for we can only assume that the cat derives pleasure from playing with (tormenting) the mouse; our assumption is, in fact, reflected in the very word we use: 'play', and we can hardly avoid the projection, because the behavior of some animals so strikingly resembles human play. Now, the biological value of play can be surmised. Most animal play behavior, when it occurs, is concentrated in the animal's 'childhood', suggesting that play serves as practice of skills that will be needed by the adult animal. In some animals, play behavior tends to disappear in maturity (in cows and sheep, for instance). Among wild beasts of prey the young engage in play (bears, lions), the adults, seldom if ever. Dogs and cats sometimes play throughout their lives, but this extension may well be a result of the way these particular animals became domesticated.

The prolongation of childhood is most marked in man. Indeed, man has been called an animal in perpetual childhood, a reference to the continued plasticity of human behavior even in adulthood. It might be conjectured that domesticated animals have developed some 'human' traits – a conjecture not as far-fetched as it sounds. We must remember that the role of natural selection in domesticated animals has been taken over by breeding, conscious or unconscious. Conscious breeding is deliberately controlled mating and survival guided by man's need or fancy for certain traits. Unconscious selection operates through man's treatment of the animals around him. The vaunted 'loyalty' of the dog may well be a consequence of such unconscious breeding (cf. p. 40). So it may have happened that some 'human' traits, such as manifestations of affection, etc., have been bred into animals who enter close relations with man. These might include the prolongation of 'childhood' observed in the play of dogs and cats.

To attribute cruelty to the cat playing with the mouse, because we assume that the cat derives pleasure from the mouse's distress, is much less warranted than a simpler assumption, that the cat derives pleasure from its play activity just as it does when playing with a piece of string. Awareness of and empathy with another creature's distress (especially if the creature is of another species) may be entirely out of range of the cat's emotional repertoire.

Saying that the cat 'derives pleasure' from its play activities is not necessarily being subjective and violating scientific standards of description, despite the strict behaviorists' austere prescriptions. Recent experiments have demonstrated the existence of localized 'pleasure centers' in mammalian brains. Given the opportunity to stimulate such a center via implanted electrodes, a rat has been known to do so to the point of exhaustion; it will also readily learn behavior patterns that lead to the stimulation of the center as a 'reward', etc. Using 'pleasure' as a shorthand term, we can now safely assume that at least mammals are guided in their behavior by a 'pleasure principle'.

Consider now a complex behavior chain that must be performed in some order. For example, the nest must be built before the eggs are laid; brooding behavior must set in only after the eggs are laid; foraging for the young, only after they are hatched, etc. If each link in the chain is guided by a 'pleasure principle', the stimulations must be so arranged that the next link can activate the (presumed) pleasure center only after the preceding link has been completed. We may speculate further (on the basis of our own introspection) that the anticipation of the pleasure to be derived from the next link in the chain contributes to the completion of the preceding link.

Consider an act of predation performed by, say, a lion. The scent of the antelope stimulates a pleasure center and guides the search behavior so that the lion follows the gradient of the scent. The sight of the antelope triggers the chase, again guided by the pleasure principle, possibly anticipating the next phase – seizure. Seizure establishes a linkage between the act of killing and the pleasure principle, which guides the lion's fangs to the antelope's throat as surely as on another occasion the same principle guides the lion's penis into the vagina of the lioness. The killing accomplished, eating begins, the culmination of the process on which the life of the lion and the continuation of his species depend.

The assumption of 'anticipation' is suggested by the fact that, normally, the chase does not occur unless the lion is hungry. We interpret this as meaning that the pleasure in performing the links preliminary to eating includes the 'anticipation' of the next link. Beasts of prey rarely kill for the sake of killing, which is what invites the invidious comparison between our behavior and theirs. But dissocation between killing and eating is by no means unknown in species other than man and so deserves attention. Normally, the dependence goes both ways. The beast will not usually chase and kill when not hungry, and, normally, will not eat unless it has killed. Exceptions to the latter rule are, of course, commonly observed; in particular, beasts of prey in captivity learn to eat what they have not killed. However, these exceptions must be attributed to a short-circuiting process, without which wild animals could not survive in zoos, as many, in fact, do not. Some animals kill without eating; well fed cats, for example. The sequence 'scent (or sight), chase (or stalk), seize, kill' stops at that point, but each of the preceding stages is still linked to the anticipation of the next, and each remains linked to the pleasure center. The behavior of 'sport' hunters can be explained in a similar way.

This idea, developed in an article, 'The Stylization of Desire' by William P. Gass,[11] calls attention to the *elaboration* of successive links in the chain that originally had biological utility only if it was completed. Thus, the ritual of the hunt used to terminate in feasting. Now it typically terminates in killing, or, with the kind-hearted, in taking photographs. Sexual behavior has periodically undergone a similar process, consummation being eliminated, as in the days of chivalry, or, as in our day, in the custom of dating, in flirtation, etc. The common denominator is the *non-urgency* of the consummation, which introduces the possibility of *choice*. Choice involves contemplation, and contemplation introduces variants, elaboration, and distortion of the patterns. The starving man eats whatever is available as foodstuff and disregards manners and ceremony. The gourmet dines rather than eats, placing great value on the choice of foods, on the order in which they are eaten, on the arrangement of the accoutrements, etc.

To some, the cat playing with the mouse and the 'sport' hunter appear cruel. The charge assumes that both derive pleasure from the suffering of others. There is not sufficient evidence to substantiate the charge, at least in these particular examples. The cat teasing a piece of string and the hunter-by-camera do not appear cruel, yet the psychological states accompanying these activities are probably almost the same as those in the cat with the mouse and the hunter with the gun. A more appropriate charge against the last two would be of callousness, failure to *identify* with other creatures. To blame the cat for this failure is, as we have seen, pointless. Against the hunter, most will agree the charge is subject to gradation. Many who view hunting with repugnance have no objection to fishing or butterfly collecting, and many a hunter who happily shoots ducks would be repelled at the idea of shooting a chimpanzee, while murder outside the paranoid world of detective fiction hardly enters any normal human being's mind. Yet, who of us has hesitated to squash a mosquito? Clearly, identification that inhibits killing is the stronger the more other creatures resemble us.

In searching for roots of man's aggressive behavior – especially large-scale and organized aggression – callousness should not be confused with cruelty. To those whose range of identification is broad, those whose range is narrower appear 'cruel', whereas 'callous' is the more appropriate epithet, and the dependence of this judgement on one's own range of identification should always be kept in mind.

Nevertheless, after these allowances have been made and after the charge of cruelty leveled against man as a species has been dismissed in specific cases for lack of conclusive evidence, there remain many other cases wherein the charge of cruelty can be amply substantiated. While callousness is simply lack of identification with others, cruelty is, on the contrary, evidence of identification with the opposite 'sign', as it were. Cruelty is the property of deriving pleasure from the suffering of others, just as empathy is sharing the suffering of others or of experiencing distress from the suffering of others. The bill of particulars charging man with cruelty is long indeed, and perhaps it is true that man is the only really cruel animal. But this may be precisely because man is also the only animal capable of empathy, since both cruelty and empathy presuppose identification with the object of brutality or of compassion. Cruelty and empathy are two sides of the same coin.

In Edward Albee's play *The Zoo Story*, a man induces another man to kill him only to establish *some* sort of affective relationship with another human being. In the narrative that leads to the shocking climax, the hero tells how a bond of intimacy was established between him and a dog after he tried to poison the dog. Russian peasant women of pre-revolutionary times are said to have considered beatings administered by their husbands as evidence of love. All such instances may be pathological, but they suggest that aggression and empathy are nearer each other than either is to indifference.[12]

In summary, the existence of an 'aggressive instinct' in man cannot be demonstrated by the conspicuous excesses of 'man's inhumanity to man'. Instances of the most depraved cruelty can be matched by instances of kindness and solidarity. Destruction of human life by humans, as in conquest, is more properly related to predation than to aggression. Although cannibalism is rare, intraspecific killing among men is, like predatory killing, incidental to other needs, not necessarily the need to kill. Finally, the unmistakable practice of cruelty for cruelty's sake depends on the same human faculty that on other occasions manifests itself in love and compassion – the ability to transcend the self and to guide one's actions by imagining how the *other* feels. That this faculty is the source of both humane and bestial impulses should surprise no one who examines man and his works. All specifically human faculties are ambivalent, and all of men's works are potentially both blessings and curses.

CHAPTER 11

Environmental Theories of Aggression

The conviction that man does what he does because he is what he is suggests a carry-over from medieval organismic philosophy.

With a shift of attention from the intrinsic 'nature' of objects to relations among objects, medieval philosophy gave way to what eventually became the scientific outlook. The syllogistic mode of reasoning with its emphasis on the identification of classes of things (which presumably reveal their nature and so explain their behavior) gave way to causal reasoning with its emphasis on relational determinants of events. The stone now appeared to fall, not because it was a 'stone', hence, being part of the earth, must seek the center of the earth as its proper place, but because there were *external* forces acting on it. These external forces, moreover, may be constantly changing. Only the *momentary* configuration of forces has an effect on the stone's motion, producing a momentary, minute change in the position and the velocity of the stone. In this resultant new situation, the configuration has again changed, so that the new configuration now must be examined to determine the next momentary change in the condition of the stone.

In other words, the behavior of the stone is envisaged in modern mechanics to be determined by the stone's *environment*, which may be constantly changing, rather than by the immutable 'nature' of the stone.

The shift of emphasis from 'inner nature' to environment as the principal determinant of behavior occurred also in viewing man. In its extreme form the environmental view was manifested in the so-called tabula rasa theory, according to which man's psyche at birth was likened to a clean slate on which experiences were accumulated as 'inscriptions'. Whatever the individual became was supposed to be determined exclusively by these external influences.[1] Specifically, the role of heredity as a determinant of psychic traits was ruled out. Clearly, the hereditary origin of certain physical traits could not be denied without disregarding conspicuous facts. It was argued, however, that the role of heredity was confined to traits having no psychological significance, such as color of eyes, skin pigments, etc. Man's skills, attitudes, beliefs, character traits, etc., were all declared to be products of environment and learning.

Theories of human behavior based on 'the nature of man' (or of certain classes of men), on the one hand, and on the environment of men, on the other, represent two extremes. It would be reasonable to assume that both 'nature' (or heredity) and environment are contributing factors to the developing psychological traits. However, the clashes between the proponents of the two extreme theories have not been simply results of controversies about 'what is true'. As frequently happens in speculations about human behavior, the extremes have been reflections of ethical, at times of political, convictions. This explains the tenacity with which extreme views of presumably scientific matters are frequently held.

On the whole (though by no means always), theories of psychological traits based on 'human nature' or rationalized in terms of hereditary determinants have been associated with politically conservative or authoritarian outlooks; those based on environmental determinants have been associated with radical, liberal, or libertarian views. Notable exceptions can be pointed out. For example, Sigmund Freud, who strongly emphasized deep-seated biological or instinctual determinants, can in no way be associated either with political conservatism or with an authoritarian bent. On the other hand, the strongly authoritarian, politically conservative Soviet state philosophy holds to the dogma of environmental determinism. Both exceptions are understandable when the context in which the views are held is examined. Freud's belief in the deep-seated destructive urges of man served to reveal the wellsprings of power appetite and the crippling effects of imposed authority, insights which hardly give support to the rationalizations of conservatives and authoritarians. Soviet state philosophy, although presently encrusted in dogma, sprang from a revolutionary outlook in which the central theme was the ability of man to throw off the restraints of established social relations and thereby to aquire freedom to transform the world, himself included.

Environmentalism is typically a reflection of scientific humanism and of its belief that science (knowledge of causes and effects) is the key to enlightenment and enlightenment is the key to the betterment of the human condition.

Environment as a determinant of behavior can be conceived in the local and in the global sense.

In the local sense, the environment of the behaving organism is the totality of stimuli impinging upon it at the given moment.[2] In this sense, the dependence of behavior upon environment can be studied by the methods of behavioral psychology. In particular, if a class of behavior patterns can be labeled 'aggression', one can list the sort of stimuli that elicit 'aggression' in a given organism. Since past experience is a factor in determining responses elicited by stimuli, they too are frequently taken into account.

In the global sense, environment includes more than the here-and-now or the here-and-now plus a history of individual experience. For a human being, this broader environment includes his mileu, the social structure or the culture in which he is immersed. The sociologist and the anthropologist are interested in this broader social environment.

Observation of animal behavior reveals a great deal about the environmental determinants of aggressive responses. One interesting finding is that the range of stimuli that evoke aggressive responses becomes broader in animals with more complex nervous systems. A rat will generally bite to protect its young, or when fighting for food, or in response to hurt, actual or anticipated. Further, biting is about the only evidence the rat gives of 'aggression'. A dog, on the other hand, can express 'hostility' in more varied ways. He can give an impression of 'sulking', even of 'jealousy'. A chimpanzee has a still larger repertoire and, unlike the dog, will actually respond to an 'insult'. For instance, if a dog is teased by an offer of food followed by withdrawal, he will look 'eager' to get the food (will whimper, wag his tail, etc.). A chimpanzee may get 'angry' and refuse to accept the food when it is finally offered in good faith.[3] And, of course, it is well known that a human being may kill another in consequence of hearing certain words pronounced.

The broadening of the range of stimuli that can elicit aggressive responses does not warrant the conclusion that the 'strength' of the aggressive instinct increases on the higher rungs of the phylogenetic scale, because the evidence tells us nothing about what other responses are elicited by larger varieties of stimuli. In fact, it is not at all clear how the strength of the aggressive instinct or of the 'destructive urge' is to be measured. If it is related to the frequency of killing one's own kind, then ants and men rate high while most other animals rate very low. Yet, the range of stimuli that evoke killing is narrow in ants and broad in primates, among whom, excepting man, the frequency of intraspecific killing is extremely low. It appears that behavioral studies shed little light on the existence or strength of the aggressive instinct. They do give information on the range of situations in which aggressive behavior is likely to be observed and how it is likely to be manifested.

Observed relations between aggressive behavior and past experience are more instructive. Kittens raised in the same cage with a mouse without an opportunity to see an adult cat kill a mouse do not generally attack their cage mates even in adulthood. Also they rarely kill other rodents. Kittens raised with their mothers and witnessing the killing of a mouse by the mother become killers in maturity almost without exception. In fact, a cat's attitude toward mice may be experimentally determined by 'childhood experience'. Cats can be taught even to fear mice if the sight of a mouse is accompanied by an electric shock to the kitten.[4]

Likewise, the willingness to fight can be strongly influenced by earlier experiences with fighting. A mouse can be made into an aggressive fighter by 'fixing' all its encounters, so that it invariably emerges an unscathed victor. These mice who 'never lost a war' become so pugnacious that they even attack females and young, which normal mice do not do. In this connection, J. P. Scott has observed that prize-fight managers in promoting their protégés are careful to match them against weaker fighters during their preliminary careers in order to build up their confidence.[5]

A frequently cited theory of human interpersonal conflict links aggression to frustration. The fundamental assumption of the theory was stated categorically by John Dollard and his collaborators: '*Aggression is always a consequence of frustration.*' From this statement it is not clear whether frustration is declared to be a necessary, or a sufficient, or both a necessary and sufficient condition of aggression. Clearly, the implications of the three conditions are different. If frustration is a sufficient condition but not a necessary one, we must expect that aggression always follows frustration but may also occur otherwise. If frustration is a necessary but not a sufficient condition, then aggression cannot occur unless first frustration occurs but need not occur even after frustration. If frustration is a necessary and sufficient condition, then aggression occurs if and only if frustration occurs. Further,

> From the point of view of daily observation, it does not seem reasonable to assume that aggressive behavior of the usually recognized varieties is always traceable to and produced by some form of frustration.[6]

This seems to cast doubt on the assumption that frustration is a *necessary* condition for aggression. The argument that follows is not a defense of necessity but of sufficiency:

> In many adults and even children, frustration may be followed so promptly by apparent acceptance of the situation and readjustment thereto that one looks in vain for the relatively gross criteria ordinarily thought of as characterizing aggressiveness . . . However the absence of overt aggressive reactions does not mean that such reaction tendencies are thereby annihilated.[7]

In other words, appearances are deceptive. Even though, following frustration, aggression is not always observed, it may nevertheless be there as a 'tendency'. To put it another way, if one sticks with the assumption that 'aggression is always a consequence of frustration', one can always find evidence for it if one looks long enough. A sufficiently diligent search is bound to uncover aggression following frustration and (one presumes) a frustration to which aggression can be traced.

Commonly, young children are not able to gratify all their desires the moment they occur and are not able to derive satisfaction from anticipating deliberately postponed gratification. Consequently, frustration is inevitable in every child's life. It is inherent in the socialization process.[8] The assumption that frustration is a *necessary* pre-condition of aggression cannot be falsified, simply because instances of frustration can always be found. Next, it is known that people learn to act in ways sanctioned by their society. Consequently, aggressive reactions must often be suppressed or directed into socially acceptable channels, perhaps in disguised form. If so, then practically every action can be interpreted as a 'tendency' toward 'aggression', perhaps sublimated. Thereby the assumption that frustration is a sufficient condition for aggression cannot be falsified, simply because 'tendencies' toward aggression can always be found, or labeled as such. A theory that cannot be falsified is scientifically worthless since it does not distinguish between supporting and refuting evidence.

The introduction of experimental *practice* into psychology has rescued many a 'theory' from the limbo of unfalsifiability. So it is with the frustration-aggression theory. Although the hypothesis as stated is devoid of theoretical leverage, it generated a great many investigations, some revealing a linkage between 'frustration' and 'aggression' in specific situations, others of questionable relevance to the hypothesis but interesting in their own right.

Linkages between conditions or events are most convincingly established by demonstrating quantitative correlations. The following experiment represents an attempt to quantify frustration and aggression and to show that when frustration increases, so does aggression. The experiment was performed on five-months-old babies during feeding. The bottle was withdrawn at various states of the feeding process. When withdrawn when only 0·5 ounce had been taken, crying began on the average 5·0 seconds after the withdrawal. When the bottle was withdrawn after 2·5 ounces had been taken, the onset of crying was delayed 9·9 seconds. After 4·5 ounces had been taken, crying followed withdrawal after 11·0 seconds on the average. The results are clear and loud: the hungrier the baby is, the sooner it starts crying after its source of satiation is taken away.[9]

If crying is interpreted as a symptom of frustration (a reasonable interpretation) and if the degree of satiation is measured by the amount of food taken (also a reasonable interpretation), then the conclusion is warranted that the degree of frustration is correlated with the degree of deprivation, a finding relevant to the problem of quantifying frustration. However, the stated conclusion is that 'as the child became more nearly satiated, frustration induced a less and less immediate *aggressive* response' (emphasis added). To interpret a baby's crying as an 'aggressive response' involves a considerable conceptual leap. A baby cries when hungry (or otherwise distressed), because the crying stimulates a normal mother to remove the cause of distress. This sort of interaction between mother and child is not confined to humans; it is observed in most mammals and birds. The interaction is a cooperative one and has been selected for in the process of evolution for its survival value. There is no evidence whatsoever that it has anything to do with 'aggression' (as if, say, the baby was deliberately crying to annoy the mother). The interpretation of a baby's crying as an 'aggression' points up the tendency to force facts into an unfalsifiable theory.

Many of the experiments suggested by the frustration-aggression theory consisted in presenting hypothetical situations to subjects and eliciting responses as to what they would do in such situations. The weakness of the evidence so obtained is obvious. Inferences of what people *would* do from what they say they would do (especially in an experiment) are of questionable validity.

In some experiments verbal responses were collected that were in part related to situations reported by the subjects to have actually occurred. Subjects were asked to record actual frustrating experiences and to rate the 'strength' of the frustration on a scale. Then they were asked to tell how they had in fact reacted and, in addition, what *would* have been the most satisfying reaction to the frustration (also rated on a scale). Finally they were asked how strong a punishment they would have expected from each of the reactions considered but not actually made. The responses indicated that anticipation of punishment reduces overt aggression and that there is a 'trade off' between the amount of satisfaction derived from an aggressive reaction and the 'cost' of anticipated punishment.[10] It must be kept in mind, however, that verbal responses in test situations may be strongly influenced by conformance to what is expected. Often an experiment of this sort serves as an instruction to the subjects about what the experimenter wants to find. In most cases, experimental subjects aim to please.

Experiments in natural settings are more promising. A particularly 'clean' experiment, illustrating so-called displaced aggression, was reported by Miller and Bugelski. A group of boys at camp was compelled to take a long, dull test, answering questions made too difficult for them. The test was, moreover, deliberately prolonged so that in the course of it the boys realized that they would have to miss Bank Night at the local theatre, to them the most interesting event of the week. Before and after the test, the boys were asked to rate ethnic minorities. Half of the group rated Mexicans before the test and Japanese after; the other half rated Japanese before and Mexicans after (N.B. experiment conducted in 1939). According to the ratings, in both samples the attitude toward the minorities was less favourable after the test than before.[11]

Anecdotal material supporting the frustration-aggression theory is, of course, abundant. A young man who is known to have hated his father and brother becomes an energetic political reformer, which provides opportunity to attack corrupt politicians, callous power figures, etc. Thus, he demonstrates both a frustration-aggression pattern and the 'displacement' of aggression into channels acceptable, at least to his followers.[12] Instances of this sort may well corroborate the theory, but they are not evidence in the scientific sense of the word. To serve as evidence, such instances must be compared with instances where young men known to have 'hated' their parents did *not* become social reformers, and also with instances where young people who did not 'hate' their parents became social reformers. Such standards of evidence are often declared to be impossible to satisfy because it is part of the theory that aggression takes on many different forms and stems from many different sources. If so, it becomes all the more facile to relate 'aggression' to 'frustration' in practically any situation, and we are again left with an unfalsifiable hypothesis.

A scientific hypothesis must contain a prediction. The less likely is the event predictable on a priori grounds, the stronger is the corroboration of the theory if it is observed. This is why the experiment in the boys' camp is impressive. Supposedly, the difference in average ratings of Mexicans and Japanese would be in the same direction in two random samples drawn from the same population (at least, if the samples were sufficiently large). That, as it turned out, the direction of the difference depended on which group was rated before and which after an experience reasonably interpreted as frustrating was a theoretical prediction of a result not expected on a priori grounds.

Several anthropological and sociological observations have been interpreted in accordance with the frustration-aggression theory. People in different cultural environments behave toward each other in different ways. In some societies there is a great deal of interpersonal, overt violence; in others, overt violence is practically unknown. A common-sense view would ascribe more aggressiveness to the people in the former society and less to those in the latter. If, however, one insists that frustration is the common lot of all children in the process of socialization, one is tempted to look for other manifestations of hostility if fighting is *not* observed. One might notice that in the non-fighting society there are more verbal assaults, quarreling, 'malicious gossip', etc. Similarly, among tribal societies, some tribes are warlike, others are peaceful. Ordinarily one might suppose that the former are more aggressive than the latter. If, however, one allows that there is in all people a reservoir of hostility accumulated in the process of socialization, one will interpret war-making as hostility directed outward and will conclude that the non-warlike people direct hostility inward towards members of their own tribes or against themselves. Such interpretations are not necessarily false, but they need to be supported by 'harder' data if they are to be taken seriously. For example, in finding that high murder rates are associated with low suicide rates, and vice versa, if it can be shown that the correlations are unlikely to be coincidental, then a case can be made for the notion that aggression will be manifested in one way or another, and that if one way is blocked, the other will be taken. Still, the relation between frustration and aggression remains an elusive one.

In the sociological sphere, the frustration-aggression theory has been used to explain criminality. Innumerable studies have revealed correlations between the incidence of criminality and low economic status. Bonger cites Hausner's finding that during peace time the criminality of German soldiers is 25 times that of civilians.[13] It is noted that during the first two years of the Nazi regime, the incidence of murders in Germany increased while thefts and burglaries decreased. It is impossible to decide whether these findings are in any meaningful way related to the frustration-aggression theory. It can, and has been, argued that poverty is a source of frustration; so is the strict discipline of the barracks, with which the Nazi regime is also associated. Nevertheless, the same data may be used against the theory with equal effectiveness. Let us say, as is commonly maintained, that children of the lower classes are subjected to fewer frustrations than those of the middle and upper classes; that soldiers, being trained to focus their hostility on the 'enemy' (real or hypothetical), might be expected on that basis to manifest less (not more) aggression (criminality) in their own society. Then the same can be said of the Germans during the Nazi regime.

The most serious flaw in relating these observations to the frustration-aggression theory appears to be, as before, the vagueness of the terms. What is criminality? And is it necessarily related to aggression? A poor man is more likely to steal (in the accepted sense of the word) than a rich man. Does this mean that the poor man is more aggressive? On the other hand, the rich man is more likely to engage in socially approved aggressive acts (say, large-scale financial operations) than the poor man. Is this an indication that the rich man is more frustrated than the poor man? Or can it be that aggression is as likely, or more likely, to be instigated by success than by frustration? Recall the mouse made pugnacious by the simple expedient of 'fixing' all his fights.

The most pronounced impact of the frustration-aggression theory has been on child rearing. Attention was called to the vicious cycle: initial frustration (unavoidable) – direct aggression – inhibition of aggression, resulting in more frustration – displaced aggression, often inducing neurosis. It was recommended that the cycle be broken at the inhibition stage, and permissiveness became a key word in the lexicon of progressive parenthood. What difference the change in child-rearing practices has made in the generations since grown up is hard to say. We are told that the present unrest among the young (frequently equated with 'aggression') is a direct consequence of exaggerated permissiveness. It is equally plausible that the aggressiveness of the discontented young (if it is aggressiveness) is a result of intense frustrations related not to child-rearing practices but to a feeling of helplessness in the face of maniacal government policies and festering social evils.

In summary, although selected instances showing linkages between clearly defined frustration and clearly defined aggressive reactions (direct or displaced) are impressive, the lack of explicit criteria for recognizing more general manifestations of either frustration or aggression makes it impossible to evaluate the extent to which the frustration-aggression theory is valid.

Introduction to Chapters 12-14

I said at the outset (p. 11) that the first task in any analysis of conflict is to identify the conflicting parties and that this task is by no means a simple one. On the basis of our introspective awareness of ourselves as actors with at least some freedom of choice and with consciously perceived goals, it seems most natural to identify individuals as the basic conflicting parties. Yet we are aware also of larger aggregates to which goals and aspirations are assigned. If we see these goals and aspirations as simply the collective manifestations of the goals and aspirations of the individuals comprising the aggregates, there is no problem. For instance, the aspirations of a State can in that case be perceived simply as the aspirations of its citizens, the State being simply an instrument for realizing these goals.

Problems arise when organized aggregates appear to acquire goals and purposes of 'their own', independent of those of the individuals comprising them. Problems arise also when the behavior of large systems seems to be determined by quasi-mechanical interactions that do not reflect *any* goals or purposes, not even of the systems. In our day, these problems are no longer of merely philosophical interest; they are set in a starkly realistic context. For instance, hardly anyone wants a senseless, genocidal nuclear war to occur. Yet the prospect of such a war, now looming, now receding, is always with us.

In the three chapters to follow, we shall examine so-called systemic theories of conflict, where not the individual psyche, molded either by inherent drives (e.g., 'aggressive instincts') or by experiences, is at the center of attention but, for the most part, *processes* not subject to control by single individuals. Some of the theories to be discussed may appear to be exceptions. For instance, in Hobbes's picture of human life as a 'war of everyone against everyone', the individual as the 'social atom' is the point of departure. In Clausewitz's theory of war, the monarch or the general appears to be a 'rational actor', pursuing well defined political or military goals. However, in Hobbes's model, individuals are not differentiated – they all have the same 'psychology' (if we can call Hobbes's mechanistic interpretations of motivation a 'psychology'). What is important in Hobbes's theory is not this 'psychology' but its systemic effect – the emergence of the absolutist State as the only viable form of social organization. Similarly, the important idea in Clausewitz's theory is the emergence of the State as the embodiment of the collective will of a nation, which then becomes the 'actor' in a Hobbesian 'war of everyone against everyone'. This war differs from the Hobbesian war in that it is conducted 'rationally' and does not lead to the surrender of autonomy by the conflicting parties (the nation states).

These systemic theories of conflict, of which we shall examine seven examples, are important for two reasons. First, they exemplify conceptions of conflict that lead to questions central in our discussion. They compel us to consider the 'psychologies' of actors larger than individuals, in particular of highly organized social 'organisms' like States. The revealed nature and effects of these clashes between large 'organisms' shed more light on the meaning of conflict in man-made environment than on conflicts between individuals. Second, the theories are important regardless of their 'objective' validity. As we have said, what people think, say, or write about conflict, particularly large-scale conflicts, is an important component of the man-made (semantic) environment and, hence, a determinant of the conflicts generated by it.

CHAPTER 12

Systemic Theories: Hobbes, Hegel, Clausewitz

In psychological theories of conflict, both the instinctual and the environmental, the individual is at the center of attention. It is he who engages in conflicts, either because he is driven by primeval urges or because his psyche has been molded by environment. Group conflicts are tacitly assumed to be summations of conflicts between individuals.

In contrast, systemic theories eschew the psychological aspect except in an auxiliary capacity. A system interacts with its environment by virtue of its structure and of relations between that structure and that of the environment. A system need not be endowed with a 'psychology', at least not with a human one. There is no need even to make any sharp distinction between animate and inanimate systems. To be sure, 'conflict' may be difficult to define without projecting anthropomorphic interpretations upon the interactions of systems. For most philosophers (all systemic theories of conflict have a philosophical flavor), this is seldom a conceptual difficulty. In particular, idealist philosophers have offered anthropomorphic interpretations of natural processes as a matter of course.

Materialist philosophers like Hobbes or Marx, who eschewed anthropomorphic interpretations of nature, avoided the difficulty by presenting conflict as it appears to men (that is, as reflected in man's psyche) as a state *imposed* on individuals by the systemic interaction.

Hobbes was a materialist in the pristine, seventeenth-century meaning of the word. As we have seen, seventeenth-century science focused its attention sharply on the world of matter, particularly on the physical laws governing the motion of matter. Hobbes's conception of the human psyche stems directly from this mechanical conception of reality.

To the materialist, living organisms are in the first instance bodies, lumps of matter. To be sure, they seem to be capable of 'autonomous' motion, but, since the motions of inanimate, material bodies can be explained by mechanical laws, there is no reason to suppose that the motions of living organisms are not governed by the same laws. This makes them akin to clockworks. What, then, distingushes living beings from inanimate clockworks? Perhaps it is the faculty of sensation, which the philosophizing materialist introspectively recognizes in himself. Sensation, too, however, can be 'explained' in the conceptual framework of mechanisms, namely as a mechanical interaction of a body with the environment or with other bodies. For instance, the sense of touch is the result of a body bumping into another body. Desires are incipient motions. Since motions are results of attractive or repulsive forces, positive desires can be explained as incipient motion due to attraction, and 'negative desires' (aversion), as results of repulsion. Desires are thus conceived as simple tropisms.

Next, in Hobbes's view, frustration of desires can be due only to the interference of other bodies (their presence in the way of one's motions). Therefore, every other body is seen to be a source of frustration. Man 'in the state of nature' is in conflict with every other member of his kind simply because he keeps bumping into them and they impede his actions. A collection of individuals is seen as a jostling crowd. Left to themselves, men would be always fighting (to remove obstacles) and would eventually exterminate each other. However, men have found a way to avoid this outcome. (How foresight and design can be derived from the mechanical model of the organism Hobbes does not say.) Men join in collectives and thereby form an artificial organism, the body politic (the State) to which they surrender their autonomy. The price of survival and of peace, then, is the total loss of individual freedom. The subject citizen has no rights vis-a-vis the State (whose power Hobbes envisages as concentrated in a sovereign), except to the extent that the sovereign chooses to grant such rights – as of property, for example; but such rights can be abrogated at any time at the sovereign's pleasure.[1]

According to Hobbes, the sovereign does have one and only one obligation vis-a-vis the subject. Since the subject surrendered his autonomy in order to be protected against aggression from his fellow men, the sovereign is obligated to protect the lives of his subjects. This obligation suggests a remarkable conclusion, and Hobbes does not shrink from drawing it. The sovereign cannot demand that a subject surrender his life, for it is precisely in order to preserve his life that the subject became a subject. Consequently, the subject can refuse to serve in war because such a service may cost him his life.[2] Note that no modern sovereign state, not even the most 'democratic' let alone totalitarian states, recognizes this right of the individual. (N.B. Exemptions granted to conscientious objectors are based on the right to refuse to kill, not on the right to refuse to die for the State.)

The conception of the State as an organism on a 'higher level' than the individual is a principal theme in Hobbes's political philosophy. However, for Hobbes, the surrender of individual autonomy to the State is a necessary evil. Having surrendered his autonomy, the individual is no longer free; he has, in fact, 'sold' his autonomy, but he still retains his individual consciousness. This construct may have been suggested by the circumstances in which Hobbes found himself. He was a staunch royalist and fled England on the eve of the Civil War. After the execution of Charles I, Charles II was considered by the royalists to be the legitimate monarch. But when Charles's cause seemed hopeless, Hobbes returned to England and submitted to Cromwell. His theory absolved him from guilt, since Charles II in exile could not be expected to protect Hobbes's life.

A very different conception of conflict, also leading to the theory of the State, is found in the philosophy of Hegel. Instead of beginning with the individual as a material body interacting via collisions with other such bodies, Hegel begins at the opposite end, as it were, with so-called 'laws of thought' which for him apparently exist and operate independently of material bodies. The process is described in his large book, *The Science of Logic*. Its main theme at first sight seems strange, the idea that contradiction is unavoidable in the process of logical progression toward the truth. Put in another way, whatever statement is made about any *portion* of the universe must carry its denial along with it. Later Alfred Korzybski put it in this way: 'Whatever you say it is, it is not.'[3] The apparent unreasonableness of this view is dispelled when we realize that by the nature of our language all our assertions are incomplete. Hegel himself did not relate his conclusions to the imperfections of language. But in arguing his case, we shall do so, because that way the kernel of truth in his system can be made more apparent.

Suppose I say of my pencil, 'The pencil is small.' It is immediately apparent that without further amplification the truth or falsehood of this statement cannot be ascertained: the statement can be either true or false, depending on what the pencil is compared with. The pencil is small compared with a lamp post, large compared with a match. In other words, both statements, 'The pencil is small' (thesis) and 'The pencil is large' (antithesis), can be true. As they stand, they are contradictory and cannot be reconciled. To resolve the contradiction, we must enlarge the portion of the world under consideration. We can say, 'The pencil is large compared with a match and small compared with a lamp post.' Now the apparently contradictory statements have been reconciled in the so-called *synthesis*, a statement about a larger portion of the world.

Take another example. Looking at a Mercator map of the world with the north toward the top, I say 'Paris is to the right of Toronto.' My friend, who is looking at the map upside-down, says 'Not so; Toronto is to the right of Paris.' The contradiction is, of course, only apparent. Realizing that 'right' and 'left' are meaningless words unless the orientation of the speaker is specified, we synthesize our points of view by agreeing that Paris is to the east of Toronto. Yet, even this statement can be contradicted; for, by virtue of the fact that the earth is round, we can say with equal right that Paris is west of Toronto. So we 'synthesize' another step by agreeing on what criterion we will use to denote 'east' and 'west'.

The fact that in practical situations the process of thesis-antithesis-synthesis can come to an end does not satisfy the demands of Hegel's system. It is true that, having specified the standards of comparison, we can agree that the pencil is larger than ... and smaller than ... However, the concepts 'larger than' and 'smaller than' involve other concepts, such as a method of measurement, the perception of the results of measurement – matters ordinarily of no concern to practical men but of great concern to the philosopher in search of 'absolute truth', the preoccupation of rationalist philosophers.

Accordingly, Hegel comes to the conclusion that absolute truth can be asserted only about the Absolute, that is, the entire universe of Being, and that this truth is a synthesis that embodies within itself all the theses and antitheses that arise in the process of contemplating parts of the universe.[4]

To most of us this conclusion may seem sterile. A philosophy that leads to the conclusion that there is only one true proposition – a proposition about the entire realm of existence – can be easily dismissed as pompous nonsense. It is, however, of interest in its own right as an expression of a fundamental question of philosophy: what is reality? Or, better put, how do we distinguish what is real from a mere appearance? This is not an empty question. We know how frequently we take appearances for reality – and the trouble we get into as a result.

Some contemplations of this sort appear to us excessively naive, reflecting only a lack of elementary scientific knowledge. In Anatole France's novel *Thaïs*, a hermit, who has sat on the banks of the Nile for a quarter of a century, wonders about the 'true nature' of the pyramids in the distance. In the morning, when the rising sun illuminates them, the pyramids appear pink; in the evening, with the setting sun behind them, they appear black. But what is their 'inmost substance', the hermit wonders.[5] Such a question seems to us to be no more than a symptom of ignorance. If the hermit knew something about the properties of light, refraction, reflection, etc., he would no longer see any mystery in the changing appearance of the pyramids. For us such mysteries are dissipated in a synthesis, brought about by scientific knowledge. But scientific knowledge itself rests on certain assumptions: for example, that 'there exists' a world independent of our knowledge; that knowledge about the world comes to us ultimately through our senses; that verification of propositions by relating them to observations is the ultimate criterion of truth, etc., etc. In other words, scientific truth is *defined* in terms of selected criteria, and those of us who refuse to go beyond these criteria are satisfied that whatever questions can be settled by the scientific method of cognition lead to true knowledge, while questions that cannot be so settled are not worth asking (or are 'meaningless', as logical positivists put it). But *this* assertion is no more than a delineation of 'legitimate' questions. It does not satisfy the philosopher who insists on asking questions beyond the pale. That not all questions are 'obviously' nonsensical will be admitted by anyone who has wondered what it 'feels like' to be a dog, or a cockroach, or, for that matter, some other human being. We can exclude questions of this sort from the range of meaningfulness by an appropriate definition of 'meaningfulness' but I doubt that such exclusion reflects a wholesome attitude. The assumption that other 'consciousnesses' besides our own 'exist', although it is beyond the range of verification in the scientific sense, is an extremely important one for human beings to entertain and underlies all existing ethical notions.

Let us therefore refrain from dubbing as nonsense all philosophical speculations that cannot be translated into verifiable propositions – the demand made of speculations in the realm of science. Extending meaningfulness to include philosophical speculations does not, however, automatically absolve all such speculations from the charge of contributing to empty verbiage. In societies where abstruse verbiage is held in awe, the established philosopher is likely to spin gigantic verbal webs without restraint. This was especially true in Hegel's Germany, where philosophy was held in the highest esteem. Confronted with a string of words produced by a revered professor of philosophy, anyone interested in philosophy was expected to fathom its meaning through superhuman effort. To plead that one did not understand it would be tantamount to admitting one's obtuseness.

It is not likely that Hegel was a charlatan like the two portrayed in Hans Christian Andersen's story 'The Emperor's New Clothes'. There is reason to believe that Hegel's avalanche of words evoked some sort of images in his mind, which he took to be a revelation of 'reality'. There just wasn't anyone around to give him 'feedback' of either comprehension or lack of it, something indispensable for keeping thought within *some* bounds of meaningfulness. By the nature of their profession, German philosophers did not often engage in any fruitful exchange of ideas. As for the students, their role was expected to be that of vessels into which the wisdom of the professor was poured.

Had Hegel confined himself to elucidating the process of cognition described above, he would have made a considerable contribution to the theory of knowledge by having shown that the acquisition of knowledge is not, as had been believed for centuries, the perception of categories and of qualities that distinguish them from each other, but an evolutionary, creative process in which entirely new concepts arise from clashes between previously established verbal categories and the impossibility of fitting into them the infinite variety of the real world. He would have given an eloquent description of the heart and soul of scientific method –

the continuing spiral of hypothesis formation ('thesis'), the attempt at verification, the ultimate falsification of the hypothesis ('antithesis'), progression to the next state through generalization of the hypothesis to include both the corroborating and the refuting instances ('synthesis').

Instead, Hegel, working within the traditional framework of philosophical thought, believed his task was to 'explain the universe' and he thought he explained it by projecting his dialectics onto something he called the 'Spirit', which supposedly pushed the universe along the path of history.

'One is tempted to suppose', wrote Bertrand Russell, 'that Spirit is trying to understand Hegel, and at each stage rashly objectivizes what it has been reading.'[6]

What, then, is this path that was blazed by the Spirit as it brought into being Hegel's conceptions of the dialectic process? According to Hegel, it was nothing less than history, now revealed as an unfolding process, a triumphant march to perfection, the process of perfection being manifested by the ever-increasing integration of human societies. At each stage another civilization plays out its prescribed role. At first it was the Orientals, to whom presumably the idea of the Absolute (God) first revealed itself: the Orientals knew that the One (God) is free. Next came the Greeks and Romans, in whose societies a class of freemen came into being, so that freedom was extended to *some*. Finally came the Germans who organized a State in which freedom was extended to everyone.[7] This last may seem an astonishing thing to say about the Prussian State in the first quarter of the nineteenth century. It must be remembered, however, that Hegel's conception of freedom was quite different from our own. Just as to the devout Catholic, 'freedom' means the freedom to obey the will of God, just as for the orthodox Soviet Communist, 'freedom' means to do what is approved by the Party, so to Hegel, 'freedom' meant the freedom to obey the State.

This conception of freedom is not altogether absurd. No one will quarrel with the definition of freedom as the unimpeded ability to follow one's inclinations. However, when a man becomes obsessed, especially with a desire to harm others and himself, we say that he is acting under compulsion. Hence, only the unimpeded ability to follow *some* inclinations satisfies our conception of freedom. The views of the devout

Catholic, the orthodox Soviet Communist, and of Hegel differ from the 'liberal' view only to the extent that the range of 'normal' inclinations (which a 'free' individual is free to follow) is defined with reference to a larger 'organism', be it God, embodied in the Church, or in the Working Class, or in the Communist Party, instead of in 'a democratic, humane society' envisaged by the Western liberal. If the essence of perfect freedom is contemplated as the state of consciousness of the One who embodies the entire universe of being, then it makes sense to picture progress as the integration of smaller 'consciousnesses' into larger ones, in which the constituent units become dissolved. We do not ordinarily think that the integration of our own cells, which gives rise to our consciousness, makes the cells 'not free', as if the cells 'wanted' to do something other than function in the interest of the survival of the whole individual but were prevented from doing so by a tyrannical brain. The perfect State, in Hegel's fantasy, appears as the embodiment of a higher form of consciousness. The dissolution of individual consciousnesses in it does not spell the destruction of their freedom but, on the contrary, creates an identification with the 'higher' freedom of the enlarged self. The same idea is evident in the Christian theological notion of 'union with God' and, perhaps, in analogous notions of Hindu and Buddhist religions (cf. the emancipation from desires in the concept of Nirvana).

Hegel's philosophy of history appears ludicrous only when we examine his concrete interpretation of it, the idea, for instance, that the Prussian State, an absolute monarchy, fulfilled the condition of integrating individual consciousnesses into a higher living entity. The notion appears outrageous when we examine the actual structure and function of that 'living system' (or any other of that kind) instead of attributing to it qualities that are supposed to emerge in its formation in accordance with Hegel's imagined manifestation of the dialectical process. To examine it this way, we must use other than philosophical tools of cognition, tools utterly neglected by idealist philosophers, like Hegel, who imagined that they could fathom the nature of the universe by following the tortuous threads of their own fantasies.

To Hobbes, the State was a device designed by man to protect him against the danger of extermination in the 'war of everyone against everyone'.[8] To Hegel, the State was a culmination of a final synthesis, the end product of a dialectical process embodied in the 'laws of thought'. Clausewitz, the foremost philosopher of war, simply took the State for granted as the acting unit in a 'war of all against all'.

'War', wrote Clausewitz, 'is an act of violence intended to compel our opponent to fulfill our will.'[9]

The key words in this definition are 'our' and 'will'. Here 'will' is not a concept derived from mechanics. In Clausewitz's conception, states are not like material bodies that come in conflict by bumping into each other, as human individuals appear in Hobbes's conception. 'Will' in Clausewitz's conception is awareness of long-term goals as well as of immediate needs. The frustration of immediate needs or desires need not automatically result in conflict. In conducting a war, a state (personified in its political leader) in the first instance calculates its power potential vis-a-vis other states, the value of what is to be gained, and the costs likely to be incurred. The 'will', therefore, is not simply a driving force, like Freud's Id or Schopenhauer's 'will'. It is directed to a specific, presumably attainable goal, and it is to attain this goal (and only for this purpose) that the state goes to war in order to compel the opponent (another state) to do 'our' will.

'Our' means that the will of the State is the embodiment of a *collective* will, in Clausewitz's conception, the will of a nation. This identification of 'State' with 'nation' and of 'nation' with a collective will is the fundamental assumption of the so-called realist conception of international relations, the offspring of Clausewitz's philosophy.

What, then, are the goals to be gained by war? These goals, says Clausewitz, are *political* and what specifically they are determines the sort of war fought and how it is fought.

... the political object, as the original motive of the War, will be the standard for determining both the aim of the military force and also the amount of effort to be made. This it cannot be in itself, but it is so in relation to both the belligerent States, because we are concerned with realities, not with mere abstractions. One and the same political object may produce totally different effects upon different people, or even upon the same people at different times; we can, therefore, only admit the political object as the measure, by considering it in its effects upon those masses which it is to move, and consequently the nature of those masses also comes into consideration. It is easy to see that thus the result may be very different according as these masses are animated with a spirit which will infuse vigor into the action or otherwise. It is quite possible for such a state of feeling to exist between two States that a very trifling political motive for War may produce an effect quite disproportionate – in fact, a perfect explosion.[10]

In this passage, Clausewitz's entire philosophy of war is concentrated. The object of a war is political, politics being understood as a process that determines power relations among political actors. The conception of power may take on different forms: it may involve dynastic ambitions, control of territory, access to trade areas, influence exerted on the internal politics of other states, etc. But power as the common denominator of all these issues remains the power to coerce – to impose 'our' will. Hence, both the means of waging war and the goal to be achieved are evaluated in the same currency – power.

Next, note Clausewitz's injunction to evaluate the political objective relative to the 'masses' to be moved, that is, relative to the means available. This amplification can be understood in two ways: (1) power must be used 'rationally', i.e., with due regard to means commensurate with goals and also to setting goals realizable by means available; (2) the state of mind of the masses (population) is a vital ingredient of the power of a State.

Since power is measured only in relation to the power of others, it follows that the 'interests' of any state (to maximize its power) are *always* opposed to the interests of all other states. Therefore, war in this conception appears as a *necessary and normal* relation among states, 'the continuation of politics by other means'. From this point of view, it makes little sense to ask why nations go to war against each other (cf. p. 56). It makes more sense to ask why at a particular time particular states are *not* at war. The answer is to be found in the circumstance that there may be times when the objectives to be gained by war are not commensurate with the effort to be expended or with the prospect of victory. Similarly, it makes sense to ask why war sometimes comes to an end even if neither side is utterly defeated. This can happen, writes Clausewitz, because one of the parties '*waits for a more favorable moment for action*' (Clausewitz's emphasis).[11]

Having said this, Clausewitz dismisses 'balance of power' as an inhibitory factor of war. A suspension of hostilities (for that is how 'peace' is to be understood in Clausewitz's conception) can last only until a 'favorable moment' arrives for one party to act, i.e., to make war.

We see, therefore, that the Clausewitzian system of sovereign states is Hobbes's 'war of everyone against everyone' writ large, with the nation states in the role of Hobbes's men in the state of nature. There is, however, a crucial difference between the two conceptions. In Hobbes's, the individual human being has completely given up his autonomy to the Leviathan (the State) in order to save himself from annihilation in the 'war of everyone against everyone'. Thus, the only thing that the State cannot force an individual to do is go to war, because by placing the subject's life in jeopardy the State negates the very reason for its existence. Not so with Clausewitz's nation state, the super-organism with whose appetites all individuals' needs and aspirations have merged. Moreover, there is no realization by the states that in the 'war of everyone against everyone' they may exterminate themselves. There is no super-Leviathan.

CHAPTER 13

Systemic Theories (continued): Marx and Lenin

In all three conceptualizations of conflict discussed in Chapter 12, the State emerges as an embodiment of a positive idea. For Hobbes, it is the (only) instrument of conflict resolution, a suppressor of the natural propensity of man to make war against all other men. For Hegel, it is the materialization of the Absolute. For Clausewitz, it is the principal actor in the political process, equated to the perpetual struggle not merely for autonomy, as with Hobbes, but for power, that is, for the enlargement of autonomy.

Marx represents a radical departure from this line of thought by calling attention to entirely different sources of systemic conflict.

As a young man, Marx was a Hegelian. Like Hegel himself, he was also strongly influenced by the democratic ideas associated with the French Revolution. The careers of the two men, however, were quite different. Hegel inherited Fichte's[1] Chair at the University of Berlin and became the philosopher of the Prussian establishment. Marx was involved in the revolutionary outbreaks of 1848 both in Germany and in France and became a political refugee, living as a lone, impoverished scholar to the end of his days.

To say that Marx was a Hegelian means that he accepted Hegel's dynamic model of the universe, rejecting the metaphysical static models in which the universe was pictured as a collection of unchanging eternal entities or categories. However, Marx unconditionally rejected Hegel's 'idealism', that is, a picture of the world in which 'thought' or 'the Spirit' or something of this sort is believed to be the fundamental reality underlying the appearance of the world. Marx was a materialist. The materialists believed that *matter* was the fundamental reality. This meant, among other things, that matter could exist, in fact did exist, before there was any consciousness to perceive it; that life was a special form of matter, and that 'mind', 'consciousness', and the like were simply by-products of the way living matter behaved.

The dispute between the materialists and the idealists reflected more than preferences for different mental images of what 'reality' was made of. It had political significance. The eighteenth and nineteenth centuries saw the final break-up of the political power of the Church and of the landed aristocracy, whose power was sanctified by the established Church. Clearly, the idealist outlook was more in harmony with religious teachings, the materialist outlook, with atheistic leanings. We are told that Napoleon, having read Laplace's treatise on celestial mechanics, asked the scientist where God fitted into his picture of the universe. 'Sire,' Laplace is said to have replied, 'I had no need of that hypothesis.'

During the seventeenth and eighteenth centuries the cosmos appeared, to those who investigated it by the now established methods of observation linked with deduction, as a vast machine which 'ran' of its own accord in consequence of the laws governing the motion of matter. The power of the method was manifested in the amazing accuracy with which future positions of heavenly bodies could be predicted. By simply reversing the algebraic sign of time, the positions could also be postdicted; not only could future eclipses of the sun be predicted but also the exact times of past eclipses, which were in accord with the observations made and recorded long ago. In this way not only did the future seem determined for all eternity, but also the past seemed to stretch into infinity. This is why Laplace 'had no need of the hypothesis' that the universe was once created or 'started'. Thereby the philosophical conception of God as the First Cause, linking concepts of religion with those of 'science', no longer seemed necessary, at least in the context of scientific explanation.

It stands to reason that people committed to the tenets of established religion would resist these ideas as doggedly as they would resist the idea of biological evolution two generations later. As was said, the forces of political conservatism were at the time lined up with the philosophical outlook congenial to the teachings of established religion; the radicals were attracted to views that found support in the discoveries of science, which dealt largely with laws governing the behavior of matter, and contradicted the cosmological doctrines of the Church. There was, however, more to the scientific outlook than preoccupation with the properties of matter. The outlook was focused not only on matter but also on *itself*, on the development of the scientific outlook as a manifestation of a progressive evolution, a steady and accelerating approach to the discovery of truth about the world.

It is this dynamic component of Hegel's philosophy that must have appealed to the young German radicals in the early nineteenth century. It only remained to clothe this philosophy in a materialist garb to make it a suitable framework of a revolutionary ideology. This is what Marx did. As his followers are fond of repeating, he turned Hegel's dialectics upside-down so that instead of standing on its head it now stood on its feet, firmly grounded in the world of matter.

There is, indeed, a dialectic process guiding the course of history, Marx declared. The driving force, however, is not the thought process of some disembodied Spirit in which ideas clash with each other as theses and antitheses, giving rise to successive syntheses. The dialectic process is an interaction of man with his material environment and of groups of men (classes) whose interests are opposed to each other. Knowledge is a consequence of these interactions, that is, of *praxis*. We have seen this idea vaguely anticipated by Hegel.[2] These are the two cardinal ideas of Marx's philosophy: one brings the philosophy of knowledge into closer relation to the scientific outlook; the other links it to a revolutionary ideology. For this reason the disciples of Marx can contend with some justification that Marx was the creator of 'scientific socialism' as distinguished from the 'utopian socialism' of the radical social philosophers who preceded him.

Let us first examine the idea that knowledge is a consequence of action rather than of, say, introspection, as it appeared to the idealistic rationalists (Plato, Descartes), or of impressions received through the senses, as it appeared to the British empiricists (Locke, Hume). The scientific method of cognition came to full maturity only when reasoning was coupled with *controlled* experiment. A controlled experiment involves a deliberate arrangement of conditions in order to 'wrest' an answer to a question put to nature. To make deliberate arrangements means, crudely speaking, to push matter around instead of recording one's impressions simply as they come. There is no question, therefore, that in this context the acquisition of knowledge is intimately connected with action. One can say more: it is associated with a willingness to act, which in turn comes from motivation. Where does this motivation come from? An answer suggests itself: it comes from a determination to *change* one's environment, presumably the characteristically human way of interacting with environment (cf. p. 51). The intimate inter-dependence of the unfolding of scientific knowledge and the growth of technology attests to the reasonableness of this interpretation of the 'dialectic process' manifested in the growth of knowledge. Not the introspective deliberations of a Spirit, but the activity of man interacting with matter is the content of this process.

Let us now examine the theory of the class struggle as the 'driving force of history'. With the growth of technology, human society becomes increasingly complex. Division of labor eventually leads to a stratification of human societies into classes. The way these classes relate to each other in the process of production (systematic production being also a characteristically human way of life) determines their relations toward each other.[3] And so it comes to pass that 'exploiting' and 'exploited' classes become distinguishable. The former typically appropriate more of what is produced, enjoy special privileges, and are exempted from the drudgery of heavy labor. The latter receive less, have more obligations than rights (if any), and are obliged to do most of the work. There are slaves and slave holders. There are patricians and plebeians. There are feudal lords and serfs. There are capitalists and workers. At each stage of human history, Marx pointed out, a particular juxtaposition of exploiting and exploited classes dominated the structure of social organization. The particular nature of exploitation reflected a particular stage of social organization, which, in turn, depended on the particular state of technology.

However, no historical stage was ever static. Every social system has nurtured within itself the seeds of its own destruction. As technology improved in the later Middle Ages, as trade increased and with it, cities grew, a new class began its rise to power within the structure of feudal society in which the pattern of exploitation was based primarily on the ownership of land. This new class, the bourgeoisie, comprising at first the craftsmen and merchants, later entrepreneurs and professionals, eventually overthrew the feudal order and reorganized society in accordance with their own interests. This was 'progress', because it released new energies and channeled them into exploration, invention, organization of production on an ever larger scale. It was in the interest of the bourgeoisie to introduce forms of social organization incompatible with those on which feudal society rested. In particular, the new modes of production demanded freer trade, wider literacy, and, above all, greater freedom of movement. The serf, attached to the soil, did not serve these needs. The idea of individual freedom became socially functional. The ideal relationship between a worker and his employer was envisaged as a contractual one rather than one based on the obligations of status. It was in the interest of the entrepreneur to be free to discharge a worker when he was no longer needed, to seek workers in a labor market instead of depending on the unproductive labor of slaves or serfs and being responsible for keeping them alive.

It was these developments which, according to Marx, brought about the type of social organization that became dominant in Western Europe in his time – the capitalist system – and, be it noted, the particular world outlook that made this arrangement seem natural and just. However, the dialectic process did not stop with the victory of the bourgeoisie and the establishment of the capitalist system. Instead, this system gave birth to a new exploited class, the proletariat, typified by the industrial worker. This class was now placed in dialectic opposition to the capitalist class, and a new class struggle ensued.[4]

Marx's account of human history ends with the prediction of the outcome of this new struggle. The capitalist system must collapse, Marx predicted, because it contains within itself a basic contradiction. Capitalist production is a cooperative process, necessitating the coordination of complex skills and vast organization of productive forces and of distribution. But, since what is produced is appropriated by the owners of the means of production, the motivating force in the productive process is not the satisfaction of human needs but the profit that accrues from it to the capitalists. Consequently, production and distribution cannot be organized rationally. The result is wasteful competition, wild fluctuation of business cycles, and a steady impoverishment of what in Marx's time was still considered the middle class – the craftsman, the small business man, the independent farmer. The efficiency of mass production makes the craftsman superfluous; the complexity of the industrial plant increases the size of enterprises, concentrating capital in fewer and fewer hands. Extrapolating the trends of his day, Marx saw capitalist society developing into one wherein a numerically negligible capitalist class is faced with an overwhelming number of proletarians. In the process of struggle with the employers (for wage increases, better working conditions, etc.), the workers will achieve 'class consciousness'. That is, they will come to understand that their miseries stem neither from the way things were eternally ordained, nor from the inability of the productive process to provide them with the necessities of life, nor even from the greed or callousness of individual capitalists; that inequities of grossly unequal distribution of wealth stem from the contradiction inherent in the capitalist system – anarchic appropriation superimposed on cooperative production. When a sufficient number of workers achieve this insight, as they must (because knowledge comes through action), they will be able because of their superior numbers to seize political power. They will then become the dominant class and will organize society in accordance with *their* interest, which is to bring the system of distribution into harmony with the cooperative mode of industrial production. The means of production (land, factories, mineral wealth, etc.) will be socialized, that is, will cease to belong to private entrepreneurs and capitalists and will become the common property of the whole society. Then no profit can accrue to anyone from production. The motivation for production will be exclusively the necessity to satisfy human needs.

To see, in all its starkness, the contrast between this view and Hegel's, one should turn attention to Marx's theory of the State. Hegel pictured the State as the incarnation of the highest stage of synthesis of the dialectic process. In Marxist political theory, on the other hand, the State emerges as an instrument of oppression used by the ruling class to keep the exploited class in submission.[5] From this conception it follows that if there were no exploiters and no exploited there would be no need for the State, and Marx actually drew this conclusion. He thought that the proletarian revolution, which, he insisted, was inevitable, would finally do away with the exploitation of man by man, because in the absence of a privileged class monopolizing the ownership of the means of production there would be no mechanism of exploitation. Once exploitation disappeared, the State, deprived of its function, would 'wither away'.

Marx carefully avoided the notion that the presence or the absence of exploitation is in any way dependent on the moral character of particular classes of people or, for that matter, on the nature of man. That is not to say that Marx was ever morally neutral. He was passionately on the side of the workers in their struggles against the entrepreneurs. However, his partisanship was expressed only in his positive attitude toward the coming proletarian revolution. He emphatically denied that this revolution would come because justice demanded it or that the final abolition of exploitation would depend in any way on a rise in man's moral stature. Marx did not deny the existence of ethical convictions and humanitarian impulses any more than the reality of cruelty and injustice in human relations. But he did not see any moral qualities as 'causes' or determinants of the nature of human relations, at least on the large social scale. Human relations and even ethical concepts themselves were, in Marx's estimation, consequences not causes of the way men related to each other in the process of socially organized production. Therefore, no appeal to moral principles or to sentiments could be effective in changing the nature of human relations. Only a change in the underlying economic relations could effect changes of attitudes. To quote the principal tenet of materialistic philosophy, being determines consciousness, not vice versa.

Marx's attitude toward prevailing ethical convictions, moral principles, social philosophies, etc., was that these are predominantly rationalizations of the class interests of those who hold the convictions. Clearly, this interpretation is not to be taken literally in each individual case. To do so would require interpreting the ideas of Marx himself as rationalizations of a bourgeois, since Marx himself never belonged to the class whose interests he championed. But Marx was not concerned with the psychology of single individuals. He was deeply interested in the 'psychology' of the whole social organism, which, in his philosophy, is the analogue of Hegel's Spirit except that it is the derivative, not the determinant, of the dialectic process. In other words, as we would put it, Marx was interested in the semantic environment to the extent that it is a *product* of what he believed to be its basic determinants, and these he took to be first, man's characteristic interactions with the physical environment, spurred by efforts to *change* the environment to suit his needs; second, man's characteristic social interactions, embodied in class struggles. These, he supposed, had been going on since human societies became stratified by class structure and would continue until the stratification disappeared in consequence of the complete socialization of the productive process. Then and only then would man become free.

The Marxist philosophy of society is a sort of analogue to psychoanalysis. Psychoanalytic theory pictures the human individual as obsessed by drives that are manifestations of unresolved conflicts of which the individual is unaware. Insight into the origins of these conflicts (through making their origins conscious) is supposed to make the individual free of obsessions and compulsions. Marxist theory pictures ideologies as manifestations of conflicting class interests of which men are unaware. 'Ideology' is used here in the pejorative sense, to mean a constrictive framework of thought that puts limits on man's ability to discover truth. Freedom, Marxists maintain, will be achieved when there are no longer any antagonistic classes, hence no compulsions to keep thought within the restrictive frameworks of ideologies. Man's energies will then be directed entirely toward molding the environment to suit his needs, which is the implicit definition of freedom.

The impact of Marx's ideas on politics has been compared to that of Newton's on physical science and Darwin's on biological science. The comparison is justifiable in view of the 'focus' provided by Marx's fusion of a theory of conflict with a theory of history. Around this focus a 'system of thought' was organized, held together by a number of key concepts in terms of which social phenomena were explained. The resulting picture of history and society resembles the pictures of physical and biological universes provided by the syntheses of Newton and Darwin.

A system of thought resembles physical systems in the sense that it is a focus of organization – it 'hangs together'. However, what makes it hang together is not physical forces or interactions but the way it shapes people's perceptions and thinking habits. Languages have already been mentioned as systems of this sort. A language 'lives' because people speak it, think it, 'hang their perceptions on it'. Religious, philosophic, and scientific systems of thought persist in the same way. In particular, their viability depends on their explanatory appeal, the extent to which people find that events make sense in terms of the concepts that bind the system together.

In addition to the explanatory appeal, scientific theories (but not religious or philosophic ones) have also predictive power. Not only do sequences of events already observed make sense when explained in terms of the concepts provided by the scientific theory; also, other events can be predicted. As was pointed out in Chapter 11, predictive power of a theory is related to the a priori *improbability* of the event predicted. In this sense, the predictive power of physical science that emerged from the Newtonian system of thought is prodigious (for instance, eclipses of the sun can be predicted many years in advance to within seconds).

The predictive power of biological science that emerged from the Darwinian system of thought did not compare with that of physical science because the theory of natural selection is stated in much more general terms than the theory of celestial mechanics. Nevertheless, the theory of evolution based on natural selection has served as a focus of ideas which later developed into theories with considerable predictive power as well as explanatory appeal: genetics, for instance.

With the Marxist system, the matter is considerably more complex. It can be argued that the emergent theory of history, whatever has been its explanatory appeal (in some quarters), has little or no predictive power. It has been maintained, for example, that specific predictions of the theory have not been corroborated, in particular, the progressive proletarization and pauperization of the masses in industrial societies and the attendant growing class consciousness in the impoverished. It must be kept in mind, however, that the predictions of Marxist theory are of a different sort from those of a natural science. Predictions by the latter are independent of human purposes and volition. Although Marx's theory of history is often called deterministic, it is not viewed as such (at least, not as mechanically deterministic) by Marxists. What Marxists claim is that the 'discovery of the laws of social development' (which they attribute to Marx) *enables* the working class to seize the controls, as it were, of the historical process. This is a 'prediction' comparable to those of technology rather than to those of pure science. Predictions of the airplane and the atomic bomb, made long before these devices appeared, did not imply that they would appear of their own accord. Only their possibility was implied by the predictions. Their realization could be assured only by the interference of purposeful human action. It is in this sense that the Marxist predictions of future social revolutions should be understood.

The appeal of Marxist theory, therefore, was in its call for action, specifically for struggle. The predictive component of the theory was a stimulant in that it guaranteed victory in the class struggle. Such predictions often turn out to be self-fulfilling.

Lenin, Marx's most ardent disciple, devoted his life to the organization of the struggle that would insure the realization of Marx's predictions. The peak of his activity was toward the end of World War I when the tsarist regime collapsed in consequence of military defeat. Lenin thought that the moment of the 'final', that is, proletarian, revolution had arrived and that this opportunity was provided by the chaos brought on by the war. His book *Imperialism*, published in 1917, was conceived as the extension of Marx's theory, namely its application to what Lenin called the 'last phase of capitalism' – imperialism. The book was written in the midst of World War I (spring 1916) and 'with an eye to tsarist censorship', as Lenin says in the preface to the edition published after the collapse of the tsarist government.

'It is painful,' Lenin continues, 'in these days of freedom, to read again these passages, mutilated by consideration for the tsarist censorship, gripped and held tight in the vise of iron.'[6]

One can sympathize with Lenin's discomfort (as with that of any author forced to write under supervision), but it may have been this very circumstance that directed Lenin's efforts toward emphasizing the purely 'objective' (that is, systemic) forces shaping the development of international capitalism. To be sure, Marxists constantly call attention to these 'objective' forces, and for this reason their theories are good examples of system analysis. However, since most of their writings are inherently polemical (Lenin's being for the most part extreme on this score), the ideal of objective analysis is often lost sight of. Considerations of censorship or not, *Imperialism* contains its share of vituperative polemics to the detriment of objective analysis. Nevertheless, the bulk of the book is devoted to a compilation of statistics purporting to show how Marx's predictions with regard to progressive concentration of capital (industrial and financial) were being realized. Further, it is shown that from the beginning of the last quarter of the nineteenth century to the outbreak of World War I the industrialized states of Europe (and the United States) 'divided the world' among them. Economic development in the various capitalist countries being 'uneven', some of the competing states got a head start in the scramble for colonial empire. The struggle for power, once centered on the European continent, shifted to Asia and Africa. The Spanish-American, the Sino-Japanese, the Anglo-Boer wars were all precursors of the explosion of 1914. Lenin's conclusion is stated most crassly in the preface to the French and German editions: '. . . imperialist wars are absolutely inevitable . . . as long as private owner-ship in the means of production exists.'[7]

As in the case of the frustration-aggression theory (cf. Chapter 11), we are left in the dark as to whether private ownership of the means of pro-duction is presented as a necessary, or a sufficient, or both a necessary and sufficient condition for imperialist wars. If both (as seems to be the most likely interpretation), one might expect that in the absence of capitalism (with which private ownership of *large* means of production is identified) no imperialist wars could take place, while, as long as capital-ism exists, imperialist wars are *inevitable*.

With regard to the first expectation, the wars waged, say, by the Roman empire appear to be an embarrassment to the theory. In fact, Lenin him-self states '. . . imperialism existed even . . . before capitalism: Rome, founded on slavery, carried out a colonial policy and was imperialistic.'[8] The editor, however, removes the apparent contradiction (the conten-tion that capitalism is a necessary condition for imperialist wars) in his explanatory notes:

> The 'imperialism of ancient Rome,' . . . must not be confused with modern imperialism . . . The difference between the imperialism of ancient Rome and modern imperialism consists in the *difference of production bases* . . . This example, among others, shows how incorrect it is to understand by the term 'modern imperialism' only a 'policy,' and not the whole system of capitalist economy.[9]

As for the contention that imperialist wars are inevitable under capital-ism (that is, that capitalism is a sufficient condition for such wars), this conclusion has been somewhat qualified in recent years by Lenin's disciples, the qualification being supportcd by appropriate quotations from Lenin.

Connections between highly developed international capitalism and war can be and have been demonstrated on reasonable grounds. What makes the Leninist thesis vulnerable is the categorical manner in which it is stated and the frequently shoddy logic with which Lenin strives to discredit rather than refute his opponents. Lenin has often been taken to task on this account, and a disdain for his polemical methods has probably been a factor in the readiness with which his theories have been rejected. In evaluating Lenin's thesis on its merits it is well to keep in mind that his prognoses (like those of Marx) are calls to action rather than predictions in the sense of natural science. If the action called for is undertaken, predictions of this sort can turn out to be self-fulfilling.

To Lenin, as to several revolutionaries of his time, World War I was a political opportunity. True, the predicted pauperization of the European masses had not taken place. Some of the benefits of the rapidly growing technology had filtered down even to the working classes, while the 'petty bourgeoisie', instead of being wiped out (as predicted by Marx), was growing in the form of the white-collar class. Moreover, the 'class consciousness' of the workers was directed to concrete economic issues rather than toward the dialectics of the historical process. In Lenin's words,

> The stratum of bourgeoisified workers of 'labour aristocracy,' who have become completely petty-bourgeois in their mode of life, in the amount of their earnings, and in their way of life . . . *support the bourgeoisie.* They are the real *agents of the bourgeoisie in the labour movement,* the labour lieutenants of the capitalist class . . .[10] [Lenin's emphasis; the last phrase is in English in the original.]

The war, however, could be readily used as concrete evidence of the 'real nature' of international capitalism. The rising standard of living in Europe was declared to be a 'bribe' financed by the super-profits of colonial exploitations. The price of accepting the bribe (in return for supporting 'national interests') was now being paid in blood at Verdun, at Ypres, and on the Somme.

Lenin's aim was to induce the European masses – in the first instance, of course, the Russian masses – to turn the 'imperialist war' into a civil war, to use the opportunity of being armed to bring about the 'final' social revolution. In Russia, the armed insurrection actually succeeded. The consequences, however, generated by forces of which Lenin, committed to an unfalsifiable theory, had no conception, were not in line with Marx's or Lenin's predictions.

CHAPTER 14

Systemic Theories (continued): Richardson and Kahn

All systemic theories by their nature represent rather high levels of abstraction since they focus on general structural features of their subject matter rather than on concrete cases. The most general aspects of structure are relations devoid of content, of the sort examined in mathematics. Quantitative relations are of this sort.

As final examples of systemic theories, we shall examine two of this extremely abstract type, Lewis F. Richardson's and Herman Kahn's.

Richardson examines what he calls 'deadly quarrels', i.e., encounters in which people kill each other. In his view, the most important classification of these 'quarrels' is according to magnitude, the number killed. As a measure of magnitude, Richardson takes the logarithm to base 10 of the number killed. Thus, a single murder has magnitude 0 ($\log_{10} 1 = 0$); a riot with ten fatalities has magnitude 1 ($\log_{10} 10 = 1$); a small war with 10,000 killed has magnitude 4; the two world wars were of magnitude between 7 and 8, while a nuclear war of magnitude 9–10 would wipe out the human race.

Richardson's aim was to examine the frequency distributions of the 'deadly quarrels' of different magnitudes in the hope that the parameters of the distribution might suggest some property of the underlying stochastic process governing the probabilities of incidence.[1] From these inferred properties one could, perhaps, derive some hypotheses about the nature of the 'system' which generates 'deadly quarrels'.

Statistical analysis of this sort sometimes is undertaken in so-called epidemiological studies. For example, by noting the distribution of industrial accidents in successive periods, it is possible to find evidence for or against the existence of 'contagion' effects whereby the occurrence of accidents facilitates further accidents; or 'anti-contagion' effects, whereby the occurrence of accidents inhibits further accidents.

One of Richardson's findings along these lines deserves attention, not that it sheds much light on the nature of 'deadly quarrels' but because it illustrates the kind of thinking typical of 'pure' systemic analysis. Richardson found that the distribution of sizes of Chicago gangs (in the golden age of gangsterism, the 1920s and early 1930s) was very similar to the distribution of the sizes of bandit raids in Manchukuo (the Japanese puppet state in China in the 1930s). On the basis of this similarity, Richardson conjectured that there was something about 'organizations for violence' that gave rise to similar statistical profiles in widely separated manifestations of the organizing process.[2]

The conclusion seems too far-fetched to be taken seriously. Yet, years later, some evidence was found that might be interpreted as a faint corroboration of Richardson's idea. Steady state distributions of group sizes can be derived from two different assumptions. According to one assumption, members can enter or leave the groups freely and do so casually (by choice). Under the other assumption, individuals can join a group but cannot leave it unless the whole group falls apart. As a consequence of the first assumption, the distribution of group sizes turns out to be quite different from that found by Richardson and, in fact, fits the distribution of sizes of observed groups gathered around swimming pools and other 'casual' groups. Under the second assumption, the distribution of group sizes turns out to resemble what Richardson found for Chicago gangs and Manchukuo bandit raids.[3] It is a commonplace observation that individuals do not 'casually' leave gangs, at least not as casually as they leave 'unorganized' groups.

It goes without saying that the relevance of this observation is exceedingly doubtful. (Do not cohesive forces operate in any organized group, not just in groups organized for violence?) But note how, in discussing Richardson's conjecture, we were led to questions that instigate further investigations. The principal value of 'pure' systemic analysis is in its question-generating potential.

Richardson's most frequently cited investigation concerns the mathematical analysis of arms races. His model of an arms race is a pair of systems stimulating each other by positive feedback (cf. p. 74). The rate of increase of the level of armaments of each is supposedly proportional to the actual level of armaments of the other. If this were the only interaction, the level of armaments of both systems would increase indefinitely at an exponentially accelerating rate. Since this is physically impossible, another interaction must be assumed. Accordingly, Richardson assumes that one's *own* level of armament inhibits its rate of growth. The resulting total system, comprising two sub-systems, has an equilibrium state; whether this equilibrium is stable or unstable depends on the relative magnitudes of the mutually stimulating and inhibiting parameters.

Richardson plotted the combined armament budgets of the Allied and Central powers during the armament race of 1908–14 and found that the growth was indeed exponential. By properly choosing the parameters, he made the predicted growth curve correspond almost exactly to the observed. However, the most interesting result was not the fit of the curve (which, because of the short duration of the process, could well have been a coincidence) but the conclusion that the theoretical equilibrium would have been unstable. The slightest deviation in either direction would have been magnified in the *same* direction, so that the postulated system *had* to move either into a runaway arms race or, on the contrary, toward complete disarmament. That it moved into the armament race, exploding into war, could have been a consequence of an accidental displacement in that direction.[4]

Again, because of the many assumptions included in the model and the paucity of data, the result cannot be taken too seriously. But it is thought-provoking. It illustrates what *may* be inherent in an international system linked by mutually stimulating interactions.

Richardson applied the same method of analysis to the armament race of 1933–9 with Germany and the U.S.S.R. as principal participants, and showed that it, too, may have been the consequence of positive feedback. His paper was published on the very eve of World War II. After that war, he started the analysis of the armament race between the United States and the Soviet Union, but he died in 1953 without having come to a conclusion about its probable outcome.

Herman Kahn's analyses were probably inspired by the work of Clausewitz, as one gathers from the title of his largest book, *On Thermonuclear War*, meant perhaps to be a sequel to Clausewitz's *On War*.

Like Richardson's classification of wars, Kahn's is essentially a quantitative one. In his book, for instance, Kahn distinguishes magnitudes of nuclear wars, which he labels World War III, IV, ... VIII. This terminology has aroused considerable indignation under the impression that Kahn is projecting in an offhand manner a sequence of recurring world wars. Actually, the roman numerals refer not to a sequence of wars but only to a sequence of magnitudes. Kahn assumes that the technology of nuclear warfare will keep developing in extent and complexity. The type of world war that would occur at a particular time would depend on the stage of technology reached then. According to Kahn's prognosis, we are now entering the era of World War VIII.[5]

Nevertheless, the connotations of the terminology are not to be dismissed, for Kahn, like Clausewitz before him, did not confine himself to description. His writings, like Clausewitz's, contain a message–two messages, in fact. One of them points out the strategic and political implications of the new type of warfare. (Clausewitz, too, stressed similar implications stemming from the new factor of nationalism introduced by the wars of 1792–1815.) The other message is a plea for 'rationality' in the face of the unknown. Kahn categorically rejects both the idea that the prospect of the horrors of nuclear war has made it 'unthinkable' and the idea that if such a war occurs it will be the 'end of civilization', perhaps of humanity. His emphasis on distinguishing gradations of magnitude is meant as an antidote to both ideas. He attempts to dispel the apocalyptic connotations of both 'nuclear war' and 'World War III', which to him are bugaboo words. I believe that the choice of notation ('World War IV', 'World War V', etc.) was meant to dissociate 'World War III' from 'finality'.

In short, Kahn appears to see his mission as one of restoring war to the status of a political instrument. Clausewitz wrote at a time when this role of war had come to its fullest fruition. A dramatic 'mutation' in the evolution of war, manifested in the sudden appearance of the atomic bomb, threatened to render this role obsolete, since it was difficult to conceive of political goals that were worth the price exacted by thermonuclear war. Kahn argues, in effect, that politics and war can be tailored to each other even in the nuclear age. The wherewithal of politics remains what it was in Clausewitz's conception – military power. The objectives of politico-military strategy also remain the same: to compel 'our' opponent to do 'our' will. Where for Clausewitz it was axiomatic that the opponent can be compelled to do our will only in consequence of military defeat, Kahn adds blackmail to the arsenal of political conflict. The costs of devastation by nuclear weapons being super-prohibitive, he argues that it may be possible to achieve political ends by the adroit use of threats.

The basic model, developed in a later book, *On Escalation*, is an extension of the quantitative hierarchy of nuclear wars, the so-called Escalation Ladder. The ladder has forty-four rungs. The rungs are separated by 'thresholds'. Passing a threshold changes the 'quality' of the conflict. Thus, the intensity of conflict can progress from verbal declarations (sub-crisis maneuvering) to 'traditional crises' where no nuclear threats are made, to 'intense crises', where 'conventional' war has already begun, across the nuclear threshold to 'limited' or 'exemplary' nuclear exchanges, and so on, culminating in the so-called 'civilian central wars'. The uppermost rung of the ladder, labeled 'spasm or insensate war', no longer 'controlled', is presumably devoid of any political significance.

The central idea of this book is that escalation, far from being the sort of process described by Richardson as being sustained by the interaction system itself, can be controlled. Indeed, a controlled process of this sort can be used as a political instrument, according to Kahn. Verbal threats, if not implemented, tend to lose their efficacy. Therefore, if threats are to be of use in gaining advantages, they must be implemented. Because of the high cost of retaliation, however, the implementation of a threat of total destruction is impractical. The Escalation Ladder, on the other hand, displays the wide latitude of 'practical' coercive actions at the disposal of the diplo-military strategist. He can presumably choose a position on the ladder with due consideration for the possible positions that the opponent can choose, and calculate the feasibility of moving up (and, presumably, on occasion, down). In this way, the diplo-military game becomes sophisticated, worthy of the minds of strategists.

Kahn takes every opportunity to point out that apparently simple situations are really complex. He decries the over-simplifications and the 'either-or' type of thinking that people fall into when they contemplate the dilemmas of international conflict in the nuclear age. With regard to arms control, for instance, he has this to say:

Assume there are two individuals who are going to fight a duel to death with blow torches. The duel is to be conducted in a warehouse filled with dynamite. One might conjecture that they could agree to leave the lights on. There is undoubtedly powerful motivation for them to do so. While both are agreed that only one is to survive, they would each like some chance of being that one; neither prefers the effective certainty of both being killed. Yet they might still disagree on: How many lights? Where? How bright? Should the one with greater visual acuity handicap himself in other ways? And so on.[6]

Equally unjustifiable in Kahn's estimation is the simplistic assumption that a nuclear attack would (or should) immediately provoke a massive retaliation. He finds gratifying progress in this respect in the thinking of American audiences that he has had occasion to address: for example, 'college students, businessmen, members of the League of Women Voters, etc.' To test the understanding of these audiences concerning modern strategic doctrine, he asks them what they think would happen if the President were notified that a large hydrogen bomb was exploded over New York City. He reports that almost no one in the audience (published in 1965) as opposed to five years previously replies that the President would immediately order an all-out nuclear attack on the Soviet Union. Instead, they conjecture that the President would address over the hot line to his opposite number in the Kremlin intelligent and searching questions of this sort:

'Why is there only one bomb? Where are the others? Why was New York City chosen? If the Soviets wanted to launch an exemplary attack, why had they not made some preliminary demands or sent a message so that we would understand what was going on?'

To keep the discussion going, these questions are answered in such a way that retaliation appears the 'proper' response. Some in Mr Kahn's audiences suggest that Moscow should be destroyed. But others object that Moscow is more important to the Russians than New York is to Americans and suggest instead the destruction of some smaller city, like Leningrad or Kiev. Mr Kahn then asks those who wanted to destroy Moscow what the United States should do if the Russians followed up by destroying Philadelphia (on the grounds that Moscow was worth more than New York City). Most of the audience feel at that point that enough is enough, that the U.S. 'had made its point' and that there was some justice in the Soviet argument that, in destroying Moscow, the U.S. had 'overescalated'.

As a result of these discussions, Kahn concludes that 'almost everyone in the U.S. who has any interest in these problems . . . learned that there are many possibilities of control in such bizarre situations.'[7]

CHAPTER 15

Systemic Theories: Summary

Systemic theories of human conflict shift attention away from the individual, his motives and reactions, to systems, particularly those systems of which individuals are components, such as nation states (in Clausewitz's or Kahn's models) or classes (in Marx's) or both (as in Lenin's model of imperialism). What, then, is the relation between the motives and reactions of the individual, on the one hand, and the actions of a larger system, on the other? Is the behavior of the system determined by the sum-total of the acts of individuals in it? Or does the action of the larger system impose certain courses of action on its constituents? Can we ascribe 'motives' or 'aspirations' to larger systems, as the exponents of the 'realist' school of international relations do when they speak of 'national interest'? And, if so, do these motives and aspirations induce facsimiles in the component individuals?

In attempting to answer these questions, we must qualify the meaning of the word 'determine'. In ordinary usage, we say one event determines another if knowledge of the first enables us (at least in principle) to predict the second. To what extent 'determinism' operates in nature is a question that has long occupied the attention of philosophers and, as is the case with most philosophical questions, this one can never be answered to everyone's satisfaction. There is, however, a form of determination that is demonstrable as such and that, at the same time, reconciles the principle with the apparently contradictory principle of 'indeterminism', or, in some cases, with that of 'free will'. This is the determinism of large numbers.

When a coin is tossed, the outcome 'heads' or 'tails' can be considered to be both determinate and indeterminate. It cannot be proved to be either. Our assumption of one or the other depends on what we conceive to be, in principle, ascertainable. The outcome of a coin toss (or the outcome of an 'experiment', as we shall refer to it) depends on the course of motion of the coin, which *presumably* depends on a great number of particular circumstances: the torque imparted to the coin, its trajectory (influenced not only by the initial velocity and by gravity but also by minute air currents), the angle at which it hits the surface landed upon, the slight irregularities of the surface at the point of contact, etc. To say that all these circumstances 'determine' the outcome is to assert the deterministic nature of physical laws, that is, to assume the principle that one is supposed to be demonstrating. On the other hand, to say that the outcome is only a probabilistic one is simply to take cognizance of our ignorance of the innumerable influences in each particular experiment.

Repeated tosses of the coin will sometimes result in heads, sometimes in tails. If the coin is thrown very many times, the ratio of the number of heads to the total number of tosses, while fluctuating, will seem to approach a constant value. This value we call the *probability* that the coin falls heads. The observed long-run constancy of the ratio is the empirical basis of the notion of probability. It is expressed mathematically in the so-called law of large numbers, which states (very roughly) that, although the outcome of a particular experiment may be one of several and there is no way of telling which will occur, in a long sequence of experiments the ratios of the frequencies of each outcome to the total number of experiments will approach constant values.

The law of large numbers applies to some aspects of human behavior. Although each resident of a city feels that he is 'free' to come and go, that, for instance, he goes to work in the morning and home in the evening of his own free will, nevertheless, *in totality*, the population behaves as if some force were moving it in one direction in the morning and in the other in the evening. Although each feels free to go out or stay in, day after day and year after year, the streets are jammed during the rush hours and virtually empty in the early morning hours.

The attention of the system theorist is often turned to certain distributions within systems. Instances already mentioned are the distribution of concentrations of substances in systems of chemical reactions (cf. p. 31) and in living systems. Many of these distributions remain constant and, in fact, define the steady states of the system. We have seen also that systems if 'left alone' tend toward steady states determined by their structure and interactions with the environment. Mathematically, this trend is often demonstrated as a deterministic one. But it can be also shown in so-called *stochastic* systems[1] in which the simple events are probabilistic but the system behaves deterministically in its totality.

As an example, take the hypothetical systems postulated in classical economics. A great number of commodity producers (or sellers) and consumers (or buyers) come together in a 'free market' to engage in trade, using money as a common medium of exchange. The 'classical' theory says that the price of each commodity will be stabilized at some equilibrium value, depending on the supply of the commodity and the demand for it. Disturbances of the equilibrium will be restored by the mechanism of the free market. If the demand for a commodity goes up, consumers will compete for the existing supply and will offer higher prices. This will be an incentive for more production, which will bring the supply in line with the demand and will reduce the price. An analogous process will restore the balance if supply departs from its 'natural' (equilibrium) value. Classical economists sometimes refer to this homeostatic mechanism as the operation of the 'invisible hand.'

The model is concerned only with the market, not with the distribution of control over the productive process. In fact, it assumes that any one or a great many of the participants can shift freely from producing one type of commodity to another as the homeostatic mechanism demands. Clearly, the mechanism would not work if only one producer produced some commodity; for, if everyone needed it, the monopolist could set the price and the supply, assuming the demand fixed, by the nature of the essential commodity. In other words, the classical model of the free market assumes really 'free' competition, which, in turn, implies that the producers are more or less 'equal'.

The results of 'free competition', however, involve not only minute fluctuations in supply, demand, and prices, but also changes in the fortunes of the producers, reflected in the accumulation of capital. In part, capital includes production facilities (machines etc.), facilities for buying large amounts of raw materials at lower prices (operating capital), etc. There is nothing in the market model that requires these facilities to be equally distributed among the producers. In fact, the trends in the distribution of capital became a question in economics quite as important as the operation of the 'free market'. Let us see what these trends might be.

Consider a system of entities of whatever nature, each characterized by size. As a result of interactions the entities suffer changes of size. Assume that these changes, whether increments or decrements, are proportional to the sizes already attained; that is, each entity suffers increments or decrements that are constant fractions of its size at the time. The steady state distribution of the relative sizes of these entities can be calculated mathematically. It can be shown that under these conditions, if size is interpreted as, say, mass, the mass of the system will be strongly concentrated in the largest units.

Distributions of this sort are observed in a vast variety of contexts, ranging from the distribution of populations by countries to the distribution of frequencies with which words occur in spoken or written language. For instance, the four most populous countries in the world (China, India, U.S.S.R., and U.S.), only 3 per cent of the existing politically recognized nations, contain over 50 per cent of the world's population (12 per cent of the countries contain over 75 per cent of the population). About 20 words in the English language ('the', 'of', 'that', 'and', . . .), less than 1 per cent of the average person's speaking vocabulary, constitute over 50 per cent of all words spoken or written.

The tremendous range of contexts in which this sort of 'lopsidedness' is observed leads us to suppose that the 'laws' governing distributions are quite independent of the nature of the entities involved, provided only that the fluctuations in size (or frequency of occurrence) to which they are subjected are governed by similar probabilistic events.[2]

Returning to the evidence marshalled by Lenin in support of the growing monopolization of capital (Chapter 13), we note that what it amounts to is that the bigger units are getting bigger still, a phenomenon observed in a wide range of settings having nothing to do with capitalism. What, then, does this observation do to Lenin's thesis or, more generally, to the Marxist thesis? It is damaging to the former in the sense that it weakens the case for attributing the trend toward monopolization to the 'rapaciousness' of the capitalist class. Capitalists may or may not be collectively rapacious or greedy. Psychological traits of entities *need* not be involved to explain the behavior of the system, which may be governed by stochastic processes. At the same time, system analysis in a variety of contexts strengthens the central Marxist thesis (sometimes obfuscated by Lenin's passionate invectives) that the behavior of the large systems may be independent of the 'wills' of the entities that constitute them.

The important contribution of Marx (and not only of Marx but of classical economists as well) has been the bringing into focus of the quasi-deterministic character of large-scale human affairs. The difference between Marx and the classical economists is that, while the latter conceived of the 'free market' as a system with a stable equilibrium, Marx saw capitalism as a basically unstable system which, because of forces *generated by itself*, must destroy itself.

This 'determinism' is to be understood not in the fatalistic sense but in the sense of putting into proper perspective the motives, wills, or aspirations of individual human beings against the background of large historical processes. Marx's predictions of the coming reorganization of society may or may not be realized. The importance of his thought is not in specific predictions but in his perspective on the nature of social change. A reorganization of society will come about, Marx insisted, not because the capitalist system is unjust or because a socialist one is more just, but because of the dynamic processes which the present system has set in motion.

Marx by no means ignored the role of psychology in the dynamics of social change. He insisted, however, that psychology was a reflection of 'material' (or, as we would say, systemic) conditions, not the reverse. In particular, philosophical outlooks (conceptions of reality) were for Marx rationalizations of class interests. This idea is all-too-easily vulgarized, as is Freud's idea that aspirations are sublimations of sexual urges. Nevertheless, the abuse of this idea in heated political polemics should not detract from its power. It can hardly be a coincidence that, during the era of slavery in the United States, southern preachers quoted scriptures to show that slavery was in accordance with the will of God, and northern preachers quoted scriptures to show the opposite. There is food for thought in the circumstance that individual freedom came to be extolled as the foundation of social justice at the time when entrepreneurs needed a fluid labor market.

Marx pays great attention to ideology, which is the 'psychology' of a social system. An ideology cannot be imposed by fiat, although some regimes attempt to do so. An ideology, according to Marx, is a natural by-product of the rationalization of a social system. It may also be a by-product of a struggle during which a new system is coming into being. At any rate, ideology is a *mass* phenomenon in which the innumerable variations of individual outlooks are submerged. It binds its adherents into 'behaving units' as surely as physical forces bind a solid body.

It is, however, one thing to recognize the important unifying role of an ideology and quite another to ascribe an ideology to a social group on the strength of the definition of that group, as, for example, 'the ideology of the proletariat', 'the ideology of the bourgeoisie'. The actual existence of these ideologies and the contention that they are even roughly coextensive with the groups 'as related to each other in the productive process' remain to be factually demonstrated, no matter how convincingly theoretical analysis leads to these conclusions. For theoretical analysis is only a particular concatenation of words. In certain areas of cognition, say, mathematical physics, the 'driving force' of the concatenations (mathematical logic) corresponds so closely to the 'driving force' of the events (physical causality) that a strong faith in the conclusions of the theory is justified. But close correspondence between the structure of theory and the structure of reality in the physical sciences is an exception rather than the rule. To ascribe tacitly a similar correspondence to a theory only one step removed from Hegel's free-wheeling fantasies is to misunderstand the requirements of a scientific theory.

Failure to come to grips with concrete realities, or, perhaps, the need to perceive reality as a projection of one's own drives, has led to the grotesque degradation of Marxist thought in Russia and to its gruesome social consequences. The irony of it is that the process falls neatly into the Marxist scheme which reveals ideology as a rationalization of interests, if only the proper generalization of the notion of 'interest' is accepted.

Comparing Richardson's and Kahn's models, we see both a similarity and a polarized difference. Both see conflict in a single dimension – that of magnitude. The *sources* of conflict interest neither Richardson nor Kahn. Their systems simply collide like Hobbes's 'men in the state of nature'. Of course, the moods of the two approaches are poles apart. Richardson is a pacifist. Conflict for him, especially lethal conflict, is simply a calamity. The wages of war is death. Why do people kill each other? Because they are caught up in forces governing the behavior of systems in collision, or because moods of hostility are contagious and spread like epidemics. The equations, according to Richardson, 'describe what happens when people do not stop to think.'

Kahn's scenarios describe what is likely to happen when people with a certain mentality *do* stop to think. Like Richardson, he does not inquire into the sources of the conflict. The conflict is given. It is inherent in the nature of colliding systems. Unlike Richardson, however, Kahn is attracted by the intellectual challenge of the global game of Chicken. In this game, he declares, it is not merely a matter of choosing to stay on the collision course or to swerve.

Chicken [he writes] would be a better analogy if it were played with two cars starting an unknown distance apart, traveling toward each other at unknown speeds, and on roads with several forks . . . Both drivers should be giving and receiving threats and promises, and tearful mothers and stern fathers should be lining the sides of the roads, urging, respectively, caution and manliness.[3]

Kahn disdains to assume the role of either a tearful mother or a stern father. He is urging the drivers to learn to play the game skillfully, to use caution when caution is called for and 'manliness' (if that is the name for it) where it pays off. In the description of the duel fought with blow torches in a warehouse filled with dynamite, he calls attention to the complex conditions and how they may be related to the advantages that may accrue to one or the other duelist. The question, what business the two madmen have fighting their crazy duel in that warehouse (more appropriately, the basement of an apartment building), remains unasked.

In short, the kind of thinking Kahn calls for is not at all the kind Richardson had in mind. Richardson assumed that thinking men would escape the determinism of massive, blind systems. Kahn imagines that the systems can be controlled and that the bold and the skillful will reap the rewards. The rewards are numerical: greater number of survivors, greater devastation wreaked on the enemy, greater economic potential in the 'aftermath' when the job of rebuilding and preparing for the next game will continue to tax the ingenuity of farsighted planners.

In summary, systemic theories of conflict cover an immense range of conceptions and attitudes, from the mystical idealism of Hegel to the austere materialism of Marx, and from the pacifism of Richardson to the sadistic enthusiasm of Kahn. All of them, however, point to the same conclusion: the 'psychology' of the system may be entirely independent of the psychology of its human components. If this conclusion is correct, we need not search the human psyche for attributes that explain the murderous tendencies of certain forms of human organization.

CHAPTER 16

A Taxonomy of Conflicts

Human conflicts can be classified in several ways: according to the nature of the participants; according to the issues, if any; according to the means employed, etc. Participants may be individuals, small groups (families, companies, gangs), large groups (ethnic, racial, political), nations, or blocs (NATO, SEATO, Warsaw Pact). The issues may be rights or privileges, control over resources, political power, or, in extreme cases, the very existence of the participants as systems. The means may range from persuasive arguments to physical annihilation.

A systematic taxonomy of this sort could be represented by a three-dimensional table (participants versus issues versus means) where the cells would be filled with examples of each type – for example, a war between two states fought for, say, control of territory, with armies as means. Such an exercise would be of doubtful theoretical value and might actually be misleading by giving the impression that conflicts can be neatly pigeonholed into readily recognizable categories. In most cases, the issues of conflicts are mixed and vague, and the means are not independent of the issues and the participants. The participants may seem to be recognizable, but only because certain conventional labels have been affixed to them. For instance, there is said to be racial conflict in the United States. Yet, it is certainly not true that every person labeled 'white' is in conflict with every person labeled 'black'. 'Racial conflict' is a label given to one vaguely defined class of events which give the impression that two racial groups are aligned against each other.

The matter is no clearer with regard to issues. In a political campaign and in an inter-nation war, the 'issues' are usually announced and widely publicized. In many cases, however, the stated issues cannot be taken seriously, because they are too often used for the purpose of rallying support rather than to define goals to be achieved. Typically, the words used to describe the issues have no clear referents.

Nor do the three aspects of conflict mentioned exhaust the list. One can well examine conflicts in their historical role and with regard to their genesis and their impact on the course of history. Marx, as we have seen, viewed class conflict in this way; to him, instances of it appeared as manifestations of the same on-going historical process, even though the participants and the issues kept changing in different historical settings.

In offering a classification of conflicts here, the categories used will relate to the sort of *systems* involved. The nature of the systems in conflict, I believe, determines the interactions between them, and, hence, the nature of the conflict and its psychological, sociological, and historical import. In what follows, then, the theoretical approach to conflict will lean frankly toward the systemic view.

The classification will be guided also by relating a type of conflict to the way it is resolved. 'Conflict resolution' is an unfortunate term because it connotes reconciliation. There ought to be a more general term designating the cessation of conflict, whether by conciliation, disengagement, or destruction of one, or both, or all of the participants, and it is in this general sense that I mean the phrase 'the way it is resolved'. Therefore, when 'conflict resolution' is mentioned, it will be specified whether 'resolution' is meant in the wide sense of cessation, or in the narrower sense of reconciliation.

First, the distinction will be made beween exogenous and endogenous conflicts. *Endogenous* conflicts are to be understood as those wherein the conflicting systems are parts of a larger system that has its own mechanisms for maintaining a steady state, which may include mechanisms for controlling or resolving conflict between the sub-systems. Thus, when two citizens of a State engage in conflict, the State (the larger system) usually has at its disposal ways of preventing the conflict from exceeding certain bounds (such as resort to violence) and, in addition, institutions for resolving the conflict (courts etc.). On the other hand, when two States are in conflict, there may be no super-system to exercise control or resolve conflict. In that case, we speak of an *exogenous* conflict. (As will be seen, whether a conflict is the one or the other may not always be easy to decide. Even an inter-nation war may have some characteristics of an endogenous conflict. A civil war is an example of the ambiguity.)

A second distinction will be made between symmetric and asymmetric conflicts. In *symmetric* conflict, the participants are roughly similar systems and perceive themselves as such. Thus, two individuals in a fight, say, man and wife, or two comparable nations at war, are typical examples of symmetric conflict. In *asymmetric* conflict, the systems may be widely disparate or may perceive each other in different ways. A revolt or a revolution is an example of an asymmetric conflict. The system revolted against 'perceives' itself as defending order and legitimacy; the insurgents 'perceive' themselves as an instrument of social change or of bringing a new system into being. Asymmetric conflicts may be either endogenous or exogenous. Political opposition to a regime is an example of the former type; colonial conquest of 'backward' peoples is of the latter.

An additional distinction, closely related to that between symmetric and asymmetric conflicts, is that between issue-oriented and structure-oriented conflict. An *issue-oriented* conflict is resolved when the issue is settled; the resolution does not involve a change in the structures of either of the conflicting systems or in the super-systems of which they are components. A *structure-oriented* conflict is not resolved unless the structure of either system or of the super-system changes.[1] The European wars of the eighteenth century were typical examples of issue-oriented conflicts. They were also symmetric. However, an asymmetric conflict may also be issue-oriented: for example, a civil suit involving a citizen and a state, or a strike where the labor union and the management are widely disparate systems. A revolution is always a structure-oriented conflict. If it is successful, a structural change occurs in the society affected; if it is crushed (in which case, it is usually called a rebellion), the revolutionary organization (a system) is usually destroyed.

Finally, we shall examine competition. The actors are typically several small systems, each in conflict with every other. Economic competition and struggles for power among individuals in organizations are typical examples. These conflicts are also symmetric but are distinguished by many participants, each pursuing his own 'interests'.

This taxonomy, like most, is no more than a formalization of idealized conceptions. In nature, there are no pure types separated by sharp boundaries, except possibly chemical elements (and even these are found upon closer examination to be mixtures of isotopic variants). The purpose of any taxonomy is to bring some order into our thinking. On occasions we see an instance of a conflict that can be distinctly categorized. In Chapter 17, specific examples are discussed. Here, for illustration, the Third Punic War can be cited as an instance of a clearly exogenous conflict, since there was no agency that could control, regulate, or resolve (in the narrow sense) the conflict between Rome and Carthage. The 'resolution' of this conflict in our extended sense of the word was the complete destruction of Carthage. On the other hand, the wars between the European states in the eighteenth century, though appearing to be exogenous, were not so entirely. Although the states were formally sovereign, not subject to external regulating power, there were internal constraints on the goals pursued and, consequently, on the means employed. The 'community of states' was a system of sorts, perpetuated in the interests of the rulers. But the preservation of the system was effected through the principle of 'balance of power', which precluded complete victory in the sense of the annihilation of any of the member states.

A case in point is the outcome of the Seven Years' War (1756–63), in which a coalition (France, Austria, and Russia) operated against Prussia under Frederick II (aggrandized in preceding, so-called Silesian wars). In 1762, Frederick was virtually defeated. He seems to have been saved from complete humiliation by a historical accident – the death of his most implacable enemy, Empress Elizabeth of Russia, and by the accession of his admirer, Peter III, who hastened to make a separate peace. Yet, when Peter himself was deposed a few months later by his wife and enemy, Catherine, Russia did not re-enter that war. It was as if something, like an 'invisible hand', which economists feel preserves competition, had intervened to restore the balance by preventing the elimination of a powerful member from the continental system.

The final partition of Poland (1793) might be cited as a counter-example – a member of the system being eliminated by concerted action of three powers (Prussia, Austria, and Russia). Nevertheless, even this instance can be explained as an attempt to preserve the system, since the rulers had a vested interest not only in a balance of power but also in the continuation of the predominant political system, essentially absolute monarchy. Poland, under elected instead of dynastic kings, was not an absolute monarchy, and toward the end of the eighteenth century was moving toward a constitutional government. These developments, coinciding with the French Revolution, were perceived by European monarchs as a threat to the existing system, and were possibly a decisive factor in the elimination of Poland as a member of the 'community of states'.

Had there been a way of establishing a dynastic monarchy in Poland, it is conceivable that a partition might have been avoided. Evidence for this conjecture may be seen in the restoration of the French monarchy after Waterloo. In fact, the arrangements resulting from the Congress of Vienna attest that the rulers of Europe were aware that the international system emerging at the close of the Thirty Years' War signified a 'community' with a common interest in the preservation of existing political structures. Further evidence for this conjecture can be seen in the formation of the Holy Alliance dedicated to the suppression of revolutions inspired by democratic ideas. The revolution in Hungary was actually suppressed in 1849 by the joint action of Austria and Russia. A later example of joint counter-revolutionary action was the intervention against the Russian Revolution (1918–20). Not only the Allies (France, England, U.S., Roumania, etc.) sent troops to help the White Guard against the Bolsheviks. Troops of the erstwhile enemy, Germany, were used to suppress revolutionary forces in the Baltic states and in Finland.

The most recent example of some joint action was the re-establishment of Germany, an erstwhile enemy, by the Western allies as a European military power, presumably as a bulwark against Russian expansion. To the extent that a strong Federal Republic of Germany was conceived also as a bulwark against Communist revolutions in Western Europe, alliance with it can be viewed as an example of joint counter-revolutionary action.

Similar ambiguity may blur the distinction between symmetric and asymmetric; and between issue-oriented and structure-oriented conflicts. The French Revolution was at first the culmination of a struggle against the established order (absolute monarchy). The intervention of monarchical powers stimulated the formation of a revolutionary citizens' army, which under Napoleon became an instrument of the French State. Thereupon the war became symmetric. It was, however, still structure-oriented, since Napoleon's goal was the transformation of the political structure of Europe.

In the early decades of the labor movement in industrialized countries, the conflict between workers and employers was not symmetric, since the coercive power of the State was largely at the disposal of only the employers. The conflict was in part structure-oriented, even when it was short of revolutionary (for example, the Chartists sought to introduce far-reaching changes into the social and political structure of England). When labor unions became legalized and powerful, conflicts became accordingly more symmetric and eventually entirely issue-oriented.

For some years after the Russian Revolution, Soviet leaders perceived themselves to be in a structure-oriented conflict with the capitalist world. Eventually, however, their attention turned to Russia's 'national interests', and Soviet conduct of foreign policy came to resemble that of other states of comparable power. Whether the so-called Cold War is issue-oriented or structure-oriented depends on how one conceives it. There are those who maintain that the conflict is between two incompatible ways of 'organizing the world' and that, therefore, one or the other system must emerge 'victorious', while the other disintegrates. There are others who maintain that the struggle is like any other struggle between two rival states, and that, given the destructiveness of modern weapons, the most prudent course would be to specify the issues of the conflict and try to settle them by peaceful means. The situation, however, is complicated by the fact that the governments of both countries must keep the structural aspect of the conflict alive, at least on the ideological level, for reasons to be discussed later.

Competition usually takes the form of legitimized conflict, regulated by rules. The actions of the participants may or may not be directed 'against' each other in the sense of attempting to prevent others from achieving their aims. In a pure *contest*, such actions are prohibited by the rules or are precluded by the nature of the situation. For instance, in a foot race, each contestant simply runs as fast as he can. He is not permitted to trip the other runners. In competitive games, certain actions designed to frustrate the opponents are permitted. In business competition, the situation is ambivalent. Business 'ethics' usually requires competition to be conducted as a pure contest, and the philosophy of free enterprise pictures it as such. In practice, however, business competition is frequently conducted as a game of strategy, where actions are undertaken not merely with a view of facilitating one's own efforts but also of inhibiting those of others.

From one point of view, the 'classical' European wars of the eighteenth century could also be subsumed under 'competition'. To be sure, each war was fought over an 'issue', but in retrospect, the separate issues lose their significance. The states were simply competing for power and prestige. Competition requires no issues. Moreover, competition is not usually resolved by a 'settlement'. Each individual war among the eighteenth-century states was 'settled', but the perpetual state of war among them (now dormant, now active) was not.

It might be mentioned in passing that the so-called struggle for existence in the biological universe is most properly subsumed under 'competition'. Still, even here there are ambiguities. Is the acquisition of a protective coloration by a species preyed upon an 'action' aimed at frustrating the efforts of the predators? Again, stress is on the inappropriateness of drawing analogies between events in the non-human universe that resemble conflict, and human conflict. The fundamental feature of human conflict is the awareness of it by the participants. Except in instances of direct encounters in combat, such awareness cannot be attributed to non-humans.

In addition to the taxonomy outlined above, I shall now offer another, based on the classification of conflicts as fights, games, and debates. The distinction here is among the various ways of perceiving the opponent.

In a fight, the opponent is perceived most clearly as an 'enemy', as one who threatens one's own autonomy simply by being present or existing. The 'normal' reaction to such a threat is an attempt to remove the perceived enemy from one's environment, by destroying him, cautioning him, or putting him to flight. (One's own flight from the presence of an enemy is, of course, an avoidance of a fight.) Attention is focused on the enemy, and actions are guided by strong emotional impulses which frequently block rational analysis. Animals as well as humans engage in fights and, of course, do not engage in rational analysis. Their actions are for the most part reactions to stimuli provided by 'the enemy' and are seldom, if ever, modified by learning; the actions persist as long as the stimuli emanating from the enemy persist. If these disappear, as for example, when the enemy flees, the fight ceases. In men, memory and learning impinge on practically all behavior patterns, so that the psychological correlates of a fight may by no means disappear when the enemy is no longer physically present. So as long as the conflict is dominated primarily by the enemy as a noxious stimulus, either present or remembered, we can speak of fights, even in human situations.

A game is characterized by an analysis of a *situation* and of *other situations* foreseen as outcomes of *decisions*, both one's own and those of an opponent. The distinction between an enemy and an opponent is crucial. Whereas the enemy is defined by associated emotions and attitudes (for example, as someone who is hated or feared), the opponent in a game is not. The attitude toward the *person* of the opponent may be neutral or even entirely friendly. The focus of attention is not on the presence of noxious stimuli in the person of the opponent but on the *situation*, which the opponent partially controls. It is desired to bring about another situation, but the outcomes of one's actions are determined only partially by one's own decisions. The decisions of the opponent also influence the outcomes. Consequently, rational analysis is an indispensable feature of game behavior. The elimination of the opponent is not a central issue; the opponent is constrained by the rules of the game just as oneself is. A more desirable situation can be brought about by adopting a *strategy*, that is, a plan of action contingent on what the opponent can do in following his own interest.

The type of conflict just described is, of course, typical of so-called games of strategy – chess, bridge, etc. The opponent in such a game is not typically a personal enemy who must be eliminated or constrained in order to safeguard one's autonomy. In fact, the opponent is more often a personal friend. The opponent *cooperates* in keeping the game going, and the process of playing the game is typically a pleasant experience. The pleasure of the experience derives from the struggle itself. Since victory in this case is meaningful only if the rules of the game are adhered to, the player's resources are mobilized toward rational analysis. The task is to bring about a desirable situation (to 'win') *within* the constraints imposed by the rules of the game, among which is the fact that the opponent is trying to frustrate one's efforts. The opponent is therefore a *necessary* feature of the environment and of the satisfaction derived from it.

A *debate* is a conflict of ideas. In *Fights, Games, and Debates*[2] I defined the objective of this type of conflict as *converting* the opponent to one's own way of perceiving or evaluating the environment; that is, of turning the opponent into a confederate. Debates are essentially exchanges of verbal stimuli. It is, of course, true that most exchanges (conventionally called debates) are not directed toward converting the opponent. For example, two attorneys confronting each other in a courtroom are not trying to convince *each other* of the justice of their respective cases. They are trying to convince someone else, in particular the judge or the jury. Similarly, debates in legislative bodies are not usually undertaken with the view of convincing political opponents. Typically they serve the purpose of demonstrating to the debaters' supporting constituencies that their representatives are espousing their causes. Debates directed by opponents at each other rather than at a third party are rare. Nevertheless, it will serve some purpose here to single out the debate as a conflict where the object is to convince rather than to eliminate the opponent (as in a fight) or to outwit him (as in a game).

In short, the fight is dominated by affective components of conflict, the game, by rational ones, and the debate, by ideological ones.

It is tempting to draw a parallel between these components and the Freudian components of the psyche – the Id, the Ego, and the Superego. The Id, represented as the pleasure-principle determinant of action, stands for the here and now, a force that guides action along the gradient of increasing pleasure or of decreasing pain, without regard for consequences. The Ego, representing rationality, guides the action along lines perceived as leading to more desirable situations, that is, in the problem-solving mode. The Superego, representing the imperatives imposed by the culture – that is, by the symbolic environment – is the manifestation of ideological commitments. Both the Id and the Superego offer resistance to rational analysis, the former, by pressure of immediate desires, the latter, by guilt associated with challenging the imposed imperatives.

It should be clear that, as in the preceding taxonomy, the three types of conflict singled out are idealizations. Only among animals are conflicts (if manifested in combats) all purely fight-like. A game of strategy or an ideological conflict are both entirely outside the scope of the psychic repertoire of non-humans. In human beings, on the other hand, conflicts are typically mixtures of these three, war being an outstanding example. In war, the enemy is typically very much a real enemy to be destroyed or constrained. There is, nevertheless, a strategic aspect of war, presenting problems that invite rational analysis and a strategic mode of action. Many wars (although not all) have also been pervaded by ideological issues. It is only for the purpose of analysis that I have separated the affective, the rational, and the ideological components of human conflict.

CHAPTER 17

Some Aspects of Endogenous Conflicts

The distinction between endogenous and exogenous conflicts, as they were defined in the preceding chapter, revolves around the presence or absence of a common authority over the conflicting parties. The distinction is an important one. In a statistical analysis of the correlates of 'deadly quarrels' made by Lewis F. Richardson (cf. Chapter 14), about the only positive finding was the apparent role of 'common government' in damping the severity of conflicts. According to our classification of conflicts into exogenous and endogenous, this effect would appear even more pronounced, since large civil wars, such as the American Civil War of 1861–6, would fall into the exogenous category, because the Confederacy had a de facto separate government, whether it was recognized as such or not.

Although the attenuation of endogenous conflicts can be partly ascribed to the restraining influence of a 'common authority', it is likely that a more direct explanation bears on the aggravating effect of different *absolute* authorities in *exogenous* conflicts, typically wars between states. For, regardless of whether a government is autocratic or democratic, it is always absolute in military operations by the very nature of these operations. Consequently, through the channels of military command, a government has absolute control over the soldier and disengages him from personal responsibility and from whatever inhibition against killing one's own kind there may be in the human psyche.[1] In war, 'the enemy' is defined with absolute clarity, and killing enemies *need* not be a manifestation of personal feelings of enmity. Obedience, not hatred, is the principal lever by which the abstract power of government is transmitted to the human agents of violence under its control.

In endogenous conflicts, 'the enemy' is defined with varying degrees of clarity, depending on specific issues and situations. Moreover, by our definition of endogenous conflict, the authority of the organizing bodies of endogenous conflict (if any) is not usually absolute. Therefore, endogenous conflict depends more on affect than does exogenous conflict. Since the participant in social strife is not normally required to behave like the soldier who must obey an absolute, legitimate authority, he must have personal reasons for seeing the distinction between friends and enemies.

The most severe endogenous conflicts are instances of lethal communal strife, as between Moslems and Hindus in India, and massacres either carried out by government agencies (as in Nazi Germany or in Stalin's Russia) or instigated by them. Systematic extermination of helpless populations by government agencies can, of course, reach monstrous proportions. In the instances mentioned, the numbers of victims were in millions. The exterminations of Communists by Chiang Kai-shek in 1927–8 and by the government of Indonesia in 1965 were of comparable magnitude.

Massacres carried out by government agencies (armies, punitive detachments, special extermination squads, etc.) do not necessarily depend on rampant hatred or sadistic lust on the part of the killers. In this respect they are akin to war. An agent of the government follows orders in these instances, just as a soldier does in war. Thus it was not necessary for all Germans involved in Hitler's extermination machine to be spurred by an intense hatred of the Jews, especially since only comparatively few were involved in the actual killings. Similarly, in Stalin's purges, though the extermination of political non-conformists and their families and of the 'kulaks' involved thousands of arresting officers, organizers of mass transport, guards in the concentration camps, etc., they were only 'doing their duty' as in war. To be sure, they were told that the victims were 'class enemies' but, as a rule, nothing about the nature of their 'crimes'. Thus, 'class enemy', like 'the enemy' in war, was a label that marked some people for destruction. Men need not hate to destroy their own kind.

Hatred is of essence, however, in communal strife and in massacres carried out by the populations themselves (not in the official capacity of hangmen, firing squads, punitive detachments, etc.). Such hatred is engendered by an internalization of the distinction between 'us' and 'them' in its most extreme form.

A famous example of a massacre instigated by a government and carried out by civilians was that of the Protestants, authorized by King Charles IX of France on 23 August 1572. The killings began at dawn on Sunday, 24 August (St Bartholomew's Day), and continued in Paris until 17 September and in the provinces until 3 October. The number of victims has been estimated at 50,000. The people who broke into Huguenot homes and killed whole families were not under orders to kill. They were given *license* to kill, to vent their rage on *someone*. The 'someone' in such cases is whoever happens to be differentiated as alien in whatever way the semantic environment singles out as significant.

When endogenous conflicts are classified as 'racial', 'religious', 'class', etc., the partition of a society into hostile groups is already implicit in the categorization, even if the classification purports to be a purely descriptive one by an impartial observer, say, a sociologist. For the use of these categories, especially in the age of literacy and pervasive mass media, is not confined to 'impartial observers'. It contributes to the structuring of the semantic environment. People identify themselves as members of specific social groups because they are told that they are members, and because they readily believe what satisfies a basic need, in this case a need to belong. 'Natural' divisions do not occur; divisions arise in people's consciousness as by-products of the semantic environment. This is not to say that 'objective' causes of social strife do not exist. They most certainly do, and it is an important task of social science to discover them. All too often, however, the line between 'objective' and 'subjective' is hard to draw. 'Objective' causes of social strife deserve the name to the extent that they are found in most societies and do not depend on the special features of particular semantic environments. Karl Marx thought he found such 'objective' causes in the class structure of all but the most primitive societies. Accordingly, the thrust of Marx's sociological theory was directed at uncovering the class roots of virtually every important form of social conflict. For instance, a Marxist tends to view 'racial' conflict in the United States as only an epi-phenomenon. Its roots, according to him, are in the circumstance that in the United States Blacks happened to have been traditionally members of an exploited *class*.

In some instances, such reduction of social strife to manifestations of class struggles seems specious. It would be stretching Marxist theory to the breaking point to interpret the 'generation gap' or the 'women's liberation movement' as instances of class struggle, although dogmatic adherence to the theory may stimulate such attempts. If a class basis of a social conflict is conspicuously absent, an orthodox Marxist may dismiss the conflict as sociologically unimportant.

Marxist theory puts allocation of resources at the basis of all major social conflicts, both endogenous and exogenous. The theory goes further in explaining the class stratification of society as a derivative of a particular mode of production and of the concomitant division of labor, which determines the system of resource allocation. There is ample evidence that allocation of resources is, in fact, an underlying issue of many, perhaps most, social conflicts. However, it is not the abstract 'issue' that guides the conflicts in their development but rather the identification of the participants with the contending social groups. The immediate criterion of identification may be several stages removed from the original issue.

The current strife in Northern Ireland is a case in point. Granted that a difference in economic and social status between Catholics and Protestants exists there, it is not nearly so sharp as differences in economic status between the highest and the lowest income strata in both populations. Nevertheless, the conflict that erupted into violence was along religious lines rather than along some economic boundary. The reason is clear: enmity between Catholics and Protestants has a long history and provides a nucleus for the crystalization of hostility. Identification of friends and enemies by a single criterion is easy, because an either-or categorization provides a boundary, while the virtual continuum of economic status does not.

The same is true of racial strife in the United States. It is sharpest in the lowest social strata, where the economic differences between Whites and Blacks are small, not large. It can be argued, of course, that here too allocation of resources is the underlying issue, competition for jobs, for instance, but this issue is not the allocation issue of Marxist theory, namely the division of surplus value between 'capital' and 'labor'.

It seems that at least two basic other sources of social conflict are discernible besides the allocation of resources, namely the struggle for power and the need for autonomy. The three may be closely interlaced or all may be derivative of a single basic issue. We leave this question aside and note only that a clear, simple identification of 'us' and 'them' is essential in every serious conflict involving aggregates, and, moreover, that such identification is *not* given a priori but must be inculcated by the semantic environment.

The struggle for power is a uniquely human component of conflict. Animals and even small children fight over the immediate and direct possession of something: a bone, a mate, a territory, a toy. In contrast, the struggle for power is not over the possession of a thing or a place but of a position or status, which confers on the possessor the power of *decision*. This definition of the struggle for power confines the meaning of the phrase to contexts determined by man-made environment, since only in those contexts can one speak of 'decisions'.

The so-called 'peck order' is established in a flock of hens by initial encounters among pairs, whereby one establishes her 'superior status' over the other. Barring infrequent reversals, the status so established is stable and requires no further 'struggle'. It manifests itself in specific, concrete situations, for instance, at the feed trough. Clearly, this sort of 'power' cannot be said to be the power to make decisions. As far as we know, hens do not make decisions binding on others.

Cows, too, have an order of precedence, for instance, in passing through a gate. Here the senior cow can, perhaps, be said to make a 'decision': she passes first; others follow. However, this primitive instance of 'leadership' is a far cry from the sort of leadership for which boys beyond a certain age fight. Such leadership involves genuine decision making – in the choice of games or other activities, for example. Here man-made environment is essential, for human activities, including children's games, are all set in a matrix of semantic (i.e., cultural, man-made) environment.

The power to make decisions is valued for its potential of enforcing decisions *without* the application of physical force. The tendency for means to become ends in human affairs applies to power in the same way as, say, to money. The usual disclaimer 'It isn't money I love; it is the things money can buy' often can be refuted by the fact that the rich accumulate fortunes far in excess of amounts that can be spent. In societies with monetary economies, money confers extensive power of decision, binding on others through contractual obligations. It is this power, specifically the awareness of having it, that makes money appear as an 'absolute good', of which it is impossible to have too much. The instrumental value of money is eclipsed by what appears to be an inherent value. The same applies to power itself. Appetite for power can be dissociated from the yearning for power to do specific things. In fact, just as the most valued use of money in the world of business is in making more money (this is the way credit, for instance, is conceived), the most valued use of power is in amassing more power, for instance, by recruiting allies. Factional strife within all organizations, regardless of whether the power won in such strifes confers any tangible benefits, provides ample evidence that power is an object of contention in its own right.

While conflicts over the allocation of resources and struggles for power are widely recognized as sources of endogenous conflicts, the third, in my opinion fundamental, source has only recently come into prominence and is not well understood – the need for autonomy. It is fundamental because autonomy involves the identification of self, and, by extension, of an extended 'self' of a group with which the self identifies. Further, this identification of 'us' has an obverse – the identification of 'them'. Once this distinction is clear, the basis for conflict is at hand. This is not to say that realization of autonomy *necessarily* either results from or leads to conflict, but only that efforts to realize autonomy are often faced with opposition, which starts a positive-feedback circle of escalation.

The strong empirical orientation of contemporary sociology, particularly in the United States, has given rise to a research method that now nurtures an entire profession, one might say an industry – public opinion surveys. As the data gathered in public opinion pools are tabulated, the respondents are identified by certain demographic or sociological categories, such as age, sex, geographic region, income, ethnic origin, religion, etc. The object is to see whether divisions of opinion on public issues are correlated with any of those categories. At times correlations are found which, while statistically significant (thus indicating *something* about the differential composition of the partisans of given social issues), are, at least in the United States, for the most part weak.

A weak correlation is usually, though not always, an indication that the conflict potential of an issue is not great. This is so because a weak correlation usually means that along other issues the alignment is different. When people who are opponents on one issue find themselves on the same side in another, they are not likely to be frozen in perpetual attitudes of enmity. It is when the divisions along several issues are strongly correlated that the interfaces of conflict become sharpened. They become sharpest when positions on issues practically coincide with some easily recognizable overt characteristics, be it race, ethnic origin, or whatever, because then friends and foes are immediately recognized. The overt characteristics 'take over', as it were, and become the determinants of the conflict.

Thus, while the crystalization of opposing camps may have been originally instigated by substantive issues where alignments just happened to coincide with some overt, distinctive characteristic, eventually the latter becomes the dominant divisive factor. It reveals not only to others but also to himself where a person 'belongs'. Since almost everyone wants 'to belong' somewhere, the distinguishing feature may mold his attitudes, bringing him in accord with those of the group with which he has been identified, and so in conflict with others.

Strong and real as the substantive issues may be, the need for identification with a group remains the strongest factor in instigating, perpetuating, and exacerbating social conflicts. So universal is the need for identification that cohesive groups are at times artificially created to provide it, such as fraternities, lodges, secret societies, etc. The existence of parallel organizations of this sort, recruited from the same or very similar social strata, speaks for the absence of 'issues' as the bases of cohesion. The only motivation for belonging is belonging. In India the castes originated from certain systematic divisions of labor. Eventually, however, the castes multiplied in the absence of any apparent social need, except the need for identification. It is said that on occasions some women in a village would start wearing their saris over the left shoulder and some over the right, thus creating a new caste division.

In its primitive form, the boundary between 'us' and 'them' is marked by instantly recognizable traits – racial features, kinship, membership or non-membership in historically established communities, etc. What is called 'integration' of populations into larger communities or 'societies' is the extension of membership characteristics to include more abstract traits, usually based on ideational components. This becomes possible only as the semantic environment increases in importance. The idea of 'nation' arose on the heels of increasing literacy and the consequent appearance of a new instrument of cohesion – the mass media in their first form, the press. Cohesion transcending national boundaries depends on ideology, that is, on coherent views concerning the nature of man, of society, of history, and of man's proper place in society, in history, and, lately, in nature. Recognition of 'us' and 'them' on ideological bases transcends overt characteristics, such as kinship, community member-ship, and nationality, and so serves the integration function. At the same time, however, because of the complementary nature of integration and differentiation, ideology introduces intra-societal conflicts. Ideological issues, however, are often obfuscated, because they arise not in a social vacuum but in a definite social matrix with identifiable groupings. Thus college and university students are a clearly identifiable group.

Because a dissident group, e.g., university students, is easily identified and because certain manifestations of the conflict engendered by it are disturbing or frightening (e.g., demonstrations sometimes erupting in violence), its ideology is the more categorically rejected and animosity toward the identified 'trouble makers' is rationalized by emphasizing the traditional values against which the dissenting ideology is presumably directed: 'law and order', 'national honor', the work ethos, etc.

The 'backlash' works both ways. The assertion of traditional values, frequently couched in homely clichés, provokes an attack on them, deliberate defiance of conventions, contemptuous dismissals of 'life styles', and so on. In this way, the rebellious young make themselves even *more* recognizable, and the conflict centers around the overt distinctions between 'us' and 'them' rather than on the often grave and vital social issues raised by a new ideological awareness. The policeman beating up a youngster is venting his wrath not on an opponent of the Vietnam War or on a protester against the hegemony of power but on the youngster's long hair, his beard, his abusive language directed against the policeman personally. Similarly, the ROTC headquarters, draft offices, computers, etc., being symbols of 'the Establishment', become objects of violence generated by impotent, heartbreaking rage against unresponsive, self-assured, self-righteous power.

The ideological component is clearly discernible in some intra-societal conflicts that seem to be conflicts about the allocation of resources. In American society a cleavage has appeared between conservationists and technocrats. Cities are shaken and city politics is animated by conflicts over location of new airports, over the construction of speedways, over new real-estate 'developments', urban renewal, etc. In the past, conflicts of this sort had clear economic underpinnings. Land values were often the principal issue. In fact, the foci of such conflicts were usually in business groups competing for development that would promote opportunities for business ventures or land speculation. Today's picture is different. Citizens band together in attempts to block what in their eyes is a degradation of the environment, the destruction of old-established neighborhood communities, the raping of landscapes, and the like.

One could argue that conflicts of this sort are still conflicts over allocation of resources, and so they are. But these struggles are not the usual ones over a division of the pie. Quality, not quantity, is the issue. The now publicized 'quality of life' is by its nature an ideological rather than an economic issue. The mobilization of effort against megatechnology stems not alone from awareness of noise and smog. Hostility to megatechnology stems also from the *potential* threat of technology, most conspicuous in its lethal military sector. Unlike smog and noise, this threat is not perceived directly by the senses but only through the semantic environment, in the rhetoric of international power politics, for instance. The guardians of 'the Button' are perceived as a threat to helpless humanity, and so are their rationalizations, their exercise of genocidal power against distant populations, their style in conducting and preparing for war as a great 'scientific' enterprise, replete with 'technological breakthroughs', or as a great business operation planned in accordance with the latest ideas of cost accounting. The source of the threat is the megalomania of power. Coupled with the publicized ecological threats, easily seen as consequences of that megalomania, the menace of entrenched power has generated fear and repugnance. Thus the technological artifacts themselves, perceived as symbols of entrenched power, become the visible, concrete objects of fear and repugnance. Countervailing ideas rise to consciousness: community instead of 'society' as the focus of identification; people rather than 'efficiency' as the proper object of concern; 'inner space' not outer space as the important area of exploration; harmony with nature, not conquest of nature as the worthy aspiration of man.

It is interesting in this connection to re-examine the storm over fluoridation that was a prominent political issue in the United States a decade or two ago. The 'rational' arguments of the opponents of fluoridation were exceedingly weak. All the warnings concerning the toxic effects of fluorides could be easily dismissed in view of the fact that fluorides are present in many natural sources of water supply, and that the object of fluoridation was simply to bring these levels up to naturally normal ones wherever they were too low to give proper protection to teeth. Anti-fluoridation campaigns often were based on demagogic appeals provoking unfounded fears. Frequently they were led by adherents of extreme right-wing groups, and their 'unscientific', obscurantist flavor was apparent. The conflict was seemingly between the 'enlightened' (pro-fluoridation) and the 'fanatical' (anti-fluoridation). Resistance against fluoridation resembled earlier outbreaks against mass vaccination and even of the bigoted opposition to the teaching of evolution. (The fact that occasionally a physician or a dentist was recruited into the anti-fluoridation camp means nothing. Individual members of any profession, or, for that matter, of any sector of society, can always be found to espouse or to oppose any cause, regardless of its merits or demerits.)

The real issue in the anti-fluoridation campaign was autonomy. To be sure, this issue was often stated explicitly and emphatically. But it was more often submerged in the demagogic antics of the anti-fluoridationists, and failed to make an impact, because the particular substantive issue of fluoridation was a poor battle ground in a struggle for autonomy. There are vastly more pervasive attacks on autonomy in American society than the control of water supply for hygienic purposes. It may well be that the issue had the appeal that it did among the people who supported it because it could in no way be interpreted as an attack on the vital supports of entrenched power, and so was politically 'safe'. The fact that adherents of the political right were found more frequently in the ranks of the anti-fluoridationists supports this conjecture. In fact, some of the more rabid manifestations of the campaign pictured fluoridation as a 'Communist plot' to poison Americans.

Another example of choosing a 'safe' issue on which to protest encroachments against autonomy comes to mind. At the time when the massive protests against the escalation of the Vietnam War were starting on American campuses (1965), a prominent professor in California found such an issue. On the war issue, the professor's identification was with the Administration, whether on the basis of conviction or of status considerations is not known. However, he started a campaign of his own, vigorously protesting the change from letters to numbers as codes for telephone exchanges. To his way of thinking, this change was an attack on autonomy by a giant corporation, concerned only with the efficiency of its operations and unresponsive to popular sentiment. (Letters used to be at least abbreviations of names of telephone exchanges, which, in turn were usually names of neighborhoods, hence meaningfully individual. Numbers are cold, impersonal, de-humanizing.)

The need for autonomy is all-pervasive in social strife. It manifests itself in what may appear as puerile petulance or in martyrdom. It raises the most intractable dilemmas of man's existence as a social being; for the need for autonomy seems to be incompatible with the need for social integration. Historically, integration of large social units (e.g., states) came about not in consequence of a 'social contract', concluded by 'naturally free' individuals, but in consequence of extensions of power of ruling groups. Consequently, clashes among constituent groups in larger social aggregates are seen not only as challenges to entrenched power but as disruptive forces threatening the continued existence of a supposedly integrated society. The American Civil War was fought 'to preserve the Union'. In our time, the genocidal civil war in Nigeria and the massacre of Bengalis instigated by the central government of Pakistan were rationalized on similar grounds. The excessive (at times pathological) concerns with 'monolithic unity' of the Party among the Soviet elite unleashed the bloody purges of the 1930s and remain the principal stumbling block to the democratization of at least the Soviet elite itself.

In general, entrenched power sees autonomous groups within the realm under its control as 'foreign bodies' to be eradicated if possible. When eradication is impossible, these 'foreign bodies' can be used to deflect actual (instead of imagined) challenges to the entrenched power of ruling groups. The tsarist government of Russia used the Jews in this way. Pogroms were usually instigated by the government when revolutionary moods approached the boiling point. The early Christians in the Roman Empire also served as convenient scapegoats.

In the 1950s, a relatively quiescent period in U.S. politics, it appeared to some American sociologists that the dialectic opposition between autonomy and social integration had been resolved in the United States.[2] The autonomy of the individual being the foundation of American political philosophy, it seemed that the autonomy of larger groups was guaranteed by the freedom of voluntary association. Since the existence of voluntary associations was not threatened and since the interests and the memberships of such groups were criss-crossed, it seemed as if all social strife in the United States was reduced to competition centered on strictly ad hoc issues, hence not rooted in overwhelming emotional and ideological commitments.

The American scene of the 1960s and 1970s has revealed the shallowness of this interpretation. The 'autonomy' guaranteed to the individual by the free market conception of society is not the issue in the intense social strife that has developed in the United States (and similar societies of the West). Even though the 'dignity of the individual' is a frequently occurring phrase in the rhetoric of dissenters, the crucial issue is autonomy of another sort, the autonomy of communities (not only geographical), the *intermediate* organic structures interposed between the power of the State (however camouflaged) and the individual – those very intermediate authorities the destruction of which Tocqueville foresaw in 'mass democratic' societies (cf. p. 92). The revolt is against the tyranny of the majority as well as against the tyranny of elites.

It seems, then, that the internal crisis of modern industrial 'liberal' mass societies and the severe endogenous conflicts engendered by it stem from a failure to provide bases of autonomy larger than the individual. In seeking to enlarge his awareness of self to larger groups, the individual becomes a participant in endogenous conflict, because, aside from 'interest groups' competing in a 'free market', no outlet for such meaningful identification is provided in a mass, homogenized society. In fact, autonomy is practically identified with competition. As C. Wright Mills put it,

In every area of life, liberals have imagined independent individuals freely competing so that merit might win and character develop: in the free contractual marriage, the Protestant church, the voluntary association, the democratic state, as well as on the economic market. Competition is the way liberalism would integrate its historic era; it is also the central feature of liberalism's style of life.[3]

The rejection of this concept of autonomy, characteristic of 'liberal' societies, is at the root of the most important endogenous conflicts within them. These conflicts are beginning to have repercussions far beyond the enclaves of 'prosperity and freedom' established by those societies.

CHAPTER 18

Internalization of Conflict

In nature, when conditions that keep a process going no longer persist, the process ceases. Such is the case when a system is disturbed from its steady state; changes go on in it as long as steady state conditions are not re-established. As soon as such conditions are restored, changes of state cease. One might compare conflict to the result of upsetting a steady state and suppose that conflict will go on until the upsetting condition no longer obtains. When animals fight, this is indeed the case. When one of the combatants is incapacitated or flees, the fight is over. In human conflicts, the situation is different. The 'enemy' in a fight is an enemy not only because one happens to be fighting him. He is identified as an enemy, regardless of time and place. Moreover, his 'identity' may be extended.

Consider the feud, a simple example of a conflict that continues because enmity has been defined by the symbolic environment of the participants. Let young Buck Grangerford explain it.

'Well,' says Buck, 'a feud is this way: A man has a quarrel with another man, and kills him; then the other man's brother kills *him*; then the other brothers, on both sides, goes for one another; then the *cousins* chip in – and by-and-by everybody's killed off, and there ain't no more feud. But it's kind of slow, and takes a long time.'

'Has this one been going on long, Buck?'

'Well, I should *reckon*! It started thirty year ago, or som'ers along there. There was trouble 'bout something, and then a lawsuit to settle it; and the suit went agin one of the men, and so he up and shot the man that won the suit – which he would naturally do, of course. Anybody would.'

'What was the trouble about, Buck? – land?'

'I reckon maybe – I don't know.'

'Well, who done the shooting? – was it a Grangerford or a Shepherdson?'

'Laws, how do *I* know? It was so long ago.'

'Don't anybody know?'

'Oh, yes, pa knows, I reckon, and some of the other old people; but they don't know, now, what the row was about in the first place.'[1]

In other words, a feud is a conflict that maintains itself by a perpetuated perception of Self and Other in terms of membership in a kinship system. The most important aspect of this conflict is that recognition of membership in the alien group is *sufficient* basis for aggression. We might be tempted to draw a parallel with the on-going 'feud' between dogs and cats and such, but analogies of this sort are superficial. The crucial characteristic of human feuds and their generalizations is that they are *culturally* transmitted, so that the distinguishing characteristics of the 'enemy' may be anything: family membership, social class, nationality, religion, political affiliation, or ideology. The origins of any particular conflict are typically unknown to the participants. The conflict is a self-perpetuating process.

The feud described above is not only internalized, so that the Grangerfords and the Shepherdsons are in perpetual conflict. The feud *as an institution* becomes incorporated into the normal environment of the people living in that culture. (Institutionalization is to a social group what internalization is to the individual.) Buck is wrong when he says that when everyone is killed off 'there ain't no more feud.' There will be another murder over a lost lawsuit because, as Buck says, anybody would know that to kill the winner is the 'natural' (i.e., institutionalized) thing to do. Thus, not only are killings in a specific feud self-perpetuating; so are feuds themselves. They occur because others have occurred before them.

Attitudes toward conflict are internalized by each individual as a consequence of his experience. They are also internalized (institutionalized) by larger systems – groups, tribes, societies, and nations. In the process of formation, positive feedback predominates. In the experience of a tribe, for instance, conflict with other tribes may have played a major role. Initial victories may have reinforced aggressive tendencies, not only by strengthening the disposition to engage in further conflicts but also by differentiating a warrior caste and according a high status to it. Thereby the aspirations of young men are directed toward achieving membership in the warrior caste, which further enhances its status. Status is maintained by exploits. Exploits improve military skill. A war tradition is established and is maintained by ceremony, epos, etc. Initially, aggressiveness may have been of survival value to the tribe, as in competition for hunting grounds or arable land. Eventually this contribution to the survival potential may have vanished but the traditions related to aggressiveness and violence may have become internalized to the extent that they can no longer be modified or dislodged. They have become part of the tribe's self-image. Encroachments against the associated values are then perceived as threats to autonomy, and are resisted.

A classical example of an internalized war culture is that of Sparta. The Hellenic tribe that settled in the Peloponnesian peninsula subjugated the local population and reduced them to slavery. Thereupon, the overriding goal of the ruling class became that of keeping the Helots in the state of slavery. In order to insure complete dominance over the numerically superior Helots, the Spartans became a completely militarized society with its concomitants – complete subordination of the individual to rigid conformity, 'Spartan' regimen extolling what were perceived as the 'masculine' virtues: physical fitness, bravery, loyalty to the tribal code, contempt for sentiment and esthetic values, etc. To us, the Spartans may appear to have been culturally impoverished, but to the Spartans, trained exclusively for war, other values were meaningless and worthless.

Few societies have been so exclusively militarized as the Spartan (some American Plains Indians may be other examples). In most, war is a specialty of a profession, outside of which other than military virtues are nurtured. However, no system of values is so stable as that related to conflict, and no institutions resemble each other so closely (regardless of their cultural setting) as military institutions. For the goals of organized conflict all converge on one: to destroy an enemy and to avoid being destroyed by him. This common adjustment to environment makes all soldiers brothers. Like scientists, soldiers all belong to the same culture.

Techniques of fighting require learning efforts, but of the sort that makes immediate sense (not like the efforts required to comprehend the abstractions of philosophy or theology). Techniques of fighting are techniques of survival, and their lessons are not lost on the survivors. Hence, a 'natural selection' of sorts operates on fighters. Above all, the military life is a life of cooperation, at times of genuine brotherhood, for soldiers are dependent on each other for their lives. The military organization thus offers the most direct and compelling channel for merging one's Self with a larger and immensely more powerful Self. All these aspects of organized conflict have been conducive to the internalization and the institutionalization of war in almost all societies.

There is the additional supportive aspect that conflict directed outward promotes cohesion and cooperation inward, within the system. Thus, the propensity for waging war may be a system's response to the necessity of safeguarding itself from internal disintegration, quite irrespective of the benefits or supposed benefits to be derived from aggressive or defensive external conflict.

This thesis is developed facetiously in the anonymous satire *Report from Iron Mountain*, but deserves to be taken at face value.

First of all [it is argued in the *Report*] the existence of a society as a political 'nation' requires as part of its definition an attitude of relationship toward other 'nations.' This is what we usually call a foreign policy. But a nation's foreign policy can have no substance if it lacks the means of enforcing its attitude toward other nations. It can do this in a credible manner only if it implies the threat of maximum political organization for this purpose – which is to say that it is organized to some degree of war. War, then, as we have defined it to include all national activities that recognize the possibility of armed conflict, is itself the defining element of any nation's existence vis-a-vis any other nation. Since it is historically axiomatic that the existence of any form of weaponry insures its use, we have used the word 'peace' as virtually synonymous with disarmament. By the same token, 'War' is virtually synonymous with nationhood. The elimination of war implies the inevitable elimination of national sovereignty and of the traditional nation-state.[2]

No less important is the role of war for commanding allegiance.

In general, the war system provides the basic motivation for primary social organization. In doing so, it reflects on the societal level the incentives of individual human behavior. The most important of these, for social purposes, is the individual psychological rationale for allegiance to a society and its values. Allegiance requires a cause; a cause requires an enemy. This much is obvious; the critical point is that the enemy that defines the cause must seem genuinely formidable. Roughly speaking, the presumed power of the 'enemy' sufficient to warrant an individual sense of allegiance to a society must be proportionate to the size and complexity of the society. Today, of course, that power must be one of unprecedented magnitude and frightfulness.[3]

In short, exogenous conflicts, by dramatizing the boundary between Us and Them, that is, by calling attention to what is outside of the system, also call attention to what is inside. The immediate results are attenuations of endogenous conflicts. Personal and group enmities are at least temporarily held in abeyance. Hatred of the enemy has an equally attractive obverse – love for one's own.

When the United States entered World War II, there was a tremendous upsurge of public morale. The last vestiges of apathy and despair generated by the Great Depression vanished. Suddenly everyone felt needed. The abundance of jobs had an exhilarating effect, not only because of the resultant spending money in the pockets of people who had never had any, but also because of the widespread conviction that wars are won by overwhelming superiority of material, and no one doubted the ability of American industry to produce it. Battles were still in the future and, at any rate, would be fought far away. In the meantime, the wheels of production were humming and every rivet was a nail in Hitler's and Tojo's coffins. Block organizations for allocating specific civil defense duties gave also young and old a sense of participation.

All these positive experiences unclouded by trauma (the war never did come to America) helped to prepare the United States public for the militarization of their society in the Cold War to follow. Not until the frustrations of the Vietnam War did resistance to militarization become conspicuous. It might be pointed out that this opposite trend gained momentum precisely because the Vietnam War did *not* contribute to internal solidarity (as did World War II) but, on the contrary, generated the most intense internal schism since the Civil War. Reasons for this opposite effect will be discussed in Chapter 20.

The efficacy of sharply defined sides in a conflict for enhancing the awareness of Self, transcending the individual, is probably responsible for the degeneration of the civil rights movement in the United States into a racist struggle. Originally the civil rights movement was an offensive undertaken jointly by whites and blacks against both the open and the covert restraints and indignities that kept the Negroes in inferior social and economic positions. Direct actions (sit-ins, marches, freedom rides) in the face of repressive measures, including murder, on the part of white supremacists and the police, created a basis for solidarity in the movement. Nevertheless, the movement fell apart.

In contrast to exogenous conflicts, where the boundary between Self and Other is clear and rigid, endogenous conflicts often fail to fix such lines. The revolutionary-minded civil rights fighters were not by any means the only ones who espoused the black cause. Many liberals, true to conventional American values, were equally staunch supporters of 'full equality for the Negroes'. It became impossible, however, to form the broadest possible coalition on that issue, for there were other issues linked to it, both positively and negatively. Shortly after the civil rights movement acquired full momentum, mass opposition to the Vietnam War developed, particularly among the young. At first, as often happens, the two causes were at cross purposes and competed for the energies and commitments of at least the white dissenters. Next, the emphasis shifted from assertions of Negro rights to assertions of Negro identity. Once identity became the issue, the conventional espousal of 'Negro equality' appeared to blacks in a different light, tinged with condescension. The white liberal now appeared to be saying to the black man: 'You have been inferior long enough. Repression and exploitation made you inferior. Come, we accept you. We shall help you fight repression and exploitation so that you will no longer be inferior to the white man, so that you can become our equal and participate fully in our superior civilization.'

In other words, the black man was promised equality as concomitant to his *loss* of identity as a black man, with the further insinuation that, of course, he wanted to lose the identity that kept him in bondage and in ghettos.

At that point, positive feedback set in. The search for identity stimulated *defensive* racial consciousness, which, in turn, made the white liberal wary, which, in turn, aggravated the distrust of whites by the blacks. Where the lines separating friend and foe become blurred, the natural tendency is to seek some conspicuous criterion of distinction and, having found it, to harden it into a permanent boundary. And there is nothing easier to harden (nor more difficult to break down) than an unambiguous boundary between Us and Them already established.

The tragedy of this transformation of a struggle for social justice into a futile ethnic one is that the search for cultural self-identity *is* a justifiable cause. Equality need not imply homogeneity, and the right to cultural distinction is no more unreasonable than the right to religious distinction. However, freedom of worship is not an issue in American society, *because* a form of worship is not a critical social distinction (as it once was). Style of life, on the other hand, is.

Does the internalization of endogenous conflict by individuals in a society facilitate or inhibit the institutionalization of exogenous conflict? Plainly speaking, do aggressive individuals add up to a warlike society? An argument for the affirmative answer might be supported as follows.

Judging by the military expenditures and by the extent of war-waging for the past twenty-five years, the United States appears as the most warlike nation in the world. This role may or may not be related to the excessive preoccupation of Americans with violence. The American nation was founded on the conquest of the frontier. In part, this conquest was accomplished by the destruction of native populations. Yet, it involved also a special ideological factor, the view that the nexus of human existence is the individual, and that the cardinal virtues of the individual are self-reliance and love of freedom: in short, the virtues of the pioneer. A man becomes a pioneer by escaping from authority, from community, from crowds. He sustains himself by marshalling all his energies (like Robinson Crusoe) to transform his physical environment. Energies generated by this outlook were mobilized in the service of invention, and the pioneer ideology was infused with the myth of technical omnipotence.

The technical omnipotence theme is most eloquently expressed in Mark Twain's American classic, *The Connecticut Yankee*. Consider the opening statement of the Yankee's story: 'I am an American. My father was a blacksmith. My uncle was a horse doctor. I can make anything.'

The Yankee is the first missionary of the 'American way of life'. He brings it to the natives of sixth-century England and *almost* succeeds in converting them, but not quite. In the end, the forces of tyranny and superstition defeat him.

The theme of escape is most clearly sounded in another of Twain's great American classics, *Huckleberry Finn*. Huck wants only to be left alone, to escape the stifling restrictions of family, community, and civilization. He too fails.

The pure obsession with conflict (a drive for mastery) is embodied in Captain Ahab of Herman Melville's *Moby Dick*. He destroys himself and others.

All of these most-representative masterpieces of American literature are dominated by a theme and a counter-theme. The theme claims that man realizes himself by asserting his absolute individuality. The counter-theme responds that the individual struggling against his milieu must fail. This basic American Tragedy pervades American serious literature, whether in the garb of whimsy as in Mark Twain, or in a cloak of mysticism as in Melville, or as an anarchistic philosophy as in Thoreau, or in the realistic novels of Sinclair Lewis. (Recall the fates of Carol Kennicott, Martin Arrowsmith, and Ann Vickers, all of whom challenge the stifling banality of provincial America, and fail.) Turning to popular literature and its offspring, mass entertainment, we see that the tragic theme has been suppressed. The perception of the dilemma of individualism (as it appears in American serious literature) is transformed into wish-fulfillment fantasy. The hero always wins.

Two heroes dominate in these fantasies, the hero of the Western and the hero of the private-eye story. I have singled out these two because they are the most indigenously American and, therefore, come closest to representing the American epic or folk tale. The marked difference between the two genres is worth noting.

The original-type Western is still a morality play. The hero acts alone, but he is distinctly on the side of 'good', fighting the forces of 'evil'. He may even represent the law; at any rate, he appears as the protector of a community victimized by greed or violent intruders.

The private eye has no ties. He owes loyalty only to the client who hired him, and his job is to fight for his client in a Hobbesian war of all against all. The setting is the American urban jungle (Los Angeles and New York are favorite locales), peopled by hoods, pimps, extortionists, gamblers, speculators, and magnates. Sometimes the private eye cooperates with police, but more often he *competes* with them. His advantage in the competition is his freedom from the restraints of the law under which the police must allegedly operate. The private eye, therefore, represents a particular wish-fulfillment fantasy: competition freed of all restrictions. The following passage is revealing.

'I hate the lice that run the streets without being scratched. I'm the guy with the spray gun and they hate me, too, but even if I am a private cop I can get away with it better than they can. I can work the bastards up to the point where they make a try at me and I can shoot in self-defense and be cleared in a court of law. The cops can't get away with it, but they'd like to ... [They] are tied down by a mass of red tape and they have to go through channels.'[4]

The portrait of the private eye, the culture type of American fantasy, emerges as that of a man entirely alone. He has neither family nor community connections and, as a rule, no friends. His working activity consists of snooping, stalking, eluding traps, setting traps, and, most important of all, combat. All of these exploits are punctuated by eating, drinking, and copulating. Actually, it is these activities together with the combat episodes that serve as the foci of the narrative in the way that arias serve as foci of an Italian opera. As in Italian opera, the plot serves only as the supporting structure for the endless repetition of the 'arias', these being meals, drinks, fights, and orgasms.

Sado-masochism is an integral trait of the private eye. (Masochistic fantasies indicate that the hero can take it as well as dish it out.) Together with cynicism (life is a confidence game), an appetite for four-inch steaks, and a limitless capacity for alcohol, cruelty is a badge of manliness.

'He held on and I knew if I couldn't break him loose he could kill me. He figured I'd start the knee coming up and turned to block it with a half-turn. But I did something worse. I grabbed him with my hands, squeezed and twisted and his scream was like a woman's, so high pitched ...'[5]

The stories of Mickey Spillane are, perhaps, the epitome of sadistic pornography. They are revealing in another way. The brutal hero (Mike Hammer) is endowed with a political complexion. It can be inferred from Hammer's description of Senator Knapp, a character whose death he is investigating:

'Les Knapp was another McCarthy. He was a Commie hunter but he had more prestige and more power. He was on the right committees, and, to top it off, he was the country's best missile man . . . Mr America. He pulled hard against the crap we put up with like the Cape Canaveral strikes when the entire program is held up by stupid jerks who go all the way for unionism . . . [Knapp was] one of the true powers behind the throne, a man initially responsible for military progress and missile production in spite of opposition from the knothead liberals and 'better-Red-than-dead' slobs . . . His death came at a good time for the enemy.'[6]

Mike Hammer's remarks about the Russians are in character:

'. . . those Reds just aren't the kind who can stand the big push. Like it or not, they're still a lousy bunch of peasants who killed to control but who can be knocked into line by the likes of us. They're shouting slobs who'll run like hell when class shows and they know this inside their feeble little heads.'[7]

The enormous success of literature of this sort, as indicated in sales volume, gives support to the frustration-aggression theory. In these stories, outbursts of violence seem to be triggered by a threat to an internalized but hopelessly obsolete world view – anarchic individualism, the internalized conflict of perpetual competition. Once this conflict had an outlet; it was possible to live in pursuit of 'success', or, at least, so it was believed. However, in the ever tighter world of interlocking relationships as the work-a-day world became ever more organized, routinized, and bureaucratized, the internalized conflict of competition, once the fountainhead of creative energy, can manifest itself only in a perpetual, compulsive baring of teeth.

Convincing as the evidence may seem that connects the murderous foreign policy of the United States with internalized conflict, it is not conclusive. No Mike Hammer ever sprouted or could sprout on German soil. The German had been traditionally law-abiding and sentimental – the very antithesis of the licensed gangster adulated in American fiction. Yet, the German's record for depravity has not yet been surpassed. One must conclude that it is futile to lump together all instances of genocide, all war-making, all paranoia, and seek a common source for all their manifestations.

The internalization of ideological conflict is in a class by itself. As remarked earlier, the distinction between Us and Them requires a recognizable distinguishing feature; such as is readily provided by kinship, behavior patterns, etc. It is also provided by a system of beliefs. Beliefs ordinarily are a by-product of membership in a culture, but the definition of 'us' can be considerably extended by codifying and formalizing the beliefs. 'There is no God but Allah' was a formula that admitted people to the ranks of the faithful. Actually, religious conversion was a symbolic recognition of authority, and, of course, it was accompanied by integration into the expanding authority structure.

The obverse of this process is the withdrawal of obeisance through the avowal of verbalized beliefs incompatible with those imposed by authority – heresy. The ruthless persecution of heretics coincides with the period when the authority of the Church in Europe had already begun to decline.

The frantic efforts to preserve 'ideological purity' when translated into a political context cease to appear as trivial conflicts over words. They are, instead, quite meaningful efforts to preserve authority, for ideological orthodoxy is an expression of submission. Whether the imposition of orthodoxy insures submission is another matter. Evidently, attacking symptoms rather than sources is a pervasive human foible.

Still, there is something to be said for the imposition of beliefs (if they can be really grafted onto the psyche) as a means of consolidating authority. The Church seems to have done this successfully during its period of ascendance. An ideology, being a system of beliefs, shares some aspects of material systems. For example, it 'strives' to maintain a 'steady state'. One of its homeostatic mechanisms is the so-called principle of cognitive dissonance. Cognitive inputs that do not fit into the system are either ignored or interpreted in a way that makes them fit, regardless of how bizarre such interpretations may seem from outside the system. If the ideology becomes codified into a doctrine, special functionaries may be appointed by the authorities (who derive their legitimacy from the ideology) to keep the doctrine 'pure', that is, to discredit any challenges to it.

In our day, at least two ruling groups base their claim to legitimacy on an ideology formalized as an unassailable doctrine. The Chinese version is said to be contained entirely in a single booklet shorter than the New Testament and considerably shorter than the Koran. The Soviet version is claimed by its champions to be derived from substantially more complex sources. At any rate, although practically nothing new has been added permanently to the Holy Writ of Marxism-Leninism since Lenin, the combined verbal output of Marx, Engels, and Lenin is sufficiently voluminous and often sufficiently sophisticated to qualify as a philosophical system of the first rank. It was the guardians of its purity who made it sterile by degrading it to the status of dogma while claiming for it the status of a scientific theory being continually developed and 'tested by life'.

The criterion of dogma is simple. A doctrine is a dogma if it is not possible to challenge any of its assertions without being immediately and categorically refuted, corrected, dismissed, or accorded the status of an ideological enemy. As far as I know, not a single assertion of Marx, Engels, or Lenin has ever been publicly challenged by a Marxist-Leninist in good standing. The practical consequences of this intellectual ossification may not be as serious as one might expect. Life goes on and makes its demands. Practices and policies are adjusted to these demands as they must be if a social or political system is to remain viable. The longer a doctrine remains ossified, the less damage it can do because it becomes progressively more difficult to translate the verbiage into action. Finally nothing remains but the ritual of reiterating the articles of faith.

However, at the time the ossification sets in, when the dogma is still taken seriously as a guide to action, the damage may be considerable and its after-effects may last for a long time.

The ossification of Marxist philosophy is in large measure attributable to Lenin himself. It was he who declared Marxist philosophy to be unassailable:

You cannot eliminate even one basic assumption, one substantial part of this philosophy of Marxism (it is as if it were a solid block of steel) without abandoning objective truth, without falling into the arms of bourgeois-reactionary falsehood.[8]

The statement was made in the course of a polemic against colleagues who sought to modify some tenets of materialist philosophy to bring it into closer correspondence with the developments in physics during the first decade of the twentieth century.

Cracking the intellectual whip was Lenin's way of building a political party with a single purpose composed of men with a single mind. He was thus extending a sound military principle (concentrated attack) to the intellectual sphere. Pragmatically, the method must be considered a success, since Lenin's goal, the creation of an elite revolutionary party organized along the lines of military discipline, was achieved. Even the next goal, the seizure of power by the elite party, was achieved. However, it is impossible to evaluate the ultimate consequences of the ideological ossification, because we cannot turn the clock back and re-run history under different conditions. It seems clear that the obsession with ideological purity and the concentration of total power (ultimately in one person) reinforced each other. Regardless of what the political and social consequences of this internalization of ideological conflict have been, the effects on Soviet intellectual life have been disastrous.

The rich experience of the revolution, reconstruction, and industrialization, and the emergence of entirely new social relations, remained unreflected in what might have been an unprecedented growth of social science. All social science being already embodied in the Holy Writ, only pious re-statements of the ossified doctrine could be used in theoretical interpretations of what was happening.

After World War II, when the ideology was threatened with contamination through unavoidable contacts with the West made during the war, witch hunts were extended even to the natural sciences. The Lysenko affair simulated the obscenities of the Moscow Trials of Party leaders, including highest ranking Old Bolsheviks in the army and politburo, conducted in the 1930s on Stalin's orders.

Eventually 'life' persisted in its demands, and most of Soviet science was emancipated from the tyranny of official ideology. Even social science began to sprout here and there on the base of empirical investigations. Literature, however, still remains under the watchful eye of ideological guardians.

Under conditions of partial relaxation, tensions usually mount. The feeling that 'something is giving way' arouses hopes. If Soviet society enters a dynamic phase of disequilibrium, one can expect that ideological conflict will play an important part in the process because of the way ideological conflict had been internalized in the formative phase of that society.

In comparing here the presumed consequences of internalized competitive conflict in the United States and of internalized ideological conflict in the Soviet Union, note that the initial effects were opposite. In the United States, internalization of competitive conflict had an 'atomizing' effect on society as reflected, for example, in the asphalt jungle nightmares of private-eye fantasies. In the Soviet Union, internalization of ideological conflict created, at first, a semblance of a society united by an orthodox faith. What we may be witnessing now is the beginning of endogenous, structure-oriented conflicts within both societies, nurtured by a revulsion against both the Hobbesian and the Orwellian visions.

CHAPTER 19

Professionalization of Conflict

Professionalization is in the first instance an aspect of specialization, hence, a consequence of the division of labor in complex societies. 'Profession', however, implies more than a skill, such as is required in any craft. The connotation of the word includes that of a high social status accorded to the specialty. Thus, in Western societies, medicine, law, architecture, journalism, banking, the performing arts, and academic pursuits qualify as professions, while manual skills normally do not. (The surgeon's and, perhaps, the musician's skills are among the exceptions.)

Meanings of words change with changing social conditions, and the blurring of class distinctions has somewhat blurred the distinction between professions and other occupations. Nowadays, 'profession' sometimes refers to any specialized, paid occupation, be it pugilism, gambling, or prostitution. To some extent, however, 'profession' has still retained the connotation of high social status, i.e., 'respectability' in the literal sense of deserving respect.

Skills to which the highest social status is accorded in most human societies are those having to do with the interpretation and manipulation of symbols. Professional training is to a very large extent verbal training, much of it administered in academic institutions through books, lectures, etc.

All work is essentially of three kinds: handling things (or animals), handling people, and handling ideas. Invariably, the latter two types of work have enjoyed higher social prestige than the first. The democratization of Western societies might have contributed to a degree of equalization if it were not for the fact that democratization went hand in hand with the mechanization of handling things and, consequently, with a decreasing social importance of the associated skills. (Note that the surgeon's and the musician's manual skills have not yet been made obsolete, which accounts for their being exceptions).

Not only technology but also science contribute to the preservation of the primarily symbol-manipulating character of the professions. For, to the extent that work becomes dependent on science, skills become more dependent on familiarity with abstract, theoretical concepts than on specific, concrete situations. In other words, skills become supplanted by knowledge.

Among the important professions in most societies is the organization and conduct of conflict. In its professional setting, of course, conflict is conducted not simply as a result of a hostile interaction but with a particular, socially approved aim in view. The professional boxer or bull fighter fights (or kills) not because he necessarily hates his opponent, but because he is a paid entertainer. This professional aspect of fighting does not preclude feelings of hostility on the part of the boxer toward his opponent, nor, perhaps, sadistic pleasure that a bull fight may give to the matador and his audience. However, the professional's performance does not depend on his feelings. They may enhance his skill, by providing additional motivation, but they may also be detrimental to it by deflecting his attention from the technical aspects of his work. Remuneration, on the other hand, is a necessary component of professional activity and, in fact, presently constitutes the legal criterion of the category 'professional'.

Similar considerations apply to a lawyer arguing a case. He, too, organizes and conducts a conflict (endogenous, issue-oriented, debate-like). He may be strongly motivated by extra-professional considerations; for instance, he may be convinced of the justice of his case and may be strongly committed to justice in general, and the strength of his conviction and commitment may be a factor in the efficacy with which he argues the case. What is *professionally* expected of him, however, is to win the case. The pressures attendant on the professional status of the attorney, therefore, are to select winnable cases, justice being at times at best a secondary consideration.

Indeed, in the so-called adversary model of the legal profession, it is assumed that the proper task of the lawyer is to protect the interest of *his* client, whether the client is the State, an individual on trial by the State, or a party in a civil suit. Professional ethics demand of the lawyer that he present the case of his client in the most favorable light, seeking out and emphasizing those aspects of the case that make his client's case appear just, and only those. It is assumed that the adversary lawyer will do the same for the other side and that the justice of the issues involved will emerge from these oppositely directed efforts. It should be noted, however, that at times the justice of the issues involved is not even a factor in the evaluation of the attorney's competence. His professional competence is rated according to his technical knowledge (of relevant precedents, points of law, etc.) and his strategic skills (selection of evidence and witnesses, forensic techniques, appreciation of the psychological state of the jurors, etc.).

We find a similar situation in the professionalization of politics. Politics is supposed to be an instrument whereby endogenous conflicts of interest are resolved. In democracies, the popular will is supposed to be reflected in the political process, as in the election of candidates committed to the support of particular policies. In order to fulfill this function (the espousal of certain policies in government bodies), the elected government official must have requisite support at the polls. Ordinarily if politics were indeed an instrument for resolving conflicts of social interests, the politician would present himself as the champion of this or that policy. His election would then signify the preponderant support of the policy by the electorate. The *profession* of politics, however, defines a political career, as does any profession. A career is a steady advancement in status accorded to the professional in consequence of his accumulated experience and competence. The rising status is usually reflected in increased authority, in rank, title, etc. The political career, exactly like any other, is marked by definite rungs; for instance, in the United States, one line of ascent is from state representative to state senator, to congressman to senator (or state governor), to president. In elective offices, therefore, the essential skill of politicians is the skill of getting elected. Experience in getting oneself or someone elected accumulates not only in the process of an individual career but also in the auxiliary professions involved, such as 'public relations'. In this way, the professionalization of politics, particularly in the United States, has paralleled the professionalization of competitive business. The *product*, whether that of politics (supposedly, 'policies') or that of business (supposedly goods and services), becomes of secondary importance, relevant only to the extent that it contributes to the success of the professionals, whether businessmen or politicians. The primary skills in these professions are directed toward activities relevant to the making of careers, say, contributing to increasing profits or expanding business, or to successfully mobilizing votes.

In short, the professionalization of conflict (whether in legal context, in business competition, or in politics) de-emphasizes the stated objectives of the conflicts and emphasizes success in conflict as an end in itself. The rationalization of business competition as a socially salutary process is often couched in terms borrowed from the theory of natural selection: competition in the market place promotes quality of commodities and services and efficiency of production.[1] But, if success in business is achieved in other ways, say, by astute use of stratagems or by manipulating mass psychology, professional competence will be directed into these channels. The adversary system of law and elective politics are supposed to serve justice and the realization of popular will, respectively. But, if success in either can be achieved in other ways, say, by adroit use of forensic skills or of demagogy, professional competence and commitment will be directed toward acquisition of the appropriate skills.

Let us now trace the effects of professionalization of organized violence, that is, the evolution of the military profession.

Primitive war was primarily direct face-to-face combat. Skill depended on the ability to wield weapons, and, since the effectiveness of weapons depended then on their weight, physical strength was a vital component of military competence. Bravery was, of course, also important, being the ability to suppress self-preserving instincts and, perhaps, whatever inhibitions against intraspecific killing may be incorporated in the human psyche. The warrior, accordingly, was strong, brave, and fierce.

The early stages in the evolution of war involved the coordination of the actions of many warriors into actions of organized units. An analogue of natural selection insured the survival of effective methods of organization and gave rise to the evolution of effective battle tactics. Coordination required coordinators, and the role of the commander came to dominate the conduct of battle. The commander at first participated in the actual fighting, so that the typical characteristics of the warrior were still manifested in his person. But other characteristics achieved equal importance – the ability to see the battle as a whole rather than the individual enemy engaged at the moment. Progressively, the role of the commander became that of a director of the fighting units rather than a wielder of weapons. Perceptive acuity and quick thinking replaced physical prowess as the primary factor 'selected for' in military competence.

As human societies became larger and more complex, so did war. In addition to battle tactics, *strategy* became an important component of military competence. Strategic problems extend beyond those of battle tactics. If tactics is the art of conducting a battle, strategy is the art of conducting a campaign or an entire war. Strategy is concerned with the disposition of forces so that battles will be fought under favorable conditions. Thus, it is concerned with the question of whether and, if so, when and where to fight a battle, hence with the preparation for battles – matters only indirectly related to the actual fighting: the organization of supply trains, road building, plans contingent on the outcome of future battles, etc.

Eventually the commander-in-chief of the total organized force did not need to be present on the battle field at all. Neither physical prowess, nor physical bravery, nor a fierce disposition helped him to become a proficient commander. His job became intellectual. He became a professional not only in the sense of providing competent service but also in the sense that his competence was embodied in the knowledge of general principles, that is, the ability to interpret and manipulate symbols.

As the growing importance of strategic principles made the organization and conduct of war a genuine profession, these principles became ever more important, because the high status accorded the professional makes what he says and thinks and writes influential. A positive feedback process sets in: the prestige of the profession turns attention to what the professionals are saying, increasing their sense of self-importance; the boost to self-confidence stimulates the output of profound-sounding verbiage, which 'fertilizes' the symbolic environment with nutrients essential for further growth of the profession.

The epitome of the professionalization of war was reached in Europe in the eighteenth century, the 'classical' period of strategic art.

At the close of the Thirty Years' War, the political organization of Europe was crystalized in a system of sovereign states, most of them absolute monarchies. That is to say, the international system consisted of autonomous sub-systems in interaction. The autonomy of each sub-system (state) was embodied in the persons of the monarchs, who viewed their domains as fiefdoms, a conception carried over from earlier feudal organization. Preservation of this autonomy meant the preservation of sovereignty over a territory and, consequently, over the subjects inhabiting it. Enlargement of autonomy meant enlargement of territory. Each monarch was in possession of an army which he used to sustain his autonomy and to encroach upon the autonomy of other monarchs. Altercations were frequent and usually led to wars.

The wars of the eighteenth century were, however, quite unlike wars of other periods, such as the wars of conquest that resulted in the emergence of the great empires of antiquity, or the religious wars of the sixteenth and early seventeenth centuries, or the total wars of the twentieth. To begin with, the cabinet war was fought for limited objectives. No monarch was strong enough to nurture an ambition to subjugate all of Europe. Each had an investment in keeping the system of sovereign states intact so that encroachments on the autonomy of others were limited and justified by specific claims, mostly dynastic ones. From this investment in the 'legitimacy' of sovereignty emerged the conception of the balance of power, whereby excessive aggrandizement of any state provoked a coalition of other states against the expanding one 'to restore the balance' (cf. Chapter 16).

Additionally, the severity of eighteenth-century wars was limited by the fact that the highly trained professional armies of the time were rather expensive instruments. The high degree of training required of the soldier was a consequence of the perfection of the 'art of war', in which the eighteenth century was a 'classical' period. Military maneuvers became highly stylized, and the military profession was practised by experts. The wave of innovation released by the introduction of gunpowder had spent itself, and victory in battle was seen as a reward for superior and refined skill in the practice of the craft. Consequently, long and intense training went into the making of a soldier. Such an army could not be readily replaced. Pitched battles then rarely lasted more than a day. The outcomes were decided when one side left the scene of the engagement. Capitulation was not a disgrace. The outcomes of one or two battles often decided the outcome of the war and, hence, the settlement of the issue in favor of one side or the other, or else by compromise. These cabinet wars were for the most part devoid of affect. To the monarchs, war was a normal, legal instrument in pursuit of specified, limited goals. To the generals it was the practice of a profession. Civilian populations were little involved (patriotism had not yet been invented).

It remains to consider the soldier of that period, the man doing the shooting and being shot at. His psyche can be understood only in terms of his training, which was essentially a destruction of his autonomy. Since tactical skill in battle consisted largely of an ability to execute intricate maneuvers, moving formations of men so as to maximize the effectiveness of their fire power in capturing or holding positions, the precision of these maneuvers depended on the strictest coordination, effected through instantaneous and stylized obedience to shouted commands. Close order drill was designed deliberately to reduce the soldier to an automaton. Although, physiologically, the soldier retained the characteristics of a living system, and his internal (biological) homeostatic mechanisms continued functioning so as to maintain the system in a steady state, his behavioral homeostatic mechanisms were disrupted. Especially, he was effectively inhibited from taking evading action in order to save his life. The soldier became an expendable part in a machine.

A human psyche cannot, however, be voided of all affect. Evidence that dehumanization was sometimes incomplete is provided in the high desertion rates. Also, some soldiers may have retained vestiges of repugnance toward killing, normally instilled in peaceful communities. Others may have developed a hatred for a generalized 'enemy', not a difficult matter considering that 'the enemy' was a source of mortal danger. However, inculcation of hatred toward the enemy was not usually part of the soldier's training in the eighteenth century. Neither the identity of the enemy nor the causes of a war were his concern. Nor is it likely that the sovereigns themselves who waged wars against each other harbored excessively hostile feelings. Their feelings toward enemy sovereigns were probably not much different from those of businessmen against competitors.

In sum, professionalization of war in eighteenth-century Europe demonstrates most clearly that large-scale human conflict can be organized on a comparatively low emotional level. The organization and conduct of war was entrusted to specialists whose commitment was to their 'art' and who could remain totally indifferent to the 'issues' over which wars were fought. The degree of the professionals' detachment can be seen in the ease with which generals left one sovereign's service to join another's, quite in the same way that business managers and lawyers switch their allegiance from one corporation to another without violating professional ethics.

The situation changed drastically during the French Revolutionary and Napoleonic Wars. During the French Revolution, large masses became motivated politically. A 'cause' appeared, epitomized in the slogan 'Liberty, Equality, Fraternity'. Loyalty to the cause was identified with loyalty to the country that was the first to overthrow the old order; thus, mass patriotism made its debut in history. The fervor of the common soldier in the French Revolutionary armies introduced a new factor into war. No longer was it necessary for authority, with the help of the cudgel, to suppress the self-preserving reactions of the soldier by reconditioning his normal reflexes. These reactions were now suppressed in consequence of the soldier's identification with a larger Self, embodied first in the revolutionary cause, then in France, finally in the person of a charismatic leader, Napoleon Bonaparte, who became the symbol of power and glory.

It was this radical change in the psychology of the soldier that gave Napoleon a formidable advantage over his opponents. The tactics of the eighteenth-century armies were limited by the necessity of keeping at least the infantry in strict formations, for only in these formations could the soldier behave as was expected of him – like an automaton. In contrast, the strongly motivated French soldier could be allowed considerably greater freedom. He could be used in skirmishes as well as formal battles, as a lone sniper as well as one of identical elements of a column. Above all, because the French soldier was not a product of many years' arduous training designed to inhibit his natural reactions, he was more expendable. Bonaparte's armies could be continually and quickly replenished.

Bonaparte was defeated when the patriotic fervor of other populaces was awakened and turned against him, as in the disastrous Russian campaign.

The Napoleonic Wars ushered in nineteenth-century European nationalism, essentially an identification of the individual Self with the nation state. This form of identification turned out to be remarkably stable, especially where bolstered by recurring national wars (as between Prussia and France) or where people speaking the same language had been under the rule of people speaking another – Italians under Austrian rule, several Slavic-speaking peoples under Austrian and Turkish rule. In these latter cases, identification of Self as the oppressed, on the part of the ruled, was strongly reinforced by linguistic and cultural distinctions. Successful struggles for national liberation instigated others. It is note-worthy that the first War of National Liberation so designated was the uprising of Prussia against Bonaparte (weakened by the Russian cam-paign) in 1813. From that war, which led to Bonaparte's final defeat, Prussia emerged as the most militant national state in Europe.

The nineteenth century, the era of rampant nationalism in Europe might be designated the 'romantic' period that supplanted the 'classical' period of the eighteenth century. Inter-nation conflict became in-ternalized, not merely institutionalized as a profession. It was this transformation that revealed to Clausewitz the limitless vistas of his beloved profession. For he understood that henceforth war would involve not merely a small segment of specialists, tending to lapse into mediocrity, their intellectual horizons circumscribed by an ossified doctrine. War was now democratized. It became everybody's business, and the 'art of war' could be nurtured by the resources of the entire nation.

Clausewitz's prophesy came to pass. The 'art of war' kept pace with the dynamism of the nineteenth century, nurtured above all by science. War became not simply the business of a profession directly related to the conduct of military operations, marches, sieges, battle maneuvers, etc., but the nexus of practically all professions, as is all too evident in the roster of personnel at the service of modern military establishments.

If the commander already in Clausewitz's time was one step removed from the battle field, the civilian professions serving the modern war machines are many steps removed. The work of a chemist 'improving' napalm is no different from that of the chemist developing a new fabric. The design of a communication system that guides passenger airplanes requires the same sort of professional competence as the design of another communication system that guides missiles with nuclear warheads. In Kahn's discussion (cf. Chapter 14) of Rung 39 of his escalation ladder (which he calls 'slow motion counter-city war'), *cities* are the wherewithal of compensation quite in the same way as money is the wherewithal of compensation in civil damage suits.

As was said, professionalism involves symbolic skills. And the nature of symbolic manipulation is such that it confers the more power the more abstract the symbols become (witness mathematics as the language of science, and doctrines as codifications of ideologies). Consequently, as there is more power to be wielded, the professions tend to be further removed in the minds of the practitioners from the concrete situations affected by their activities. A banker or a stockmarket tycoon may never see more money than is in his pocket. Likewise, a military commander-in-chief can sustain a successful career without ever seeing a corpse. While that was true of a commander already in the nineteenth century, at least he had then to *imagine* the battle field. And, although his professional framework of thought effectively insulated him from emotional involvement with the flesh-and-blood events on the battle field, he could at least appreciate the gravity of these events. Clausewitz himself specifically warns against flinching from bloodshed:

> Let us not hear of Generals who conquer without bloodshed. If a bloody slaughter is a horrible sight, then that is a ground for paying more respect to War, but not for making the sword we wear blunter and blunter by degrees from feelings of humanity, until someone steps in with one that is sharp and lops off the arm from our body.[2]

Clausewitz appeals to toughness, but at least he recognized that war is a bloody business. This is no longer necessary for modern strategists to do. The accessory activities of war have become so dominant that their end result recedes beyond the horizon of imagination. The vast bulk of war activity today is production, planning, organization, communication, logistic calculations, calculations of capabilities, etc., etc. – activities that differ in no way from similar activities in the ordinary work-a-day world of an industrialized society.[3]

It is for this reason that repugnance toward war has not kept pace with its hyper-growth. And even when repugnance begins to make itself felt, as in the United States, where it is emerging as a result of the frustrating war in Southeast Asia, there is no longer a clear target at which (justifiably or not) the antagonism can be directed.[4]

After the debacle of World War I, there was such a target in Germany: the military itself, identified not only professionally but also by caste (the aristocracy still furnished the bulk of the professionals). Popular resentment was not sufficient, however, to discredit the military profession even there; six years later (1925) Field Marshal Hindenburg (chief commander of the Central Powers in 1916) was elected president with the support of the Social Democrats.

The grumblings against the 'military-industrial-complex' in the United States today are not likely to rise above the level of rhetoric, because the 'complex' is not a profession whose activity one could regulate, circumscribe, or altogether prohibit. For this reason, also, the clamor for 'civilian control of the military' has no bearing on the hypertrophy of the war profession – mainly because it is now civilian politicians no less than generals who, literally, call the shots.[5] Note also that critics of the 'military-industrial complex' now are forced to extend the phrase to 'military-industrial-labor' and further to 'military-industrial-labor-academic' complex. In short, just as the 'democratization' of war in the nineteenth century made war everybody's business by contributing to the internalization of conflict on the level of the nation state, so the hypergrowth of the war machine has made war everybody's business by extending the 'art' of organized violence to encompass practically all professions.

A profession is said to be supported because it serves some need of a society. However, when a substantial fraction of the society becomes 'professional', or at least sees itself as such (as in predominantly middle-class societies), the 'needs of the society' include as an important component the professional career needs of its members. Then the professions still appear to be serving the 'needs of society' by serving the career needs of their own professionals. (This development is not confined to the professions. The social utility of an industry is now predominantly judged by the jobs it provides, not by the need or usefulness of its product.) The war profession achieves thereby added immunity. Being all-pervasive, it serves career needs of not just the military, but, one is tempted to say, practically everybody. At any rate, the line separating the war professions from the peace professions can no longer be drawn. The once encapsulated system has diffused throughout its environment, like a solute in a solvent, like a cancer in a body. Surgery is useless. Successful chemotherapy presupposes a substance lethal to the cancer but not to the host.

It appears, therefore, that the professionalization of conflicts that have become dysfunctional presents a more serious threat to man than the internalization of such conflicts. Internalized conflicts are linked to affect and depend for their 'nourishment' on heroic traditions, on memories of grievances, on ethnic prejudices, on insecurity, or on clashes of values. Thus, although the eradication of long-standing feuds or enmities among human groups may be difficult, the obstacles are apparent and, in principle, removable. The deaths of Romeo and Juliet reconciled the Montagues and the Capulets. The wounds of communal strife eventually can heal. Racism and ethnocentrism do occasionally yield to enlightenment and mutual understanding, especially if the roots of these attitudes atrophy. The professional war maker, on the other hand, is largely immune to such attitude changes, precisely because for him conflict is dissociated from affect. Hence, his conscience is disengaged and is more difficult to reach than that of a passionate hater. His defense is his self image of the 'dispassionate scientist'. Lynchings, pogroms, and massacres are crimes of passion. The organization of 'civilized' war is preparation of a pre-meditated crime.

In discussing the 'acceptability' of different weapons, W. H. Oldendorf writes:

> The more closely this approaches the basic effects of fang and claw, the more readily ... accepted ... explosive weapons seem so *right*, and the quietly lethal weapons so wrong.[6] [Emphasis in the original.]

There is still another aspect to 'quietly lethal' weapons that accounts for the greater revulsion against them than against 'violent' weapons. The problem posed by the inventor of a more powerful bomb does not involve the image of a human victim. The parallelism of developing a more effective chemical or biological weapon does. The inventor of such a weapon may, for example, be searching for a strain of a filariasis parasite that can be transmitted directly from man to man without an intermediate host. Or he may invent a plastic fragmentation bomb, more effective because plastic fragments, unlike metal fragments, cannot be detected by X-rays, thus defying the surgeon's efforts to save the wounded. Or he may 'improve' napalm, which depends for its effectiveness on the impossibility of shaking or washing off the burning droplets. His task is to frustrate efforts of living human beings to escape destruction or to save lives.

This sort of 'science' represents, perhaps, the ultimate degree of dehumanization, a direct consequence of the professionalization of war.

CHAPTER 20

Conflict Resolution

Both endogenous and exogenous conflicts have always been considered 'problems', but of different kinds. The Bible cites fratricide as the first murder, a traumatic event. Other killings, including massacres, are chronicled as exploits.

Since men live in cooperative groups, and cooperation is disrupted by excessive endogenous conflict, if a cooperative group exists at all, this must be because some limits on conflict within it have been imposed, indeed, internalized. On the other hand, the continued existence of a cooperative group may be threatened by other groups, and these threats are often met by aggressive or defensive action. In such inter-group struggles, survival advantage, at least in the short run, accrues to the victorious. Therefore, the 'problem' of exogenous conflict, as it appears to the conflicting groups, becomes one of conducting it effectively, not that of inhibiting or suppressing it.

The boundaries of a 'cooperating group' are not fixed by nature, however. The tendency has been for these groups to become larger. Families coalesced into clans, clans into tribes, tribes into nations. This coalescence was the result of two factors, first, the extension of the range of possible cooperation by the technology of production and communication; second, the advantages accruing to the larger cooperative groups in conflicts with other groups. Thus, while inhibitions of endogenous conflicts extended over larger domains, inhibitions of exogenous conflicts did not keep pace. Big political systems, like nations, may have successfully suppressed at least large-scale lethal conflicts inside their boundaries. But nations did not thereby become less aggressive than, say, tribes or clans with respect to each other.

Coalescence has now gone beyond the nation as a unit. By the 1950s the world appeared to many, including most authoritative public figures, political scientists, and the like, as partitioned into two hostile blocs of nations. From each side it appeared that the problem *within* the bloc was that of consolidating cooperative arrangements (NATO, the Common Market, the Warsaw Pact, Comecon, etc.). At the same time, it appeared to the same people that the problem of inter-bloc conflict could be solved only by insuring that one's own bloc was stronger than the other, militarily, economically, and politically.

Nevertheless, it is impossible to ignore the fact that organized, violent conflict has become so destructive and lethal that it cannot be justified on either utilitarian or moral grounds. Also, the range of possible cooperation now appears to be the entire globe. Accordingly, the idea that every conflict is amenable to 'peaceful resolution' has become ascendant not only in the pacifistically oriented religions but also in science.

It is maintained that 'a science of conflict resolution' can be developed by applying the methods of investigation current in existing sciences to the study of the genesis and the epidemiology of human conflicts; further, that understanding these 'causes' of conflicts will provide us with the knowledge of how they can be prevented, alleviated, or resolved. Conflicts – at least, the severe ones like ethnic and racial enmities and wars – appear in this view as aberrations of normal (i.e., cooperative) human relations in the same way as diseases appear as aberrations of normal physiological functions. Just as understanding these aberrations made scientific medicine possible, so, it is assumed, understanding the etiology of conflicts will give rise to a science of conflict resolution, applicable to the restoration or further enhancement of cooperation among men.

Clearly, ideas about approaches to conflict resolution depend crucially on the models of conflict that are supposed to represent its most important features. If one believes the source of human conflict to be in man's aggressive instinct, then depth psychology seems to be the proper theoretical framework in which to formulate therapeutic proposals, such as releasing the individual from compulsions imposed by 'instinct', sublimating his aggressive impulses, etc.

If conflict is seen as a manifestation of aggression, but aggression is traced to specific experience (frustrations, for example), then the modification of the symbolic environment so as to remove sources of excessive frustrations seems to be a reasonable approach. The key to world peace appears, then, to be in finding appropriate child-rearing methods.

Endogenous conflicts among religious, ethnic, and racial groups are traceable to prejudices, crystalized around 'stereotypes', images of the supposedly prevalent representative members of the hated or despised group. Often education or re-education is offered as an antidote to stereotyping.

Control of internal violence by governmental authority, recourse to courts of laws, and the like, suggests that an effective system of international law may eventually solve the problem of inter-state war. Several prototypes of 'world constitutions' are on record.[1]

A great deal is also being said about what is called 'conflict management'. The underlying idea is the usual 'realist' model of the international system in which states appear as actors with conflicting interests. Occasions for the clash of interests are 'issues'. Conflict between two states is assumed to be aggravated in proportion to the number and importance of issues on which their interests clash. According to one approach to conflict management, it is important to 'fractionate' a conflict, that is, to examine the issues singly instead of collectively. In this way, the conflict is kept closer to concrete situations and is prevented from developing into matters of 'principle', or into ideological conflict, levels on which it may be impossible to resolve it.

The clearest formulation of the 'fractionation' approach was made by Roger Fisher. Each 'issue', in Fisher's conception of an international conflict, is a separate bargaining situation. There are two sides, each with a different evaluation of the consequences of settling the issue one way or another (or not settling it). The first step toward settling the issue is to make a list of these consequences, attaching to each a 'value'.[2]

Fisher puts the stress on concreteness. The bargainers must have a clear idea of who will be making decisions relevant to the issues, who will gain or lose by the particular decisions made. The bargainers must also specify exactly the demands they are making on each other, as well as offers for complying with the demands, and threats of sanctions for non-compliance. They must specify when the presumed advantages or disadvantages will accrue. Finally (but only when all concrete aspects have been spelled out), the bargainers can appeal to the rightness, propriety, or legitimacy of their demands.

If such a concrete formulation is made, the conflict is representable as a *game*. The word is used here in its technical sense, as in the theory of games. Essentially, game theory is the branch of decision theory applied to situations involving two or more decision makers whose interests do not coincide. Decisions lead to outcomes, and the interests of the players are reflected in the (generally different) values that they assign to each possible outcome. The interdependence of the players is reflected in the fact that no one player controls the outcomes by his decisions. Moreover, he knows that each of the outcomes depends not only on what he does but on what the others will do. Each player is also aware of the values assigned by every player to every one of the several outcomes.

The simplest conflict being between two parties, we shall examine the representation of such conflicts as *two-person games*. Such games can be represented by a rectangular array, a *matrix*. The horizontal rows of such a matrix represent the several decisions available to one of the players, called Row. The vertical columns represent the decisions available to the other player, called Column. The 'cells' of the matrix, that is, the intersections of the pairs of decisions, represent the outcomes, and the numerical entries in these cells are the respective values assigned by the players to the outcomes. An example of such a game is shown in Matrix 1. The rows R_1, R_2, R_3 represent the actions open to Row; the columns C_1, C_2, C_3, the actions open to Column. The entries in the lower left corners of each cell are the 'payoffs' to Row; those in the upper right corners, to Column.

Note that in the game represented by Matrix 1 the sum of the payoffs is zero regardless of the outcome. This means that the more one of the players wins, the more the other loses, so that the interests of the two players are diametrically opposed. Such games are called *zerosum*.

One might suppose that a conflict represented by this game could be resolved by a compromise. For instance, Row might be induced to choose R_1 as his action, and Column to choose C_3, so that both would neither win nor lose. But if the game represents the total situation of interest, that is, if the issue represented by the game is the *only* issue, there is no reason for Column to accept this compromise. Note that by choosing C_2 Column can *assure* for himself a win of at least 2 units regardless of what Row does. It is also true that Row, by choosing R_3, can prevent Column from gaining more than 2 units. In a way, therefore, the outcome in cell

$[R_3C_2]$ is a sort of 'resolution of the conflict'. This resolution is effected without the intervention of third parties and without the invocation by either party of principles of fairness or justice. The outcome is purely the result of the relative power positions of the players. Each has a *best* strategy which he will use if he is 'rational', that is, attempts to maximize his gains (or minimize his losses) and consequently (because the game is zerosum) to maximize the losses (or minimize the gains) of the other player. Moreover, the choices indicated are the 'best' available to each player, provided each not only is himself 'rational' but also knows that the other is equally 'rational'. In game theory, it is proved mathematically that a 'best' strategy is available to each of the two players in every two-person zerosum game.[3]

	C_1	C_2	C_3	C_4
R_1	8 / −8	5 / −5	0 / 0	−11 / 11
R_2	10 / −10	3 / −3	20 / −20	−15 / 15
R_3	−6 / 6	2 / −2	−2 / 2	10 / −10

Matrix 1

The situation is quite different in conflicts represented by games that are not zerosum (*non-zerosum games*), where the payoffs do not necessarily add up to zero in every outcome and in which, therefore, the interests of the two players are not necessarily diametrically opposed. It is to this situation that Fisher addresses himself in his approach to conflict management.

An example of a 'non-zerosum' conflict is shown in Matrix 2, a highly simplified version of so-called eyeball-to-eyeball confrontation between two powers, exemplified, say, by the Cuban missile crisis of 1962.

	C_2	D_2
C_1	0 0	10 −10
D_1	−10 10	−1000 −1000

Matrix 2

Assume for simplicity that each side has two options: C – to yield; D – to stand firm and go to war if necessary. Assume, first, that the value of yielding (if the other also yields) is zero to both; next, that yielding unilaterally is worth −10 (through loss of prestige etc.), while making the other yield unilaterally is worth +10 (gain of prestige etc.). Finally, assume that going to war is disastrous for both, say −1000 to each. This is the simplest version of the game of Chicken, whose 'sophisticated' version was discussed by Herman Kahn (cf. p. 172).

Here a 'rational' player would have difficulty deciding what to do. The prudent decision seems to be to yield. But, if this decision is prudent and the other party is 'rational', can one not count on *his* yielding, so that by making an irrevocable commitment to stand firm can one not gain 10 units? On the other hand, might not the other be thinking in exactly the same way? If so, then both have made an irrevocable commitment (in the expectation that the *other* is 'rational') that results in disaster.

	C_2	D_2

	C_2	D_2
C_1	1 1	10 −10
D_1	−10 10	−1 −1

Matrix 3

An even more peculiar situation is represented in Matrix 3, a simplified version of the disarmament problem. Here, examination of the matrix shows that it is to the advantage of each power to remain armed (choose D) *whatever* the other does. For, if the other disarms (chooses C), one gains an advantage (+10) by remaining armed. If the other remains armed (chooses D), one must also remain armed in self-defense (otherwise one stands to get −10). Yet it is to the advantage of *both* powers to disarm, since both get +1 in the upper left cell and −1 in the lower right.

In non-zerosum games, conflict resolution involves more than a 'balance of power' resulting from the 'most rational' choices by the two parties as in zerosum games. For, in a non-zerosum game, an arbitrator can often point out to *both* parties the advantages of a compromise solution. In the case of the eyeball-to-eyeball confrontation (Matrix 2), it is clearly to the advantage of both parties to choose C. This choice can also be rationalized by each player as a 'prudent' one. However, in the disarmament case (Matrix 3), while it is to the advantage of both to disarm, the 'prudent' choice is to remain armed, which is worse for both (if both choose it) than the 'imprudent' choice. The arbitrator can get the parties out of this trap by calling attention to this. Even without an arbitrator, if the parties can freely communicate, they can point out to each other the symmetry of their situations and the advantage of coming to terms.

Conflicts represented by Matrix 1 (zerosum games) are by their nature exogenous. The parties to the conflict have no common interest. Conflicts represented by Matrices 2 and 3 may be exogenous or endogenous. In the exogenous case, even if the two have a common interest, say, to effect the outcome in the upper left cell rather than the one in the lower right, they cannot achieve the advantageous outcome since to do so requires a co-ordination of their choices and, perhaps, the enforcement of an agreement. If such coordination is possible, or if provisions for enforcement exist, the conflict is by definition endogenous (cf. p. 175) because the parties either have a common set of values or are subject to a common authority.

Note that the conflicts represented by Matrices 2 and 3 are symmetric: both players are in the same positions. Game theory also provides 'solutions' of asymmetric conflicts, in which the positions of the participants are different. Consider the game represented by Matrix 4.

	C_1	C_2
R_1	5 0	0 5
R_2	-1 -2	-2 -1

Matrix 4

Examining the payoffs, we see that it is to Row's advantage to choose R_1 regardless of what Column does, since Row's payoffs are negative in both cells of R_2. Similarly, it is to Column's advantage to choose C_1 regardless of how Row chooses, since Column's payoffs are bigger in both cells in the left-hand column than in the corresponding cells of the right-hand column. The outcome of both of these rational choices is the upper left cell, where Row gets nothing while Column gets 5.

This outcome may seem manifestly unfair to Row, but there is no way for him to improve it without Column's cooperation. If the two can come to the bargaining table, the situation is different. For then Row can threaten Column with the possibility that he may choose R_2, where Column gets at most -1. To be sure, Row also stands to lose (whatever Column does) by choosing R_2, but, being in a position to threaten damage to Column, he may get Column to make a concession, namely to cede a portion of his gain. Note that in this situation it is apparently to Column's advantage *not* to come to the bargaining table, for without the opportunity to communicate his threat, Row cannot get Column to make a concession.

Assuming that Column is forced to bargain, game theory provides a 'solution' to this game, based on the relative bargaining positions of the two players, which, in turn, depends on 'what the players can do to each other if agreement is not reached.'

It turns out that, in the game represented by Matrix 4, Row is 'entitled' to 2 units out of the 5 that they two can jointly get. Row's bargaining position is weaker than Column's; he can threaten to cause a loss for both, but in repeated plays of this game it is *up to Column* to allow Row to get an occasional payoff of 5, which Column can do by switching his choice to C_2. There is no other way for Row to get the big payoff. It turns out that if Column chooses C_2 40 per cent of the time, it no longer pays Row to carry out his threat.

The method of calculating the 'compromise' is based on a number of assumptions. One is the assumption of symmetry. Although the bargaining positions of the players are different in this particular game, it is nevertheless assumed that *in principle* the players are equal in the sense that if their positions in the game were interchanged the game would have to have the same solution. This symmetry is analogous to 'equality before the law'. The verdict in a civil suit is not supposed to depend on *who* is the plaintiff and who the defendant but only on the merits of their respective cases.

Another fundamental assumption underlying the solutions of this sort is 'non-comparability of utilities.' This assumption amounts to saying that the 'solution' of a two-person bargaining game should be independent both of the unit in which the payoffs of either are expressed and of the zero point to which the payoffs are referred. This independence, in turn, implies that it makes no sense to add the payoffs of the two players. (If one does not know whether two lengths are measured in the same units, the 'sum' of the two numbers representing the lengths has no meaning.)

The third fundamental assumption is that the solution of the bargaining game must be such that *both* players cannot do better in that game. This amounts to saying that the players are 'collectively rational'. For if they are and can coordinate their choices so that *both* can do better, they will.

The final assumption is called 'independence from irrelevant alternatives'. This means roughly that if the game is enlarged by adding more outcomes – which, however, do not affect the threats that the players can make against each other nor offer solutions better for both players – then the original solution should not be affected.

It turns out that these four assumptions prescribe a unique solution to every bargaining game of the sort described.[4]

Now, if these assumptions were satisfied in real life and if every two-party conflict could be defined by specifying precisely the outcomes available to each party, along with the utilities of the outcomes to each, then the problem of resolving any such conflict could be solved, provided only that the rationality of the players would involve a commitment to a 'reasonable' solution, one that takes into account the relative power of the parties as reflected in their bargaining positions. It goes without saying, however, that hardly any of the four assumptions, reasonable as they appear, are often satisfied in real-life conflicts.

In real-life situations the symmetry of the players cannot be assumed, because how the players *define* themselves is often a substantial issue of the conflict. Many conflicts are asymmetric and structure-oriented and cannot be represented by a symmetric issue-oriented model.

Comparison of utilities of different players – a factor excluded in the game-theoretic solution – is sometimes at the very root of conceptions of social justice and thus of real-life conflicts. The vaguely stated principle of social welfare, 'the greatest good to the greatest number', involves the assumption that what may be a small sacrifice for some may insure a large benefit for others and is therefore justified.

In life, conflicting parties are all too often observed to be quite unable or unwilling to take action of benefit to both, or to eschew action detrimental to both.

Violations of the 'irrelevant alternatives' principle are repeatedly observed in elections offering more than two candidates, where the weakest candidate by his mere presence on the ballot may influence the outcome, even though the possibility of his being elected had never come into consideration.

From the point of view of the practising decision maker, the most crushing indictment of the game-theoretic approach to conflict resolution is that it is seldom possible to even define the conflict as a game without over-simplifying it beyond recognition. The range of actions available to each party seldom can be specified precisely, and it is even more difficult to assign numerical payoff values to outcomes, especially intangible ones involving prestige, future prospects, etc.

Still, in my opinion, this particular criticism of the game-theoretic approach misses the point. The purpose of formulating an issue-oriented conflict as a game *is not that of resolving the conflict by 'solving the game'*. It is that of *displaying the structure of the conflict* and thereby exposing features of it that may be concealed by rhetoric. In particular, appreciation of the peculiar structure of some of the so-called mixed-motive conflicts represented by non-zerosum games may change the conflicting parties' perception of their situation.

The most serious shortcoming of the game-theoretic approach to conflict resolution lies, I believe, elsewhere. First, because game-theoretic formulations often presuppose an audience of decision makers (rather than arbitrators), the emphasis tends to be on 'how to bargain effectively' rather than on 'how issue-oriented conflicts can be resolved'. The jacket of Fisher's book (illustrated by Robert C. Osborn) shows a fencer with a carrot attached to his foil. The book is distinctly a how-to-do-it book addressed to negotiators. The chapter titles reflect the orientation: 'Think First About Their Decision'; 'Give Them a Yesable Proposition'; 'Improve What Happens to Them if They are Good'; 'Make the Most of Legitimacy', etc.

A frankly strategic approach to techniques of negotiation must ultimately become self-defeating, because, in suggesting how to gain advantages in a bargaining situation, it suggests also how to resist the stratagems. As a result, on another level, bargaining tends toward a zerosum game.

This 'degradation' of the bargaining process has been carried to extremes by some professional strategists who serve the military establishment. Some of these students of conflict seem to be fascinated by blackmail as a key to diplomatic success. Both the offensive and the defensive uses of blackmail are discussed at length in the literature on diplomilitary strategy. The offensive techniques are those of demonstrating to the opponent that your threats are made in earnest. For example, Kahn's 'exemplary' nuclear attack of limited scope has the purpose of convincing the enemy that you will not shrink from taking ultimate measures. (The practice of sending the kidnap victim's severed finger to the family has a similar purpose.) Another way of demonstrating 'resolve' is to convince the opponent that you could not renege on the threats even if you wanted to, because the matter is no longer in your hands. The so-called Doomsday Machine has been suggested (perhaps facetiously, but one can't be sure) as a device of diplomacy designed to do just that. The Doomsday Machine is a cache of nuclear explosives buried on the territory of its possessor. Since it need not be airlifted, there is no limit to its size. It can be big enough to blow up the planet. The machine is programed to explode upon the receipt of a pre-set signal; for instance, the disturbance resulting from a nuclear explosion on the territory of the possessor or, for that matter, *any* disturbance associated with some act prohibited to the enemy. The effectiveness of this device depends on the inability of the possessor to deactivate it. Attempts at deactivation automatically explode the machine, so that it is immune even to the enemy's conquest of the territory on which it is located. Likewise, the possessor of the Doomsday Machine is immune to attempts to intimidate him into deactivating it.[5]

An effective defense against blackmail is denying to the blackmailer the opportunity to communicate his threat (cf. p. 232). In this way, the *blocking* of communication channels is presented as a negotiating strategy. As with any other stratagem, this one can, of course, be readily learned and adopted by the opponent, with dubious effect on the efficacy of 'bargaining' as a method of conflict resolution.

The other shortcoming of the game-theoretic approach to conflict resolution is that preoccupation with it may obfuscate rather than clarify the structure of the conflict. As explained on p. 234, the non-zerosum model of conflict, while it may serve to point out the areas of common interest among the participants, seeks to present the conflict as issue-oriented. It is not equipped to analyze asymmetric, structure-oriented conflicts where the actual 'issue' is neither the conflicting nor coincident interests of the conflicting parties, but the *structure of the system* in which they are immersed.[6] Thus, a revolt of slaves against their status as slaves cannot be 'settled' by a compromise whereby the slaves are accorded better treatment, or whatever. Once the *structure of the system* becomes the real issue, offers of this sort will be seen only as attempts to preserve the structure and will be rejected as long as the revolt can be sustained.

To take another example, the opponents of capital punishment will categorically reject all proposals to make executions more 'humane', to allow the condemned more 'privileges', etc. Issues like slavery and capital punishment simply cannot be settled by compromises. They touch upon the very *existence* of the challenged institutions, not on the way they function. From the point of view of an abolitionist (whatever the institution he seeks to destroy), 'improvements' only make matters worse because they may render the offending institution more acceptable to some. There are, then, conflicts where refusal to settle by compromise is not always an 'unreasonable' position, because the impossibility of compromise is inherent in the very nature of the conflict.

Finally, preoccupation with strategic thinking – the mode associated with the 'rational manipulation of the environment' – often blocks the formulation of conflicts on the genuine level of debates, where the object of a party to the conflict is to effect a change in the perception of the *opponent* (rather than of an audience). An effective debate presupposes a common set of values and a core area of agreement, and, further, the willingness to analyze the sources of the disagreement. Often such analysis leads to the discovery of areas of ignorance in one or both opponents; of different assignments of weights to the same facts; of different hypotheses concerning the consequences of actions, etc. In this way, a genuine debate frequently leads both parties to new insights and possibly to a synthesis of their apparently opposite positions.

Debates on scientific questions, when properly conducted, are of this sort. In areas of knowledge where deduction is rigorous (in the exact sciences, for example), resolution by synthesis is always possible. In mathematics it is inevitable: every debate about a mathematical question must end either in concession by one side or in a recognition of errors on the part of both. Therefore, in scientific debates so-called forensic techniques are utterly useless. To what extent genuine debate can be extended to conflicts involving values is an open question. But it is almost certain that some debate-like conflicts could be lifted to the level of genuine debates if it were not for the deeply ingrained habit among symbol manipulators of viewing all conflicts as tests of shrewdness, considered a major virtue in the world of internalized competition.

It remains to consider the systemic approach to conflict, subsumed under so-called peace research. This approach is based on the assumption that war is an affliction that now and then descends on portions of the human race. The 'problem of war' appears here analogous to the 'problem of disease', with which medical science has coped fairly successfully. The analogy suggests that 'the problem of war' could be 'solved' if enough research were done on the etiology of war; for, then, prophylactic or therapeutic measures could be designed on the basis of reliable knowledge, quite as prophylactic and therapeutic measures against diseases were developed on the basis of research in biochemistry, bacteriology, physiology, etc.

Richardson (cf. p. 159), one of the pioneers of peace research, in his *Statistics of Deadly Quarrels*, calculated statistical correlations between indices of severity of wars, on the one hand, and a large selection of other indices, some pertaining to individual conflicting units, some to relations between them, such as the existence or non-existence of a common language, a common religion, etc.[7] It is noteworthy that hardly any of the indices examined by Richardson could be shown to be related to either the incidence or the severity of wars. The one possible exception is that the influence of a common government on conflicting groups is a pacifying one, a finding that could be expected on common-sense grounds. The principal value of Richardson's negative results in this area is that many other presumed 'correlates of war' also turned out not to be correlates at all, either as facilitators or as inhibitors of war.

Further researches on the 'correlates' of wars and other conflicts have been undertaken by several authors.[8] The findings reveal no *outstanding* correlates. Thus, if one does not wish to conclude that war is a purely random phenomenon (that is, give up the search for correlates), one must assume that the 'causes of war' (if they can be talked of at all) are exceedingly complex. This conclusion should surprise no one who takes the analogy between war and disease seriously. An attempt to single out 'correlates of disease' by a statistical analysis would surely produce a similarly fruitless result.

A somewhat more promising approach is that of recording the time course of some index in periods immediately preceding crises or wars. Armament budgets, studied by Richardson, have already been mentioned. Other indices, directly related to the symbolic environment, have been singled out by a method called *content analysis*. The idea is to examine the statistical profile of the verbal outputs of communication media, diplomatic exchanges, and such sources, with special attention to frequencies or intensities of words, phrases, and statements that reflect the level of hostility of the entire system. The reading of these indices is somewhat analogous to taking the temperature of a patient or the bacterial count of the water supply or the pollution index of the atmosphere or the meteorological indicators of a gathering storm.[9]

The purpose of all these readings might be to take advantage of warning signals in initiating proper measures to avert a danger. Extending the notion to include indicators of departures in the international system from a steady state is motivated by the hope that, once the significance of the indices as warning signals is established, appropriate measures can be taken to prevent an international catastrophe. Whether this hope is well-founded depends, of course, on the existence of appropriate agencies or institutions empowered to undertake the necessary measures, and on the efficacy of the measures. In the medical setting, the institutions exist – medical services, public health agencies, etc. Natural phenomena, like storms, earthquakes, etc., usually cannot be averted, but their disastrous consequences can be avoided by due regard to warning signals, again because appropriate social organizations exist. Moreover, even if effective measures are not known, in some cases institutions exist ready to apply the results of research in creating such measures. For instance, if the long-awaited cure for leukemia should be discovered, therapeutic procedures would be very quickly established in medical practice; improved methods of fighting fires are constantly being adopted by municipal fire departments, etc.

The question before us is, where are the institutions empowered to take appropriate measures if a 'cure for war' is ever discovered? There have been attempts to create such institutions, such as the League of Nations, the World Court, the Security Council of the United Nations, etc., but their power to avert or stop wars has on most occasions been shown to be grossly inadequate. It has been so far impossible to increase their power because this can be done only by curtailing the power, indeed, the autonomy, of national states, including, of course, that of the Great Powers wherein the greatest war-making potential is concentrated. Moreover, all these supra-national bodies were created with the express proviso that the sovereignty of at least the Great Powers shall remain sacrosanct, as reflected in the unanimity rule governing the decisions of the Security Council. As long as the 'security' of the Great Powers is equated with autonomy, and autonomy with military might, it is hardly realistic to expect the existing supra-national bodies to exercise a significant stabilizing control over the international system, even if systemic peace research produces reliable knowledge about how such control can be exercised.

In sum, while conflict management and peace research may contribute to the solution of the formidable problems posed by conflict in man-made environment, both are subject to severe limitations.

Conflict management in the sphere of structural conflicts (cf. p. 176) is of questionable effectiveness, because in focusing on specific issues it ignores the deeper underlying sources of such conflicts – the structure of the situation itself. Conflict management is somewhat analogous to the treatment of the symptoms of a disease rather than of the conditions in which the disease is rooted. Further, the notion that some conflicts may be *necessary* to remove the underlying causes is beyond the conceptual scope of conflict management. Techniques of conflict management may be effective where misconceptions or irrelevant commitments exacerbate a conflict that is predominantly issue-oriented and can be settled to the satisfaction of both parties, in the sense that the settlement is preferable to continuation of the conflict to both (or all) of the conflicting parties. A genuinely neutral arbitrating or conciliating agency is essential in such cases.[10] Conflict management undertaken by one of the parties (especially the dominant one in an asymmetric structural conflict) amounts to no more than a utilization of stratagems, quickly recognized as such. In this context, it is likely to be counter-productive.

The most important achievement of peace (or conflict) research so far has been to establish a field of inquiry where war is examined as a phenomenon instead of a skill, as it appears in the work of 'military scientists'. In his monumental work, Quincy Wright[11] presented the first comprehensive study about war on the global and historical scale. The avowed ultimate goal of peace research is to uncover the 'causes of wars', so as to enable man to throw off the curse of perpetual self-inflicted destruction. The limitation of peace research so conceived is in the circumstance that there are no institutions empowered to make use of the knowledge about 'causes of wars' in the way medical institutions make use of knowledge about the causes of disease. If and when such institutions come into being, the frequently cited analogy between peace research and medical research will be more justifiable.

Peace research could even now play a major role with regard to war if knowledge about conditions directly related to the organization and conduct of wars (for instance, the very existence of war-making institutions and of the interests served by them) were made available to ever-widening publics. Then this knowledge might modify the semantic environment that perpetuates the popular support or the legitimacy of war-making institutions and of the social, economic, and political systems that have brought them into being.

In other words, as long as war continues to be institutionalized, the most valuable result of peace research would be a change in the conception of war, from that of a political instrument or a natural catastrophe or a disease to that of organized crime.

CHAPTER 21

Prospects

Men of good will, tempered by a sense of political realism, insist that proposals for change should be addressed to actors who are in a position to make the changes and that the proposed changes should be of the sort that can be at least considered by decision makers. I agree that any proposed action should be addressed to an actor who is empowered to undertake it and who perceives the outcomes to be in accord with his interests, values, or commitments. I part company with the 'political realists' by rejecting the assumption that proposals for actions should be tailored to the needs and perceptions of *presently* effective actors – the power figures and the power institutions of our day. For such accommodation means a tacit acceptance of, in fact a reinforcement of, the currently dominant values, perceptions, and social roles. Such acceptance detracts attention and energies from the central problem presented by power conflicts which, in the present man-made environment, degrade the quality of human life and threaten man's very existence.

Consider the 'five steps for world change' proposed by U Thant, then Secretary General of the United Nations, an organization theoretically dedicated to the interests of mankind as a whole.

1. The world must radically change from the present course of national divisions and antagonisms to a course of common concern and unity of purpose.

2. Membership in the United Nations should be universal. All qualified nations should be part of a world-wide system of security and solidarity.

3. Claims to exclusiveness of political and social systems (that is, of exclusive possession of truth, principles of social justice, etc.) must be abandoned. 'No rigid system, however well established on a few sacrosanct principles, is able to cope with all the problems of our diverse, complex and constantly changing society.'

4. Cooperation should replace confrontation between the two super-powers, the United States and the Soviet Union.

5. Total man should be nourished 'not only by material aspirations but deeply entrenched in morality, tolerance, unselfishness and understanding for his fellow men.'[1]

Prescriptions of this sort entail much more than the design and execution of programs. They entail a radical change in the *perceptions* of values, system boundaries, and social roles. The perceptions of people in positions of power and of those who serve power in professional capacities are especially difficult to change, not only because the prerogatives of power are not easily relinquished but also because people in power are often convinced that in exercising power they are discharging awesome responsibilities. The absolute monarchs of the Christian world typically saw themselves as the executors of Divine Will. The Spaniards, while enslaving the Indians of the Americas, also baptized them, intending thereby to save them from eternal damnation. Colonial conquests of the nineteenth century were represented as civilizing missions. Contemporary colonial wars are advertised as 'defense of freedom'.

To what extent the policy makers fall for their own pitch in specific instances is hard to say. The practice of *realpolitik*, while sometimes requiring a smoke screen in the face of hostile public opinion, need not be 'ethically' justified in private councils of decision-making. However, in matters of ideology and of 'national defense', the power elites probably do see themselves as guardians of welfare and security.

In defending corporate capitalism, for example, U.S. policy makers are quick to point out that the highest 'standard of living' in the world was first achieved in the most capitalist society of all. They will insist that the 'exploitation of labor by capital' has long been supplanted by a partnership between the two. To extend the notion of 'exploitation' to the deliberate stimulation of appetites for whatever is marketed (regardless of the effects of such stimulation on the physical or mental health of the 'targets') requires a different perception of man and his needs. The 'market model' of democracy precludes such a perception.

Likewise, the defender of the Soviet political system will vehemently deny the existence of 'exploitation' in the U.S.S.R. on the grounds that exploitation results from private ownership of the means of production and that, therefore, the abolition of the latter has automatically terminated the former. To extend the meaning of exploitation to include the imposition of a uniform ideology (for easier manipulation of the masses) requires a different perception of autonomy, incompatible with the perceived historical mission of the 'first socialist state'.

The professional serving the military establishment, whether or not he wears a uniform, may be genuinely convinced that a reduction of military 'capability' would jeopardize the 'security' of the country. If pressed, he may admit that the only justification for the existence of a military machine with a genocidal potential is the existence of another such machine. To face the question of what justifies the existence of *both* machines is to answer it: military establishments provide justification for their existence by reference to their own existence. The answer reduces the military profession to a monstrous absurdity. It is not easy to see oneself in the service of absurdity.

The central obstacle, therefore, to the 'steps to world change' proposed by U Thant, and reflecting the aspirations of millions, is the practical impossibility of changing the perceptions of those in whom the power to make such changes is concentrated. The impossibility stems from the very condition of entrenched power maintained by the symbolic environment, the source of 'legitimacy' of the existing power institutions.

In a way, the problem is a recurrent one. It has been repeatedly 'solved' throughout history in the sense that long-established 'legitimacy' of power structures dissolved when the symbolic environment changed so that it could no longer nurture their 'legitimacy'. It is not, therefore, unreasonable to expect that the present centers of power will also eventually lose their legitimacy.

The question is how this loss of legitimacy can come about. In the past, entrenched power elites were ousted by defeat either in war, or by armed uprisings led by newly emerging power elites. War, having become what it is, can no longer be viewed as a precursor of a welcome 'new era'. Recent historical experience with elite-led revolutions indicates, first, that they require a large following driven to desperation by deprivation and oppression (a condition not met in 'advanced' societies); second, that the consequences of entrenched power are not eliminated thereby.

Perhaps, instead of being overthrown and supplanted by other power, entrenched power can be eroded. The most brutal power depends, in the last analysis, on the prevalent conviction that it is 'legitimate'. Even usurped power supported by terror is effective only because of an internalized belief that might is right. Erosion of power occurs when it no longer evokes awe or loyalty or admiration or a vicarious superiority; when it begins to elicit repugnance and, above all, contempt.

The ferment now pervading the 'advanced' societies is indicative of just such changes in attitudes toward power. The ferment is not of the sort that can crystalize into a countervailing power base so as to bring another 'class' to the top of the social pyramid 'to organize society in accordance with its interests', as the Marxists picture social revolutions. Nor is it confined to the neglected and the dispossessed. It pervades also the materially comfortable strata, especially the vastly expanded university student populations, where, in spite of factional rivalries and doctrinaire fixations, there is agreement on one damning charge against the 'establishment' – that preparation for participation in the social 'mainstream' destroys the autonomy of human beings. And they are right. The 'mass' states, both the 'democratic' and the authoritarian variety, have rendered meaningless the autonomy of human beings by destroying the 'intermediate authorities' (cf. Tocqueville's prophecy, p. 93) that bind people into communities. The 'pluralism' of American society, glorified by the ideologues of market-place democracy, has substituted corporate units and 'interest groups' for communities.[2] At the other extreme, Soviet bureaucracy suspects treason in every inclination of a citizen that can conceivably be construed as a challenge to the hegemony of prescribed social organization or prescribed State ideology.

It is this persistent, at times desperate, at times pathetic, search for a basis of autonomy that has been dubbed the 'alienation' of the young. Because there is no satisfactory model to emulate, the 'alienated' young grope for a life style and are sometimes driven to escapism, hedonism, nihilism.[3] Distrust of organization and of the discipline it involves prevents them from becoming a political force to be reckoned with. Nevertheless, if disdain for power, the refusal either to strive for it or to submit to it, is indeed the common denominator of the 'revolt of the young', they may yet contribute significantly to the erosion of entrenched power in two ways.

First, the self-assurance of elites depends in no small measure on the guaranteed availability of replacement cadres, the modern analogue of dynastic continuity. Although the 'alienation' of a sector of youth has not seriously depleted the pool of recruits, numerically speaking, it has 'polluted' that pool. In the United States, for example, it is no longer true as could formerly be assumed (accurately or not) that the *entire* young generation aspires to the presidency or to affluence or to respectable professional status or to officialdom. In many cases, the rejection by the young of the standard ambitions seriously impairs the self-esteem of the high and mighty, as when they experience it within their families. Thereby, the self-image of the elites – an important component of power – is tarnished.

Second, the new climate provides a basis for changing alignments throughout the world, cutting across the old bonds of loyalty or conformity. The emerging alignments are of the powerless against the powerful. Brutal onslaughts by entrenched power, be they against the helpless Vietnamese, Bengalis, or Czechs, ignite outbursts of indignation in the United States, in Western Europe, and in Japan. They nurture seeds of doubt (or cynicism) in authoritarian states, where the self-assurance of the elites depends on the perpetuation of a monolithic ideology.

Specific effectiveness of this sort of erosion is difficult to estimate, but it has certainly contributed to the malaise of the power elites. The failure of the U.S. intervention in Southeast Asia was as much the result of domestic opposition as of the dogged resistance of the Vietnamese. The 'collective decision' to invade Czechoslovakia is said to have passed by a single vote, a situation unthinkable under Stalin's autocracy. A repetition of Vietnam, say, in Brazil, or of Czechoslovakia, say, in Roumania, appears highly unlikely.[4]

To forecast long-run effects is equally difficult. Marx could project a 're-organization of human society' because for him the history of human society was essentially the history of Western Europe. Present-day 'futurologists' think in global terms; yet, characteristically, they single out special aspects of the 'future'. The following 'problems' were offered for consideration at a conference sponsored by the American

Academy of Arts and Sciences in 1966[5]: the inadequacy of existing government institutions for dealing with radical social change; population density and its effects; the structure of intellectual and educational institutions; the control of natural and human environment; the problem of leisure, a consequence of supplanting human labor (both physical and mental) by machines; the state of the international system.

Contemporary differences in the visions of the future stem from different conceptions of ways to deal with these problems. There is a sharp division between two camps. One includes the technocrats, accustomed to seek technical solutions to problems posed by existing authorities, without reference to their far-reaching implications. Thinking in this camp is governed by the conviction that the 'problems' with which humanity is faced, including those attendant on conflict in man-made environment, can be dealt with adequately within the existing frameworks of power and authority. The other camp includes those who maintain that the technocrats are concerned with the wrong problems. The central problem, the opponents of technocracy insist, is not how to get more of everything nor even how to use power 'rationally' to realize goals inherited from the past. The problem is how to set *new* goals, wherein the quality of human life is central. These sharp critics of continued reliance on 'techniques' insist that a radical re-examination of basic values is imperative if civilization or even mankind is to have a future at all.

This ideological conflict is rapidly growing in prominence. It cuts across the old lines of 'free enterprise' versus 'planned society'; technocrats serve both 'capitalist' and 'socialist' establishments while most of their opponents accept neither a market economy nor central planning as a basis for re-organizing society. Unlike the technocrats, the latter do not address themselves to carefully selected problems that can in principle be solved within existing institutional structures. Their aim is to effect radical changes of perception as a prerequisite to *posing* problems they consider relevant.[6]

If the 'new humanism' is to emerge as a positive ideology (not merely a critique of existing ideologies and practices), two dilemmas must be resolved. The first concerns the 'dialectic opposition' between autonomy and cooperation; the other resides in the opposition between man as a molder of nature and man as a part of nature.

The first opposition is not the familiar one between 'freedom of the individual' and 'the demands of organized society'. The boundary of the autonomous unit is not fixed in the human psyche. At times it has appeared to be the individual, as in the flowering of the Renaissance or as in the contemporary 'liberal' outlook. But these are only particular manifestations of aspirations to autonomy. At other times and in different cultures the 'natural' boundary of the Self was not that of the individual but of various types of human groups. If the 'new humanism' is concerned with the extension of autonomy and with protecting it against entrenched power, then the autonomy of all groups that clamor for it must be recognized and supported. This presents problems, because wherever there is awareness of Self, there is also awareness of Other. Inclusion implies exclusion. Realization of autonomy all too frequently leads to aspirations of self-aggrandizement and so to destructive conflicts. We can expect, for example, that in consequence of 'nation-building' in Africa, rivers of blood will flow in senseless wars both 'internal' (suppressing rival domestic autonomies) and 'external' in emulation of erstwhile European masters.

Apparently, the solution to the autonomy-cooperation dilemma lies in nurturing multiple identifications. Personal autonomy *need* not conflict with devotion to family, with identification with community, with a culture, with humanity, or with nature. In addition to these 'concentric' identifications, 'cross-identifications' should be nurtured, that is, with like-minded persons or communities far removed on other dimensions. The world scientific community, indifferent to national, religious, or cultural barriers, is a conspicuous example. Exclusive identification (egocentrism, ethnocentrism, nationalism) breeds strife, in the course of which autonomy is starved rather than nurtured. It is characteristic of tyranny to demand exclusive identification with a power system, typically a State.[7]

The other dialectical opposition is between controlling the non-human environment and living in harmony with it. Here it is not a question of fratricidal strife within mankind or of the dehumanization of humanity in the rarefied atmosphere of global strategies. The question is whether the broadening Self can reach beyond Man. The poisoning of the environment by the works of man has become a burning issue of our day, and the wielders of power have hastily and nervously acknowledged the 'problem'. What is required, however, is not just putting filters on car exhausts, stopping the testing of nuclear bombs in the atmosphere, or cleaning up the lakes, rivers, and seas. These are 'safeguards' like the 'safeguards' put on weapons systems. What is more fundamentally involved is the curbing of man's power appetite, the abandonment of man's arrogant self-image as the lord of creation.

There is a crucial distinction between the right to autonomy and the appetite for power. When a craftsman masters his materials, he exercises his autonomy. He does not destroy the autonomy of another as he creates organization out of a lump of matter. The urge to create is as inherent to the human psyche as the urge to use language, and it *must* manifest itself in the modification of man's environment. As cooperating units become larger, the modification of the environment becomes necessarily more pervasive. The process is irreversible, because the modified environment can support more people; as more people populate the earth, they come to depend on the modified environment that can support them. The anti-technocrats, appalled at the evils accompanying the sprawling growth of technology and its ugly excreta, condemn it in the same terms that pacifists condemn the burgeoning weapons systems. Yet, while dismantling the weapons systems can do no harm except to entrenched power, dismantling the supportive technology of production and communication *must* reduce the population dependent on it, and such reduction would most likely be traumatic (through plagues, starvation, etc.) In other words, the 'withdrawal symptoms' may be fatal.

Even if modification of the environment brought about by technology could be reversed comparatively painlessly, the reversal would entail a contracting of the boundaries of cooperating units and, hence, a narrowing of identification. For all the harm it has done, megatechnology nevertheless represents cooperation on a scale unprecedented in history. To be sure, many anti-technocrats, distrustful of large-scale social organizations, might welcome the narrowing of boundaries of autonomy and identification. At the same time, however, they yearn for the *extension* of Self boundaries to include the non-human environment, and sometimes hold up pre-industrial man as a model – the modern version of the eighteenth-century Noble Savage.

The Self of pre-industrial man may have included the natural environment in his vicinity, but it definitely did not include human groups other than his own (mostly kin). The Noble Savage probably massacred his fellow men as ruthlessly as we do. He just lacked the means to do it on so grand a scale.

The fault is not in the extension of the boundaries of cooperative systems, which necessitate an expanding technology. The fault is in the consolidation of power, whereby not the boundaries of the autonomous Self but the boundaries of a conquered domain are extended. Uncouple the growth of the Self from the growth of power, and the contradiction between creative modification of the environment and living in peace with nature will disappear. There is no reason why technology (as such), even on the grandest scale, cannot be an extension of the craftsman's or the artist's creativity and so be in harmony with human autonomy.

The crucial question is whether the need for autonomy and the appetite for power *can* be separated, so that the former can be nurtured while the latter can be curbed. Anthony Storr sees the two drives as the manifestation of 'aggression' under different conditions. Aggression (shorn of the component of hostility) is, in his view,

... necessary for development, for separateness, for the achievement of differentiation ... [but] Competitive aggressiveness ... is characteristic of immaturity ... Aggressiveness is at its maximum when dependence (and hence inequality) is at its maximum; as development proceeds it becomes less important till, at the point of maximum development, only so much aggression exists as is necessary to maintain the personality as a separate entity.[8]

Transposed to the level of humanity, this would mean that man's destructive aggressiveness against nature may be a manifestation of a need to assert his autonomy in the immature stage of humanity. When man's autonomy is fully established, that is, as his capacities have become more fully realized, only so much 'aggression' may be expected to remain as is needed to guarantee the maintenance of the human race as an autonomous entity. (In system-theoretic terminology, this would mean to maintain a steady state.)

On the other hand, the same author, addressing the problem of providing 'substitutes for war', is disturbed by the prospect of 'millenniary pacifism'.

The affluent society cushions us against hunger, against disease, against destruction, and in doing so deprives us of any opportunity to test ourselves to the limit, to struggle or to die . . . To wait until senile decrepitude puts an end to one's protracted plush existence is not necessarily an agreeable prospect.[9]

No less important than the distinction between autonomy and power is the distinction between pacific equilibrium (or 'millenniary pacifism', as Storr calls it) and steady state. Isolated systems tend toward thermodynamic equilibrium in which all gradients have disappeared and nothing else happens (cf. p. 29). Open systems (as all living systems are on whatever level of organization) are maintained in a steady state only by constant activity. As Lewis Carroll's Red Queen says, 'it takes all the running you can do to stay in the same place.' The achievement of a steady state on this planet, which must include all of nature, will require effort, knowledge, and cooperation on a scale far larger than what has been mobilized to conquer (or rape) nature. It takes more technical knowledge, not less, to provide for the restoration of the natural environment as nourishment and energy are extracted from it. And it takes more organization, not less, to do so on the global scale.

The formidable dilemmas posed by conflict in man-made environment, whether of man against man or of man against nature, are rooted in the widespread failure to distinguish between autonomy and power. By denying autonomy to others – human beings or even to other living things (on the scale of the entire biosphere) – the unbridled appetite for power strangles what is *human*. Therefore, if Man's uniqueness is embodied in his *awareness* of his autonomy as the most precious gift of evolution, men must address themselves to the task of dismantling the fortresses of entrenched power.

NOTES

1. The So-Called Struggle for Existence

1. Jean Baptiste Lamarck (1744–1829) stated the 'law' of inheritance of acquired characteristics in his *Histoire naturelle des animaux sans vertèbres* published in 1815: 'All that has been acquired, laid down, or changed in the organization of individuals in their life is conserved by generation and transmitted to the new individuals which proceed from those which have undergone those changes.' As for the origin of the changes, Lamarck supposed them to result 'from the supervention of a new want [*besoin*] continuing to make itself felt . . .' George Bernard Shaw, whose ideas about biology were not influenced by evidence, dramatized Lamarck's ideas in his play *Back to Methuselah*.

2. 'Population control' in nature is not confined to such external constraints. There are also constraints internal to the species. For example, increase of the density of a population in relation to the available food supply may decrease the number of young surviving and may even, through some psychological mechanism, itself a product of natural selection, modify the behavior patterns of the organisms so as to decrease fecundity. Perhaps the periodic 'mass suicide' of the lemmings is an instance of such control. Whatever be the nature of the constraints, we see in them the operation of an important system property – *negative feedback*. It is the type of control exercised by the governor of a steam engine. If the engine runs too fast, the centrifugal force of the flywheel lifts a jacket that reduces the inflow of steam to the cylinders, thus reducing the speed, which, in turn, increases the flow of the steam. This kind of built-in, seemingly 'automatic self-control' is called a 'homeostatic control'. The principle of homeostasis is discussed in detail in Chapter 2.

3. From Tropism to Behavior

1. Jack P. Hailman, 'How an Instinct is Learned', *Scientific American* 221, 6 (1969), pp. 98–106.

2. 'The architectural nest is simply a more permanent expression of

living activity gradients and its morphological attributes enable us to detect the results of the dynamic physiological events more readily.' A. Emerson, 'Social Coordination and the Superorganism', *American Midland Naturalist* 21 (1939), pp. 182–209.

4. Learning

1. Demonstrated by B. F. Skinner and his laboratory assistants in an educational film, viewed 1963 at the Institute for Programmed Learning, Ann Arbor, Michigan. Professor Skinner and his colleagues also 'taught' a pigeon to bowl during a lull while they were doing war-time research (1943). This episode is recounted in B. F. Skinner, *Cumulative Record* (New York: Appleton-Century-Crofts, enlarged edition, 1961), p. 132. See also, in this same work, Part VIII, '"Superstition" in the Pigeon', pp. 404–12, and 'How to Teach Animals', pp. 412–19.

5. From Signal to Symbol

1. Again exceptions have been noted. Monkeys have been taught to peel potatoes, and there is evidence that they can transmit this skill to their young. Monkeys also give some evidence of understanding the rudiments of 'syntax', experienced through arrangements of colored blocks. In fact, the more we learn about the living world, the less justification there is for denying the continuity of the non-human and human psyches. Nevertheless, there is no denying the tremendous gap between non-human and human ways of life attributable directly, probably exclusively, to culture transmitted by symbolic language and thus acquiring its own evolutionary potential.

7. Evolution and Survival

1. J. Fisher, 'Interspecific Aggression', in *The Natural History of Aggression*, ed. J. D. Carthy and F. J. Ebling (London and New York: Academic Press, 1964), p. 12. Before the present geological period the 'longevities' of bird and mammal species were much greater. The shortened life span may be a reflection of accelerated evolution of these classes.

2. Various estimates are in essential correspondence with some minor differences. Sources: R. Thomlinson, *Population Dynamics* (New York: Random House, 1965); H. Kahn and A. J. Wiener, *The Year 2000* (New York: Macmillan, 1967); *Man's Impact on the Global Environment* (Cam-

bridge, Mass.: Massachusetts Institute of Technology Report, 1970).

3. '[H]uman beings possess a most remarkable capacity which is entirely peculiar to them – I mean the capacity to summarize, digest, and appropiate the labors and experiences of the past . . . to use the fruits of past labors and experiences as intellectual and spiritual capital for developments in the present . . . And because humanity . . . lives in the present . . . for the future, I define humanity . . . to be the time-binding class of life.' A. Korzybski, *Manhood of Humanity* (New York: E. P. Dutton, 1921).

4. G. G. Simpson, *The Meaning of Evolution* (New York: New American Library), Chapter 4.

5. It must be admitted that the idea of complex behavior patterns evolving by synthesis of simpler patterns is beset with difficulties. Suppose we conceive of 'nest building' as a composite of two patterns, picking up twigs and weaving them into the nest. It is difficult to imagine that birds of some species spent some thousands of years just picking up twigs until a mutation 'gave one of them the idea' of weaving a twig into the nest. On the other hand, in the evolution of scientific ideas something of this sort does seem to happen. The 'atomic' theory of Democritus and Lucretius and the 'monadic' theory of the Pythagoreans lay dormant for over two thousand years until it was formulated rigorously by Dalton in 1808 in the context of chemistry. By that time it was provided with the fertile soil of experimental chemistry, and sprouted. Whether anything analogous happens in biological evolution is an intriguing question.

6. N. Rashevsky has developed some mathematical models of such processes in *The Mathematical Biology of Social Behavior* (Chicago: University of Chicago Press, 1951), Chapters XI–XIII.

8. The Idea of Progress

1. The theorem that a young slave is led to 'demonstrate' (by answering Socrates' leading questions) is that the square on the diagonal of another square has an area twice that of the latter, a special case of the Pythagorean theorem. It is noteworthy that the only question which Socrates asks about the 'background' of this slave is whether he speaks Greek. (Cf. Plato, *Meno*.)

2. J. W. von Goethe, *Faust*, Part II, Act I, Scene II.

3. Here we interchange 'figure' and 'ground' (cf. p. 16), and man is pictured as the 'environment' of evolving artifacts. Note that man's 'perceived needs' are not necessarily survival-enhancing.

4. A. Comte, 'Plan of the Scientific Operations Necessary for Reorganizing Society', in *On Intellectuals*, ed. P. Rieff (Garden City, N.Y.: Doubleday & Co., 1969), pp. 255–6.

5. S. Amos, *Political and Legal Remedies for War* (London, Paris, New York: Cassell, Petter, Galpin & Co., 1880), pp. 6–7.

6. ibid., pp. 15–16.

7. ibid., p. 14.

8. ibid., p. 230.

9. A. Comte, op. cit., pp. 256–7.

10. A. de Tocqueville, *Democracy in America* (New York: Harper & Row, 1966), Vol. 1, p. 378.

9. *A Day in the Lives of Mr A and Mr Z*

1. A contributing factor to the rapprochement was the rise of Urania as a new military power hostile to both.

10. *The So-Called Aggressive Instinct*

1. Cathy Hayes, *The Ape in Our House* (New York: Harper & Bros., 1951). Since this effort was reported (1951), much progress has been achieved in 'teaching apes to talk'. A formidable difficulty is of purely anatomical nature. Apes do not have an efficient apparatus of oral articulation. The difficulty is by-passed by teaching them sign language, whereby they acquire a much larger 'vocabulary' than Viki, the chimpanzee adopted by Keith and Cathy Hayes. Nevertheless, a 'vocabulary' is not the same as a language with a syntax. Dogs have a vocabulary of signs. They assume clearly distinguishable postures that can be reasonably interpreted as 'Give me some of that' or 'I love you' or 'I suspect you' or even 'I am sorry!' What a dog cannot say, nor, to my knowledge, any non-human, is something like 'If you give me some of that, I shall love you; if not, you may be sorry.'

2. D. Freeman, 'Human Aggression in Anthropological Perspective', in *The Natural History of Aggression*, ed. J. D. Carthy and F. J. Ebling (London and New York: Academic Press, 1964), p. 115.

3. K. Lorenz, *On Aggression* (New York: Harcourt Brace & Co., 1966).

4. J. Fisher, 'Interspecific Aggression', in *The Natural History of Aggression*, op. cit.

5. P. H. T. Hartley, 'An Experimental Analysis of Interspecific Recognition', *Symposia Soc. Experim. Biol.*, *Cambridge* No. 4, pp. 313–36.

6. J. Fisher, op. cit.

7. The suggestiveness of the term 'war' may be seriously misleading here. An ant's responses to another ant seem to be rigidly mechanical and can be analyzed into stereotyped components, precluding any basis for assuming a planned course of action characteristic of human behavior. (Cf. D. I. Wallis, 'Aggressive Behavior in the Ant, *formica fusca*', *Animal Behavior* 10 (1962), pp. 105–111; 267–74.)

8. Cf. R. Ardrey, *The Territorial Imperative* (New York: Atheneum, 1966). The author goes so far as to relate the institution of property and nationalism to the 'instinct' for protecting territory (see pp. 103, 191).

9. Cf. *Animal Populations in Relation to Their Food Sources*, a Symposium of the British Ecological Society, Aberdeen, March 1969, ed. A. Watson (Oxford and Edinburgh: Blackwell Scientific Publications, 1970). In Part IV, General Discussion, see especially the remarks of V. C. Wynne-Edwards (p. 423) and A. Watson (p. 433). Also, D. E. Davis, 'The Role of Density in the Aggressive Behavior of House Mice', *Animal Behavior* 6 (1958), pp. 207–10.

10. Stanislaw Andreski, for example, points out that in 'every warlike polity . . . there are elaborate social arrangements which stimulate martial ardour by playing upon vanity, fear of contempt, sexual desire and fraternal attachment, loyalty to the group and other sentiments. It seems reasonable to suppose that if there was an innate propensity for war-making, such a stimulation would be unnecessary.' S. Andreski, 'Origins of War', in *The Natural History of Aggression*, op. cit., p. 130.

11. W. P. Gass, 'The Stylization of Desire', *New York Review of Books*, 25 February 1971.

12. 'Hate is not the opposite of love; apathy is . . . To live in apathy provokes violence [and] . . . Violence is the ultimate destructive substitute which surges in to fill the vacuum where there is not relatedness . . . When inward life dries up, when feeling decreases and apathy increases, when one cannot affect or even genuinely *touch* another person, violence flares up as a daimonic necessity for contact . . . To inflict pain and torture at least proves that one can affect somebody.' Rollo May, *Love and Will* (New York: W. W. Norton & Co., 1969), pp. 29–30.

11. Environmental Theories of Aggression

1. Like any other theory that enjoys at least temporary vitality, the environmental theory of psychological determinants contains a solid kernel

of truth. At least one important aspect of human behavior can be definitely said to be unrelated to biological make-up, namely the particular language learned by the child (cf. p. 171). The child will learn to speak the language or languages of his speech community regardless of his hereditary background, and the child growing up without other human beings will not learn to speak at all. The few recorded cases of so-called 'wolf children' (presumably abandoned and surviving for a few years in a wild state) corroborate this assertion. That the complete dependence of language behavior on learning was not always understood is evidenced by an experiment said to have been proposed by King Frederick II of Prussia. That amateur scholar assumed that a child deprived of speech stimuli would speak the 'original language of humanity', which Frederick supposed was either Hebrew or Greek. Accordingly, he is said to have ordered some babies to be reared in complete silence in order to find out which of these two languages they would start to speak.

2. The conception of behavior as 'responses to stimuli from the immediate environment' is an extension of the mechanistic point of view toward psychology (cf. p. 35).

3. E. B. McNeil, 'The Nature of Aggression', in *The Nature of Human Conflict*, ed. E. B. McNeil (Englewood Cliffs, N. J.: Prentice-Hall, 1965), p. 16.

4. ibid., p. 19; also Z. Y. Kuo, 'The Genesis of the Cat's Response to the Rat', *Journal of Comparative Psychology* 11 (1930), pp. 1–35.

5. J. P. Scott, *Aggression* (Chicago: University of Chicago Press, 1958).

6. J. Dollard *et al.*, *Frustration and Aggression* (New Haven: Yale University Press, 1939), p. 1.

7. ibid., pp. 1–2.

8. It is believed by some that frustration is not only unavoidable but essential to the maturation of self-hood: '. . . the frustration of finding that all wants are not immediately satisfied leads to the discovery that one is dependent upon others: the frustration of finding intransigent objects to the realization that one has physical limitations and that there is an external world with which one is not coexistent, and over which one's power is limited.' A. Storr, *The Integrity of the Personality* (Harmondsworth and Baltimore: Penguin Books, 1963), p. 81.

9. R. R. Sears and P. S. Sears, 'Minor Studies of Aggression: V. Strength of Frustration-Reaction as a Function of Strength of Drive', *Journal of Psychology* 9 (1940), pp. 291–300.

10. L. W. Doob and R. R. Sears, 'Factors Determining Substitute

Behavior and the Overt Expression of Aggression', *Journal of Abnormal and Social Psychology* 34 (1939), pp. 293–313.

11. N. E. Miller and R. Bugelski, 'Minor Studies of Aggression: II. The Influence of Frustration Imposed by the In-group on Attitudes Expressed Toward Out-groups', *Journal of Psychology* 225 (1948), pp. 437–42.

12. H. D. Lasswell, *Psychopathology and Politics* (Chicago: University of Chicago Press, 1930).

13. W. A. Bonger, *Criminality and Economic Conditions* (Boston: Little, Brown & Co., 1916), p. 517.

12. Systemic Theories: Hobbes, Hegel, Clausewitz

1. '. . . nothing the sovereign representative can do to a subject, on what pretense soever, can properly be called injustice or injury . . .' T. Hobbes, *Leviathan* (Oxford: Basil Blackwell, 1957), p. 139.

2. '. . . a man that is commanded as a soldier to fight against the enemy . . . may nevertheless . . . refuse, without injustice; as when he substituteth a sufficient soldier in his place . . . And there is allowance to be made for natural timorousness, not only to women, of whom no such dangerous duty is expected, but also to men of feminine courage.' ibid., pp. 142–3.

3. A favorite device of Korzybski was to invite his listeners to give a 'complete' description of an apple while he pointed out features they left out (cf. *Science and Sanity*, 2nd edition, Lancaster, Pa., and New York: International Non-Aristotelian Library Publishing Co., 1941, p. 471).

4. G. W. F. Hegel, *The Science of Logic* (London: George Allen & Unwin Ltd, 1929), Vol. II, Section 3, Chapter III.

5. Philosophers in search of 'certainty' were evidently profoundly disturbed by the ephemeral or 'contradictory' nature of 'appearances'. Some, like Hegel, resolved this tension by boldly proclaiming the identity of opposites. In this, Hegel was anticipated by Heraclitus of Ephesus (530–470 B.C.) who declared: 'The road going up and the road going down are one and the same thing. Good and evil are one and the same thing. Doctors who cut and burn ask for a fee for doing so.' Source: F. Enriques and G. De Santillana, *Storia del pensiero scientifico* (Milan and Rome, 1932), Vol. 1, pp. 64–9. Quoted in E. Carruccio, *Mathematics and Logic in History and in Contemporary Thought* (Chicago: Aldine Publishing Co., 1964), p. 23. In George Orwell's *Nineteen Eighty-Four*, this sort of 'dialectics' ('doublethink') is caricatured in the brutal slogans adorning the Ministries: 'Love is Hate'; 'Freedom is Slavery'; 'War is Peace'.

6. B. Russell, *History of Western Philosophy* (New York: Simon and Shuster, 1964), p. 784.

7. C. J. Friedrich, 'Introduction' to G. W. F. Hegel, *Philosophy of History* (New York: Dover Publications, 1956). Hegel expresses the pinnacle of perfection achieved by the German states thus: '... the formal principle of philosophy in Germany encounters a concrete real World in which Spirit finds inward satisfaction and in which conscience is at rest.' Hegel, op. cit., p. 444.

8. T. Hobbes, *Leviathan*, Part I, Chapter 4.

9. C. von Clausewitz, *On War* (Harmondsworth: Penguin Books Ltd, 1968), p. 101.

10. ibid., pp. 109–10.

11. ibid., p. 111.

13. Systemic Theories: Marx and Lenin

1. J. G. Fichte (1762–1814), one of the principal architects of the German idealist tradition in philosophy, an apostle of German nationalism during the Napoleonic Wars.

2. The central idea that emerges from Hegel's image of thought contemplating itself is that knowledge is a result not of a passive reception of stimuli from the outside world (as it appeared to British empiricists) but of inner tension arising from the clash of contradictions, an echo of Heraclitus's dictum, 'War is the father of all things.' John Dewey's 'instrumentalism', although expressed in altogether different context, is based on a similar idea.

3. K. Marx, *A Contribution to the Critique of Political Economy* (Chicago: C. H. Kerr, 1913), pp. 11–13.

4. K. Marx and F. Engels, *Manifesto of the Communist Party* (New York: International Publishers, 1934).

5. 'The State is the product and the manifestation of the *irreconcilability* of class antagonisms. The State arises when, where, and to the extent that the class antagonisms *cannot* be objectively reconciled. And, conversely, the existence of the State proves that the class antagonisms *are* irreconcilable.' V. I. Lenin, *The State and Revolution*, Collected Works, Vol. 21 (New York: International Publishers, 1932), p. 154 (emphasis in the original).

6. V. I. Lenin, *Imperialism, The Highest Stage of Capitalism* (London: Martin Lawrence Ltd, 1933), p. 7.

7. ibid., p. 10.
8. ibid., p. 75.
9. ibid., p. 125.
10. ibid., pp. 13–14.

14. Systemic Theories: Richardson and Kahn

1. A stochastic process is a mathematical model of a system that passes from state to state (cf. p. 36) in accordance with some 'law' governed by probabilities.

2. L. F. Richardson, *Statistics of Deadly Quarrels* (Pittsburgh: The Boxwood Press; Chicago: Quadrangle Books, 1960), pp. 114–19.

3. An illuminating discussion of the distribution of group sizes is found in J. E. Cohen, *Casual Groups of Monkeys and Men* (Cambridge, Mass.: Harvard University Press, 1971). See also J. S. Coleman and J. James, 'The Equilibrium Size Distribution of Freely Forming Groups', *Sociometry* 24 (1961), pp. 36–45; W. J. Horvath and C. C. Foster, 'Stochastic Models of War Alliances', *Journal of Conflict Resolution* 7 (1963), pp. 110–16.

4. L. F. Richardson, *Arms and Insecurity* (Pittsburgh: The Boxwood Press; Chicago: Quadrangle Books, 1960), Chapters II, III.

5. H. Kahn, *On Thermonuclear War* (Princeton: Princeton University Press, 1960), pp. 311–14.

6. H. Kahn, *On Escalation: Metaphors and Scenarios* (New York, Washington, London: Frederick A. Praeger, 1965), p. 16 fn.

7. ibid., pp. 185–6.

15. Systemic Theories: Summary

1. See note 1 on Chapter 14.

2. G. K. Zipf has gathered voluminous data on rank-size distributions and attempted to subsume them under a general 'law', which he called 'The Principle of Least Effort'. His theoretical discussion is marred by a commitment to a fixed idea and by lack of mathematical competence, but his pioneering efforts have inspired many interesting investigations. (Cf. G. K. Zipf, *Human Behavior and the Principle of Least Effort*, Cambridge, Mass.: Addison-Wesley Press, 1949.)

3. H. Kahn, *On Escalation: Metaphors and Scenarios* (New York, Washington, London: Frederick A. Praeger, 1965), p. 12.

16. A Taxonomy of Conflicts

1. For a discussion of this aspect of conflict, see, for example, J. Galtung. 'A Structural Theory of Aggression', *Journal of Peace Research*, 1964, No. 2, pp. 95–119.

2. A. Rapoport, *Fights, Games, and Debates* (Ann Arbor: University of Michigan Press, 1960), Part III.

17. Some Aspects of Endogenous Conflicts

1. Whether a civilian government exercises control over the military command is immaterial. The power of the military command over the people actually doing the fighting is absolute in either case.

2. Daniel Bell, *End of Ideology* (New York: The Free Press, 1960).

3. C. Wright Mills, *Power, Politics, and People*, Collected Essays ed. Irving Louis Horowitz (New York: Oxford University Press, 1963), p. 263.

18. Internalization of Conflict

1. Mark Twain, *The Adventures of Huckleberry Finn*, Chapter XVIII.

2. Anonymous, *Report from Iron Mountain on the Possibility and Desirability of Peace* (New York: The Dial Press), pp. 38–9.

3. ibid., p. 44.

4, 5, 6, 7. All quotations are taken from M. Spillane, *My Gun is Quick* and *The Girl Hunters* (New American Library, Signet paperbacks, 1962).

8. V. I. Lenin, *Materialism and Empirio-criticism* (New York: International Publishers, 1927).

19. Professionalization of Conflict

1. In extending the idea of the 'survival of the fittest' to the social sphere, the exponents of Social Darwinism provided a rationalization of social inequality. One excerpt will suffice:

The class distinctions simply result from the different degrees of success with which men have availed themselves of the chances which were presented to them. Instead of endeavoring to redistribute the acquisitions which have been made between existing classes, our aim should be to *increase, multiply, and extend the chances* [emphasis in the original] . . . Such expansion is no guarantee of equality.

On the contrary, if there be liberty, some will profit by the chances eagerly and some will neglect them altogether. Therefore, the greater the chances the more unequal will be the fortune of these two sets of men. So it ought to be, in all justice and right reason . . .

W. G. Sumner, *What Social Classes Owe to Each Other* (Caldwell, Ohio: Caxton, 1952; first published in 1883).

2. C. von Clausewitz, *On War* (Harmondsworth: Penguin Books Ltd, 1968), p. 345.

3. The dissociation of war from violence is dramatically reflected in comments such as these:

'It sure is a funny way to fight a war. I mean, I have yet to even see Vietnam or Laos. I get up in the morning, have breakfast and fly off. And man, I don't see anything – just clouds, sky and sun.

'I get the coordinates on the map, drop my load, and I'm back in time for beer and lunch in the base restaurant complete with air conditioning. After a nap, I usually spend the afternoon swimming.

'I'm living with this Thai chick. Sometimes we go out at night to a bar, or I go play cards. Usually, though, I just stay around the house, reading or screwing.' – American B-52 pilot, Uttaphao Air Force Base, Thailand

'There was this hippy passing through here a couple of weeks ago. He was a kind of nice guy. But you know what? He accused me of being a war criminal.

'I could kind of see his point. I mean, my job is sticking fuses into bombs. I could understand how he could see it that way.

'But, man, I just don't feel like a war criminal. I mean, I never would think of killing anybody. But my job is just a job, you know? Like screwing a bulb into a socket.' – ordnance technician, Udorn Air Force Base, Thailand

cf. *Liberation*, Spring 1971, p. 36.

4. A perusal of *The Pentagon Papers* (New York: Bantam Books, 1971), published first in the spring of 1971 by the *New York Times*, gives an impression of constantly shifting and vanishing foci of responsibility. Now the military opposes starting anything and is pushed into it by the State Department or the White House; now the military wants to go all-out but the 'industrial' lobbies say no; now the elected representatives of the people declare against the war and vote appropriations for it; now the 'hawks' want to pull back, and the 'moderates' want escalation, etc.

5. The irrelevance of the question of military versus civilian control of policy has been argued forcefully by Gabriel Kolko:

Even if personnel are less crucial than the inherited duties of specific offices, and to which *all* must conform, it is also a statistically verifiable fact that many in the ranks of key decision-makers in the federal political structure are indeed drawn from the interlocked world of big banking, corporate law, and giant industry. Sixty per cent of the key foreign policy decision-making posts during the period 1944–60 were filled by men from this element, and another 15% were held by career government men who later transferred into the economic world. A more extensive Brookings Institution study, covering 1933–65, revealed that 63% of all Cabinet Secretaries and 86% *of the Military Secretaries* were either businessmen or lawyers prior to appointment. [Emphasis added.]

G. Kolko, 'Power and Capitalism in 20th Century America', *Liberation*, Winter 1971. In other words, agencies where foreign policy is made can refute any allegation of being under 'military control'. The point is that the military-business world is one.

6. W. H. Oldendorf, 'On the Acceptability of a Device as a Weapon', *Bulletin of the Atomic Scientists*, January 1962; quoted in R. E. Osgood and R. E. Tucker, *Force, Order and Justice* (Baltimore: Johns Hopkins University Press, 1967), p. 217 fn.

20. Conflict Resolution

1. Cf. G. Clark and L. B. Sohn, *World Peace Through World Law* (Cambridge, Mass.: Harvard University Press, 1964). Also Q. Wright, 'Toward a Universal Law of Mankind', *Columbia Law Review* 63 (1963), pp. 440–46.

2. R. Fisher, *International Conflict for Beginners* (New York: Harper & Row, 1969), Chapter 5.

3. The notion of 'strategy' in this context includes so-called 'mixed strategies' in which a player chooses among the available strategies in accordance with certain probabilities. A 'best' mixed strategy prescribes the particular probabilities of choice. For a discussion of this topic, addressed to a reader with quite modest mathematical background, see A. Rapoport, *Two-person Game Theory: The Essential Ideas* (Ann Arbor: University of Michigan Press, 1966), Chapter 6.

4. Thus, it is not quite accurate to say that Row is entitled to 2 units of the 5 which they can *jointly* get. More accurately, Row is entitled to 'get his way' (i.e., to the realization of the outcome in the upper right corner of Matrix 4) 40 per cent of the time. This is clear from the remarks immediately following the somewhat misleading statement.

5. The basic paper on the theory of two-person non-zerosum games, where communication, bargaining, etc. are permitted, is J. F. Nash, 'Two-

person Cooperative Games', *Econometrica* 21 (1953), pp. 128–40. For less technical discussions of game theory as a tool of conflict resolution (in more general contexts), see A. Rapoport, 'Conflict Resolution in the Light of Game Theory and Beyond', in *The Structure of Conflict*, ed. P. G. Swingle (New York: Academic Press, 1970); also A. Rapoport, *N-Person Game Theory: Concepts and Applications* (Ann Arbor: University of Michigan Press, 1970) and *Two-person Game Theory*, op. cit., Chapter 8.

5. H. Kahn, *On Thermonuclear War* (Princeton: Princeton University Press, 1960), pp. 145–53.

6. J. Galtung, 'A Structural Theory of Aggression', *Journal of Peace Research*, 1964, No. 2, pp. 95–119.

7. L. F. Richardson, *Statistics of Deadly Quarrels* (Pittsburgh: The Boxwood Press; Chicago: Quadrangle Books, 1960), Chapters V–IX.

8. For example, R. J. Rummel, 'Dimensions of Conflict Behavior Within and Between Nations', *General Systems* VIII (1963), pp. 1–50; J. D. Singer and M. Small, *The Wages of War, 1816–1965: A Statistical Handbook* (New York: John Wiley & Sons, 1972).

9. For example, R. C. North, 'Perception and Action in the 1914 Crisis', *Journal of International Affairs* 21 (1967), pp. 103–22; O. R. Holsti, R. A. Brody, and R. C. North, 'Measuring Affect and Action in International Reaction Models: Empirical Material from the 1962 Cuban Crisis', *Peace Research Society Papers II* (1965), pp. 170–90.

10. The absolute arbitrating power of the umpire is a consequence of an *advance* agreement of the 'conflicting parties' (the players) to abide by his decisions. In general, the effectiveness of 'conflict management' is directly related to the authority of the arbitrating or conciliating agency.

11. Q. Wright, *A Study of War* (Chicago: University of Chicago Press, 1942). L. F. Richardson and P. A. Sorokin (P. A. Sorokin, *Man and Society in Calamity*, New York: Dutton, 1942) were the other two prominent pioneers of peace research.

21. *Prospects*

1. Toronto *Globe and Mail*, 25 May 1971.

2. Cf. P. F. Drucker, *Men, Ideas, and Politics* (New York: Harper & Row, 1971), Chapter 8 and 11.

3. At times, the acute need for a model to emulate drives the 'politicized' groups to 'Maoism', or even to neo-Stalinism, as in West Germany.

4. Unfortunately, these apparent curbs (if they are such) by world public

opinion on brute force give little cause for optimism. The much more diffuse and covert power of mammoth international corporations (the power to exploit world resources and to allocate productive effort and capital) is more immune to the sort of pressures that can under certain circumstances be brought to bear against politico-military power.

5. *Daedalus* 96 (1967), pp. 653–4.

6. For a cogent statement of the anti-technocrat position, see Jacques Ellul, *The Technological Society* (New York: Alfred A. Knopf, 1965). A somewhat less extreme position is presented in L. Mumford, *The Pentagon of Power* (New York: Harcourt, Brace, 1970).

7. I believe that the suppression of the Jewish *cultural* community is not a case of 'classical' antisemitism, directed against the individual Jew (hence, vehement and often sincere denials of antisemitism in the U.S.S.R. by the Soviets). The position of the Jew in the Soviet Union is different from that of other nationalities, identification with which can be fitted into the scheme of Soviet patriotism, since the national 'republics' are under central political control. The Jewish community is world-wide and its cultural roots go far deeper than Russian history. The Soviets can say with some justification that they 'emancipated' indigenous Asiatic cultures from tsarist oppression. Jewish culture, on the contrary, flourished under oppression, and as *a culture* owes nothing to the Revolution. For this reason, the Jews more than any other Soviet nationality are suspected of divided loyalty, and justly so. What is oppressive is that multiple loyalty should be so intolerable.

8. A. Storr, *The Integrity of the Personality* (Harmondsworth and Baltimore: Penguin Books, 1963), pp. 56–7.

9. A. Storr, 'Possible Substitutes for War', in *The Natural History of Aggression*, ed. J. D. Carthy and F. J. Ebling (London and New York: Academic Press, 1964), p. 141.

INDEX

abstraction, 27, 49, 159, 212 (*see also* cognition)

aggression, as 'masculine' virtue, 199; from frustration, 126–31, 206; learned from experience, 126; in animals, 112, 125; in children, 132; in predation, 111, 112; internalized, 199; positive aspects of, 249; reinforcement of, 126, 198; theories of, 112–32, 198

aggression, in context of biology, 113, 116, 118, 199; of ethics, 113; of psychology, 117

aggressive instinct, 109–22, 225

Albee, Edward, *The Zoo Story*, 122

alienation of youth, effects of, 244–5

allegiance, rationale for, 200, 218 (*see also* loyalty)

Amos, Sheldon, 89, 254

Andreski, S., 255

animal communication, 49; verbal, 47, 55; control of, 60; technology, 101

Ardrey, R., 255

Aristotle, 80

arms race, 160–61; – control, 163

asymmetry, organismic, 33

authority, 80, 184; absolute, 184–5; erosion of, 92, 195, 201, 244; escape from, 203; denial of, 207; submission to, 207 (*see also* [The] State)

autonomy, individual, 136, 145, 195, 199, 244; in Western democracies, 195–6; national, 216, 238–9; need for, 187–9, 193–4; personal vs. group, 247; relation to cooperation, 246–7; surrender of (*see* Hobbes); vs. integration, 195; vs. power, 248–50

'backlash', 191

bandwagon effect, 75

behavior, 31, 34–5; afferent–efferent, 42; environmental determinants of, 123, 130; forced, 59; 'instinctive', 45, 109, 255 (*see also* homeostasis, tropism); learned, 42, 53, 126, 256; manipulation of, 90, 243; natural, 43, 53; pre-arranged (imprinted), 35–6; reflexive, 43; sexual, 111, 120; stereotyped, 110; triggering of, 35–6, 53, 119 (*see also* conditioning)

behavioral psychology, 125

behaviorists, 18

Bell, Daniel, 260

Bellamy, Edward, 93

'belonging'-ness, 190

biological (innate) mechanisms (*see* homeostasis, tropism)

Bonger, W. A., 131, 257

Brody, R. A., 263

Bugelski, R., 129, 257

business 'game', 180

'cabinet wars' (*see* Wars, 18th-century European)

capitalism, 150, 155–6; – international, 157

causality, 19, 37, 85, 123, 152, 171

[a] 'cause', 200

cause–effect, 124

Clark, G., 262

class consciousness, 151

class struggle, theory of, 149–40, 155 (*see also* conflict)

Clausewitz, Carl von, theory of war, 133, 144–5, 162, 219–20, 258

cognition, by analogy, 18; projection, 17, 18, 35, 111; objectivization, 19;

More about Penguins and Pelicans

Penguinews, which appears every month, contains details of all the new books issued by Penguins as they are published. From time to time it is supplemented by *Penguins in Print*, which is a complete list of all available books published by Penguins. (There are well over four thousand of these.)

A specimen copy of *Penguinews* will be sent to you free on request. For a year's issues (including the complete lists) please send 30p if you live in the United Kingdom, or 60p if you live elsewhere. Just write to Dept EP, Penguin Books Ltd, Harmondsworth, Middlesex, enclosing a cheque or postal order, and your name will be added to the mailing list.

Note: *Penguinews* and *Penguins in Print* are not available in the U.S.A. or Canada

Leviathan

Hobbes

Edited by C. B. Macpherson

From the turmoil of the English Civil War, when life was truly 'nasty, brutish, and short', Hobbes's *Leviathan* (1651) speaks directly to the twentieth century. In its over-riding concern for peace, its systematic analysis of power, and its elevation of politics to the status of a science, it mirrors much modern thinking. And despite its contemporary notoriety – Pepys called it 'a book the Bishops will not let be printed again' – it was also, as Dr Macpherson shows, a convincing apologia for the emergent seventeenth-century market society.

On War

Clausewitz

Edited by Anatol Rapoport

In his famous treatise *On War* (1832) Carl von Clausewitz may be said to have distilled Napoleon into theory. He is best remembered for his pronouncement that war is a continuation of politics by other means and for his observations on total war: but modern strategists who profess to apply his doctrines would do well to read him again. For Clausewitz, as Professor Rapoport contends, made a distinction between judicious and injudicious war, and the relationship he detected between war and politics really means that war can only be waged in certain circumstances.

PELICAN CLASSICS

Essay on the Principle of Population

Malthus

Edited by Anthony Flew

The Reverend Thomas Malthus's blunt identification of the ultimate demographic choice – starvation or restraint – has guaranteed his fame, even if his analysis of how population checks are always operating has often been misunderstood.

This volume presents both the full text of Malthus's original polemic of 1798 and his final restatement of 1830, *A Summary View*, addressed in part to 'those who have not had leisure to read the whole work'.

Today there is a torrent of books asking whether we can 'prevent the Malthusian nightmare becoming a reality', and in his introduction Professor Flew (besides assessing the impact of Malthus on both Darwinism and Marxism) examines how far his argument does, and does not, stand up to the refutations that have rained upon it for a century and a half.

PELICAN CLASSICS

The Origin of Species

Darwin

Edited by J. W. Burrow

The Origin of Species is at the root of man's present attitude
to himself and the universe: no one book since the *Summa* of
Thomas Aquinas has made a comparable impact. Written for
the general public of the 1850s, it remains, in the words of
Dr Burrow's helpful and entertaining introduction, 'easily
the most readable and approachable of the great revolutionary
work of the scientific imagination'.

Man and Environment

Crisis and the Strategy of Choice

Robert Arvill

What will the world look and be like tomorrow? Must the landscape be an extension of today's spreading deterioration? More air fouled by noise and poisoned fumes; more water polluted by chemicals and oil slicks; more land crushed under the sprawl of towns, super-highways, airports, factories, pylons, and strip-mines? Is man bound to build a stifling steel-and-concrete hell for himself? Or can effective steps be taken now to preserve our open-spaces, seashores, and life-sustaining elements from the assaults of technology?

This is a book about man – about the devastating impact of his numbers on the environment and the decisions and actions he can take to attack the problem. The author is an expert on conservation and planning. Land, air, water, and wildlife are treated by him as both valuable resources in very short supply and as precious living entities. He contrasts present management of these resources with man's future needs. British experience and examples from all over the world illustrate the critical and practical aspects of the problem. Past conservation programmes are reviewed and evaluated, and the book offers a complete set of proposals for regional, national, and international action on environmental protection. The approach is farsighted, informed, urgent.

Shape of Community

Realization of Human Potential

Serge Chermayeff and Alexander Tzonis

Technology is creating an ever-expanding environment which is becoming increasingly hostile to the natural one. The conflict between the natural and the man-made has reached a point of unprecedented crisis: life's total habitat is endangered. One of the most devastating threats is created by transport and communications which destroy meeting places and the sense of community.

Affluent societies in their narrow-minded preoccupation with quite material gains are losing sight of long-term consequences which, however, are tragic to man's survival. The simple remedial steps that are being taken now have become ineffective and obsolete.

Shape of Community is a manifesto urging the re-thinking of technology as a catalyst of human evolution, rather than simply as a blind destructive force. It proposes a design methodology and an urban model that may lead to a peaceful coexistence of man and nature, and man with man within the community.

Human Identity in the Urban Environment
Edited by Gwen Bell and Jaqueline Tyrwhitt

By the year 2000 there may be over 1,000 cities in the world with a million or more inhabitants. Already thirteen areas deserve the title of 'megalopolis', including the eastern seaboard and the Great Lakes complex in the United States, the smaller denser area of England, and the huge population surrounding the Rhine.

How is man to remain human in the coming wilderness of steel, concrete and tarmac?

It is to this problem that this collection of more than forty essays is addressed. The governing factors of nature, the needs of man, society, buildings and construction, and the networks of transport and communications provide headings for articles by W. H. Auden, C. A. Doxiadis, Bertrand de Jouvenel, Margaret Mead, Buckminster Fuller, Arnold Toynbee, C. H. Waddington and a number of architects, planners and sociologists.

Finally the editors have assembled a group of articles which provide a case study of the greatest complex of all, the Tokaido megalopolis in Japan, where nearly 70 million people live.